JavaScript™
Goodies

by Joe Burns
Andree Growney

EARTHWEB PRESS

QUE®

Macmillan Publishing
201 West 103rd Street   Indianapolis, Indiana   46290

JavaScript™ Goodies

Copyright © 1999 by Que

International Standard Book Number: 0-7897-2024-8

Library of Congress Catalog Card Number: 99-63133

Printed in the United States of America

First Printing: June 1999

00   7 6 5

Trademarks

Warning and Disclaimer

Executive Editor
Tim Ryan

Development Editor
Tiffany Taylor

Managing Editor
Jodi Jensen

Project Editor
Heather Talbot

Copy Editor
Mike Henry

Indexer
Heather Goens

Proofreader
Mona Brown

Technical Editor
Michelle Wyner

Interior Design
Louisa Klucznik

Cover Design
Aren Howell

Copy Writer
Eric Borgert

Layout Technicians
Ayanna Lacey
Heather Miller
Amy Parker

About the Authors

Joe Burns, Ph.D. is a professor at Southeastern Louisiana University where he teaches graduate and undergraduate classes in Web design and Internet-mediated communication. Joe is the Webmaster of HTML Goodies (`http://www.htmlgoodies.com`), a site devoted to teaching HTML and Web design that serves up close to four million pages every month to almost a quarter-million individual readers. He is also an Internet consultant for EarthWeb in New York City. Joe first became interested in the Internet while studying for his Ph.D. at Bowling Green State University. There he created HTML Goodies and first began teaching computer classes. Joe is currently working on the viability of delivering university-level classes over the Internet and the effect of teaching in a Web-based environment. Joe lives in Hammond, Louisiana, with his wife Tammy, and two cats, Chloe and Fido.

Andree Growney is currently a software engineer at TERC, a non-profit educational research and development company in Cambridge, Massachusetts, where she does Internet applications development. She has been working with computers for more than 20 years. A former programmer and systems analyst, she became infatuated with the Web early in its development. She was formerly the Webmaster at Susquehanna University in Selinsgrove, Pennsylvania, where she also taught client/server and other database-to-Web related courses.

EarthWeb Press

EarthWeb Press is a co-publishing partnership between EarthWeb and Macmillan Computer Publishing. Our mission is to serve Web developers, programmers, and IT professionals by giving them the technical information they need to build tomorrow's systems.

EarthWeb Inc. is the leading provider of Internet-based online services to the Information Technology (IT) community worldwide. Through its flagship service, `developer.com`, and its other integrated business-to-business online services including Datamation and ITKnowledge, EarthWeb addresses the needs of IT professionals for content, community, and commerce.

More than 150,000 technical resources can be found on EarthWeb's online services, including

- The full text of hundreds of technical books
- 375+ proprietary tutorials
- In-depth explorations of the newest technologies
- Technical discussion boards led by industry experts
- Hard-to-find specialized IT products
- Technical job listings

For more information on EarthWeb, visit the corporate site at `www.earthweb.com`.

Macmillan Computer Publishing (MCP) is the world's largest computer book publisher. The books published in our two leading imprints, Que and Sams, help computer users and programming professionals deal with the complexities of new technologies. Macmillan Publishing is much more than a print publisher—we are a multimedia content provider. Our information is available not only as bound books, but also as multimedia software products and online interactive Web sites. Our Web site includes

- BetaBooks (`www.mcp.com/betabooks/`): see cutting-edge books in progress before they publish.
- Resource Center (`www.mcp.com/resources/`): get code, utilities, Web links, and other support materials for our books and the technologies they cover.
- Personal Bookshelf (`www.mcp.com/personal/`): register for access to five of our published books at a time for free.

For more information about MCP, please visit our main site at `www.mcp.com`.

Contents at a Glance

Contents

Chapter 6   Mathematics, Random Things, and Loops   139

Chapter 7   Clocks, Counts, and Scrolling Text   167

xiii

Dedication by Joe Burns

This book is dedicated to my wife, Tammy, who never seems to think anything is outside of my grasp. Plus, she found that missing equal sign in Chapter 7 that kept me at bay for two hours.

Dedication by Andree Growney

To my husband, Wally, with all my love.

To Kristen, Todd, Eric, and Diann, for whom my love and admiration grow daily.

And in loving memory of my mother, Bess Schwedersky, who eyed computers suspiciously, but always supported me in whatever folly I chose to pursue.

Acknowledgments by Joe Burns

First and foremost, many, many thanks to Andree Growney who went into this project with me knowing full well that it might never become anything more than a series of Web pages. Hey, Andree! We got a book!

Tim Ryan deserves another pat on the back for editing another *Goodies* book. He's gone to bat for me twice now and it resulted in two books. How about three, Tim?

Thanks to Tiffany Taylor for content editing. Compared to the *HTML Goodies* book, this was painless. Ditto the painless comments from Michelle Wyner at Netscape. Your tech editing was great. You pointed out concerns in a helpful manner and I probably used your words more times than I should have.

Murry, Jack, Jen, Colby, Mike (How the heck are ya?), Lindy (book, book, book), Chris, and all the people at EarthWeb deserve lunch on me … as long as I can put it on the company's tab. More Italian this time around?

Larry Augustine deserves thanks for allowing me to sit in my office at work and write when I should have been taking care of a radio station. I know you knew. Thanks for giving me the time.

Thanks to Ken Kopf for being there when I was at the end of my JavaScript rope. You helped more than you know.

Thanks to Mom and Dad for playing cheerleader after the last book and now for this one. Every person in Cleveland who came into contact with them was forced to listen to stories of their son, the author.

Dave … I'm a teacher because I wanted to be just like you.

Acknowledgments by Andree Growney

A special thank you to our publisher, Tim Ryan, and to everyone at Macmillan who helped with the production of this book.

Thanks also to our wonderful technical and content editors, Michelle and Tiffany.

Special thanks to Mike Greene at EarthWeb for his encouragement.

Many, many thanks to my co-author Joe Burns, for bringing me on board, and for the rare pleasure of laughing out loud while reading a computer book!

Tell Us What You Think!

As the reader of this book, *you* are our most important critic and commentator. We value your opinion and want to know what we're doing right, what we could do better, what areas you'd like to see us publish in, and any other words of wisdom you're willing to pass our way.

As an Associate Publisher for Que, I welcome your comments. You can fax, email, or write me directly to let me know what you did or didn't like about this book—as well as what we can do to make our books stronger.

Please note that I cannot help you with technical problems related to the topic of this book, and that due to the high volume of mail I receive, I might not be able to reply to every message.

When you write, please be sure to include this book's title and author as well as your name and phone or fax number. I will carefully review your comments and share them with the authors and editors who worked on the book.

Fax: 317-581-4666

Email: java@mcp.com

Mail: Associate Publisher
            Que Corporation
            201 West 103rd Street
            Indianapolis, IN 46290 USA

An Introduction
by Joe Burns

Welcome to *JavaScript Goodies*. The purpose of this book's 55 lessons is to get you started writing your own JavaScript events.

If you've tried to learn JavaScript through a textbook or from the Internet, my guess is that you found it quite difficult. Me, too. After a while, the text melded into a large block of strange hieroglyphics equal to the Rosetta stone. I always felt like I was deciphering the text rather than reading it.

Learning JavaScript is literally learning a new language. The text might look like English, but the construction of the sentences is quite different. This book will teach you JavaScript by coming at the language from an entirely new perspective. Instead of getting all the commands and then building a script, we'll start with the script and tear it down to its individual commands. In the process, you'll learn JavaScript programming.

Why Now?

I used to get email at my HTML Goodies and Java Goodies Web sites all the time asking, "When are you going to put together a series of lessons for writing JavaScript?" Most readers of my sites know that I already have primers for HTML and for creating advertising banners. So why not JavaScript? Good question!

In an effort to put lessons together, I bought the books, read them, read them again, and gave up. JavaScript books, at least the four I've bulled through, are dry and hard to follow. They're textbooks. We all know how fun those were to read. So, in an effort to not have to write JavaScript lessons at all, I created the Java Goodies Web site at http:// www.javagoodies.com. (It's right now being combined with JavaScripts.com to create one giant JavaScript repository.)

The purpose was to create the largest possible download source for JavaScript. I figured that instead of teaching you to make your own JavaScripts, I would supply you with as many ready-to-go scripts as I could. Well, it seemed like a smart idea at the time. Now Java Goodies has more than 600 scripts, and readers still want JavaScript lessons. I should have seen it coming.

My Co-Author

Andree Growney used to be the Director of Instructional Technology Support Services and Webmaster at the university where I worked, and is a bit of a wizard at this JavaScript stuff. One day I asked if she would be interested in putting a book together on how to write JavaScript and posting it to the HTML Goodies Web site to test it out. To my great joy, Andree said yes. So we got started.

We sat in her office and brainstormed until we came up with 30 different JavaScript topics. Our thinking was, "If you grasped these 30 lessons, you're well on your way to writing your own scripts." We then set to work creating scripts for each topic idea. I wrote the tutorials for my scripts, Andree wrote for hers. We edited each other's work.

I finally set it all to hypertext and it hit the Net in August 1998 as the HTML Goodies 30-Step JavaScript Primer series at http://www.htmlgoodies.com/primers/jsp/.

Wow! What a response. The bulk of the email from the site didn't concern the content or the teaching method as much as the format for teaching JavaScript. Email after email stated, "I understand this."

Mission accomplished.

How You Will Learn

My own method of learning the JavaScript language is the method these lessons—and hopefully you—will follow. I didn't set out to learn JavaScript following this book's method. It just happened that way. Let me explain.

Every script submitted to the Java Goodies site arrived via email. Usually the email transmission does quite a number on it. Scripts always arrived bent, folded, and mutilated, and it was my job to put them back together so they will work again. After doing that a couple hundred times, I found I was using my reference books less and less. I could look at a script and see what the problem was. Error messages stopped sending me into a rage. Commands were becoming familiar. Formats and structure started to become friendly.

I was learning JavaScript. But I was learning it backward from the approach described in the books I had read. Everything I had seen to that point gave the commands and then built the script. So I thought, let's go the other way. Let's start with the script fully finished, and then tear it apart. If we keep doing that over and over with new scripts, readers are bound to see patterns and common structures.

Forget trying to write from scratch right off. Let's get the readers altering finished scripts. There's a phenomenal sense of accomplishment if you can look at a script and alter where its output appears, or change the color of the text, or make numbers add up in different fashions.

With that sense of accomplishment comes the desire to learn more, to write a brand new script. The next thing you know, you're writing JavaScript.

You see, there's more and more research showing that teaching by lecturing doesn't work. When you read a textbook, you are essentially being lectured. These primers are going to come at the subject from a different angle.

A professor of mine liked to say, "Tell me and I forget. Show me and I remember. Involve me and I learn." The purpose here is to involve you.

Once the go-ahead was given to turn the JavaScript Primers into a book, I knew 30 wouldn't be enough to satisfy the reader. The online users are right now screaming for the lessons to be expanded. So I almost doubled the number of lessons. This book has 55 different scripts that we'll break down for your entertainment.

Each of these 55 lessons will display one JavaScript and tear it apart so you can see how it works. You see, you have to be taught *why* something works, not just be shown that it works. Case in point: David Copperfield doesn't close the door on his assistant, open it, and exclaim, "Son of a gun! She's gone again!" He knows why she disappeared. All you know is that he shut the door and she went away. You both know that the box works, but only he knows *why* it works. He will be in a better position to create another trick, whereas you'll just keep closing the door, hoping it'll work.

The Format of the Lessons

As I said before, this book contains 55 lessons in 9 chapters. Each will follow the same format:

1. First, you'll get a brief concept statement regarding what the script is supposed to do and what the example is supposed to teach you.

2. Next, you'll see the script in text form.

3. Third, you'll see the script's effect. This book is fully supported online. I'll tell you how you can get all the scripts in the book into your own computer in a moment.

4. Fourth, we will tear the script apart, looking closely at the building blocks used to create the whole. The purpose is for you to be able to read a JavaScript as you would a sentence.

5. Finally, each lesson has an assignment. You'll be asked to alter the script you've just worked on so that it will be a little different, or a lot different. Either way, you will be asked to create 55 new scripts from the 55 we give you.

Then at the end of each chapter, you'll find a review lesson. We'll stop, quickly review the JavaScript commands you've learned up to that point, and then use them to create a whole new script. This is where this book will hopefully start to come to life for you.

I've been a college professor for a number of years now, and the hardest thing to teach students is that there comes a point where they have to look at the building blocks I've shown them, and use those blocks to build something that is fully their own. Just mimicking what I show you here is not enough. You need to build something new.

Examples and Assignments

This is a book. You knew that. But we want this book to have an interactive feel to it. You should be able to see the JavaScripts in action. When you finish an assignment, you should be able to see a possible answer, and be able to look at the source code to see how it could be done.

In an effort to help you do that, the wonderful staff at HTML Goodies and Java Goodies—me—has put together a packet that contains all this book's examples and assignment answers. How often do you get the answers up front? Just don't cheat and look before you try to do the assignment yourself, okay?

You can use the examples and assignments packet one of two ways.

First, it's all available online at http://www.htmlgoodies.com/JSBook/. Log on to the Internet and use your browser to look at the pages as you need to. You'll find an easy-to-follow chart of the examples and assignments by lesson. I'll also offer a direct URL to the required page right here in the book. Keep in mind that these pages were created for your use. Feel free to download one or all of them by clicking on File and choosing Save As. Just remember they are HTML pages, so be sure to save them with the .html extension.

Second, you can download the entire packet of examples and assignments and install them right on to your own computer. It's very easy to grab and install. The packet contains all 55 scripts found in the book along with all 55 assignments. It's available in zip-file format. Follow these steps:

1. Log on the Internet and point your browser to `http://www.htmlgoodies.com/JSBook/JavaScriptGoodies.zip`.

2. After you have the packet, unzip its contents into an empty folder on your hard drive.

3. Use a browser to open the file `index.html` and you'll see links to all the examples and assignments.

Let's Get Started with JavaScript

Be careful going through these lessons. Often a student will want to roll through the earlier lessons as quickly as possible. Most of the time that leads to commands being jumbled up in the mind. Your brain needs time to digest all of this. If I may make a suggestion: Don't do more than two or three lessons a day.

Students tell me they read the entire chapter, but cannot remember what they read. That's because getting to the end was the goal, not getting the most out of the reading. Speed kills. Give your brain time. Here's an example. You read all of this, right? Well, without looking back up the page...tell me the name of my co-author. I've written it three times now.

You rolled before you crawled, before you walked, before you ran. Give your brain time to roll around the easy scripts.

Andree and I wish you the best of luck with your future JavaScripts.

The Basics

This chapter contains the following lessons and scripts:

- What Is JavaScript?
- Lesson 1: Printing Text on a Web Page
- Lesson 2: Error Messages
- Lesson 3: Object Properties
- Lesson 4: Chapter Wrap Up and Review

The purpose of Chapter 1 is to get you started on the right JavaScript foot. In this chapter you'll learn how to work with JavaScript, and how to create JavaScripts that print text to your HTML page, fix error messages, and tell the world what time it is.

What Is JavaScript?

First off, JavaScript is not Java. It's easy to get confused and think that Java and JavaScript are one and the same. Not so. Java is a programming language developed at Sun Microsystems. JavaScript, on the other hand, is a programming language created by the good people at Netscape.

With Java, you create fully standalone programs that must go through a somewhat complex process of writing, compiling, and being referenced in your Web page. JavaScript, on the other hand, is simply text that you type into your Web page much as you type in HTML tags and text. In order for JavaScript to work, the Web page it is in must be viewed with a browser that understands the JavaScript language, like all Netscape browsers 2.0 and above. Internet Explorer browsers have trouble with advanced JavaScript commands found in JavaScript version 1.1 and 1.2. The scripts in the book however, stay at the JavaScript 1.0 level and will run on both browsers. When writing JavaScript, remember that *JavaScript is not HTML*! I am often asked whether one is simply a different version of the other. Nope. The following sections outline the differences.

JavaScript Is Case Sensitive

In HTML, the tag <B> works the same as the tag <b>. That's because HTML doesn't differentiate between upper- and lowercase characters. Not so in JavaScript. You must pay very close attention to the capitalization of commands. Placing an uppercase character where a lowercase one should be will cause an error.

Beware of Line Breaks and Spaces

HTML is very forgiving in terms of spaces and line breaks. It doesn't matter how many spaces you leave between words or paragraphs. In fact, there's no reason why you couldn't write an HTML document as one long line or skip 20 lines between every word. It doesn't matter.

The opposite is true in JavaScript. It makes a big difference where each line ends. There are some times when you can break a line of JavaScript, but not very many. Following is a single line of JavaScript:

```
document.write("<FONT COLOR='RED'>This Is Red Text</FONT>")
```

Those commands must all stay on one line. If you change this line to look something like this:

```
document.write("<FONT COLOR='RED'>This Is Red Text</FONT>
")
```

the code will not work properly and cause an error. (We'll get into errors and fixing them in Lesson 2.) Also, an extra space between two commands (or anywhere else a space doesn't belong) will cause an error.

Don't Set Margins

Whether you're writing or editing a script, you *cannot* allow margins to get in the way. Always edit your work in a text editor that has no margins. I don't mean margins set to their widest point. I mean *no margins*. You should be able to write off of the right side of the text screen for miles. Doing it any other way is going to cause you problems.

And now with some of the basics out of the way, let's get right to your first JavaScript!

Lesson 1: Printing Text on a Web Page

This first script is meant to introduce you to the very basics of creating and placing a JavaScript on your page. Simply type the following JavaScript into any existing HTML page of your Web site:

```
<SCRIPT LANGUAGE="javascript">
document.write("<FONT COLOR='RED'>This Is Red Text</FONT>")
</SCRIPT>
```

The concept of this script is to use JavaScript to place text on a Web page, as illustrated in Figure 1.1. In this case, the text will be red.

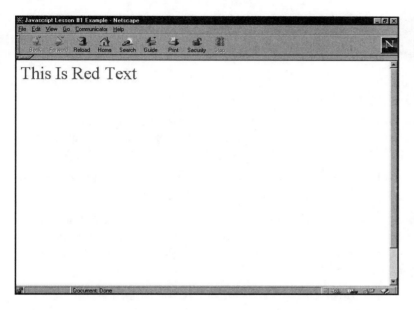

Figure 1.1
Putting red text on your HTML page.

 To see the script working on your own computer, open Lesson One's Script Effect or point your browser to http://www.htmlgoodies.com/JSBook/lesson1effect.html.

Deconstructing the Script

Let's start at the top. The first line of the script looks like this:

```
<SCRIPT LANGUAGE="javascript">
```

That's HTML code to alert the browser that what immediately follows is going to be a JavaScript script. That seems simple enough. All JavaScripts start with this same command. We're writing this script in JavaScript version 1.0. Because there is no number following the word javascript, the browser assumes by default that the following code is in JavaScript 1.0.

But what about that LANGUAGE="javascript" deal? Do you really need that?

Yes. There are other types of scripts: VBScript, for example. Using that LANGUAGE attribute will keep it all straight in the browser's mind.

Because we're only dealing with three lines of text here, allow me to jump right to the end. The command

```
</SCRIPT>
```

ends every JavaScript. No exceptions. Now, put that on a brain cell. That's the last time those two commands will be discussed. Remember, start with <SCRIPT LANGUAGE="javascript"> and end with </SCRIPT>. Moving forward...

Now we hit the meat of the script:

```
document.write("<FONT COLOR='RED'>This Is Red Text</FONT>")
```

This script is simple enough that you can just about guess what each little bit does, but let's go over it anyway so that we're all speaking with the same common terms.

The document holds the contents of the page within the browser window including all the HTML code and JavaScript commands. If it helps you to simply think of document as the HTML document, that's fine.

That document will be altered by write-ing something to it. What will be written to the document is inside the parentheses.

Now some terms. In JavaScript, the document is what's known as an *object*. The write that follows, separated by a period, is what is known as the object's *method* (an action to be performed on the object). So the script is basically saying, take the object (something that already exists) and write something to it.

The double parentheses are called the *instance*. The text inside of the parentheses is called the method's *parameters*, or what will be done when the method is acted upon the object. Are you with me so far?

Notice that what is inside of the parentheses is encased in double quotation marks. In HTML, quotation marks are not always required. In JavaScript, they are. You must use them. And not only that, there's an exact way of using them.

The text inside the double quotation marks is simple text: It will be written to the screen exactly as shown. Note that there are HTML flags within the double quotes. That's fine. The script is just going to write it all to the page.

But there are couple of things to be concerned about when using a `document.write()` JavaScript command.

- You should recognize the text as a FONT flag that will turn text red. Notice that single quotation marks appear around the HTML attribute code: `<FONT COLOR='RED'>`.

  You see, if you use double quotes, the JavaScript will think it's at the end of the line and you'll only get part of your text written to the object. You know you didn't mean that double quote to mean the end of the line, but the script doesn't. You'll most likely get an error message telling you something is wrong.

  Some people get around this concern by not using any quotes around HTML attributes. They write the previous command this way: `<FONT COLOR=red>`. Either way will work, but if you decide to write using quotes around HTML attributes, remember this: Inside of double quotes...use single quotes.

- When writing text within the instances of double quotes, be careful not to use any words that are contractions. For example:

  ```
  document.write("Don't go there!")
  ```

  That line of code is going to produce a JavaScript error. You know that the single quote above doesn't denote an attribute, but JavaScript doesn't know that. It thinks you've started an attribute and when it doesn't find the ending single quote, an error will result.

How Did the Text Become Red?

So, did the JavaScript actually turn the text red? No. The HTML did that for you. What the JavaScript did was write the code to the page. There it displayed and was shown as red. The JavaScript was simply the delivery device. Neat, huh?

One More Thing

Look at this code and its result, shown in Figure 1.2.

```
<SCRIPT LANGUAGE="javascript">
document.write("This is the text that will be written to the page.");
document.write("But even though these lines of text are on different lines");
document.write("in this script, they will not reproduce the same way on the");
document.write("HTML document.");
</SCRIPT>
```

Figure 1.2
Multiple document.write
statements run together.

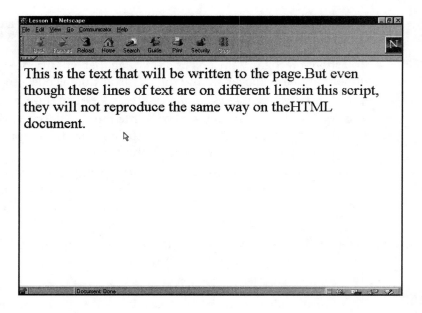

Notice how all of the lines run together when written to the page even though the text is written in four lines. The reason is that the document.write statement just writes text to the page. It does not add any breaks when its lines stop.

There is a command, writeln, that will add a br to the end of a line when used. The format looks like this:

```
document.writeln("text to a page");
```

However, good JavaScript form suggests you create your own line breaks by using the HTML <BR> flag. writeln is rather buggy, and doesn't always work correctly depending on the type of browser the user has.

How about that? The first lesson is over and you've already got two very useful commands under your belt. Better yet, you know how to use them.

Your Assignment

Each time you do an assignment, you'll need to copy the script described in the lesson so you can paste it into an HTML document and play with it. You probably already noticed this, but you can always copy and paste the script right from the sample Web page. If you're going online to see the examples, go to http://www.htmlgoodies.com/JSBook/ lesson1example.html.

Alter the script above so that it will produce two lines of text, one red and one blue. *But* you must do this by writing more JavaScript commands, not by simply adding more HTML to the instance. Make the two bits of text write to two different lines rather than simply following each other on the same line.

 You'll find one possible answer by clicking on Lesson One Assignment or pointing your browser to `http://www.htmlgoodies.com/JSBook/assignment1.html`.

Lesson 2: Error Messages

You know what I've found missing from the myriad of JavaScript books I've read? A description of how to deal with error messages. I guess the assumption is that you'll get all your code right the first time and never see one. Welcome to reality.

If you've ever attempted to write or install a JavaScript on your Web pages, you know these little jewels are part of the fun. Just when you think you get it right, boom! Something like Figure 1.3 pops up.

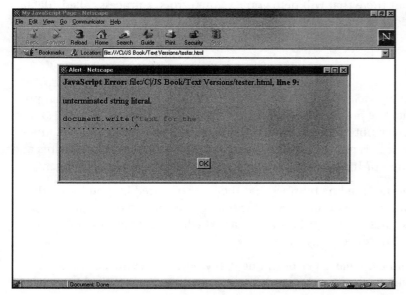

Figure 1.3
A JavaScript error.

This lesson is intended to tell you what to do when you encounter error messages. I've worked through thousands of them. Now you're starting to write JavaScript, and you'll get your share of them too.

It is said that the best way to fix errors is to avoid creating them. That's a great deal easier said than done. However, you can up your chances of getting fewer error messages by writing in a text editor that does not have margins. Also, allow each line of JavaScript to remain on its own line. There's no need to break longer lines in two. In fact, doing that will probably throw errors. That said, I'll bet you get errors just about every time you start to play with this new language, so let's get into how to repair them.

The Two Types of Error Messages

There are basically two types of errors you can produce.

- A *syntax error* means that you've misspelled something, or the JavaScript is not config-ured correctly.
- A *runtime error* means that you have used an incorrect command and the JavaScript doesn't understand what you're trying to do.

Either way, they both mean the same thing. Somewhere, something's messed up.

Now, there are programs out there that will help you fix your errors, a process called "debug-ging," but I still prefer to do it by hand. I wrote it and I want to fix it. And it's actually easier than you think.

Fixing the Errors

The wonderful thing about a JavaScript error message box is that the little window that pops up tells you where and what the problem is. Look at the error message box in Figure 1.3. It's a syntax error, meaning I have not configured the script correctly, and the error is on line 9. What's more, the error message is pointing at the problem area. See the long line of dots and then the little caret pointing up? It's like the browser is saying, "Here's what I don't get."

When an error message denotes the line number that the error occurred in, you locate that line by counting down from the top of the HTML document, not the top of the JavaScript. You must also count blank lines. You might also have a text editor program that offers to find a specific line for you. Those are really helpful.

For instance, the document below has an error in line 9. It would be a syntax error because the instance was not allowed to close on the same line it started on. See how the last word and parenthesis were jumped to the next line?

```
<HTML>
<HEAD>
<TITLE>My JavaScript Page</TITLE>
</HEAD>
```

```
<BODY>

<SCRIPT LANGUAGE="javascript">
document.write("text for the
page" )

</SCRIPT>

</BODY>
</HTML>
```

After you've counted down and you're actually at the line that has an error, you need to decide what to do. More times than not, if it's a syntax error:

- The line has been truncated. That means it has been chopped off early, like the example above.
- Something is misspelled.
- You have used a double quote where a single should go. That's called using unbalanced quotes.
- You're missing a parenthesis.

If the error is runtime, the error message is pointing at a command that doesn't logically follow in the sequence. For instance, you might have used the code `document.wrote` instead of `document.write`.

Dealing with Multiple Errors

Nothing gives me heartburn faster than running a script and getting multiple errors. All you can do is sit while a whole slew of gray error boxes pile up on your desktop. I used to think multiple boxes meant there were actually that many errors. But it's not always so.

JavaScript is an extremely logical language that likes to work in a linear fashion. Let's say you have 10 errors throughout a long script. When the error messages pile up, the error that the computer found last in the script will be sitting on top of the pile of boxes. Don't go after that last error. It probably doesn't exist.

You see, the first error in the script might very well be creating all the other errors. If you forgot to put a command in the third line of code, every subsequent line that needs that command to work will claim it has an error. So, fix the errors in sequence from bottom to top. I have found many times that a script threw 20 error boxes, but fixing only the first error—the one on the bottom of the stack—solved all the problems.

Now that all of that is said, those of you who are using Netscape Navigator 4.5 or higher might notice something a little different in terms of errors. The good people at Netscape have added a new JavaScript Console feature that will give you a great deal of help when you encounter errors.

To read more about the console and what it can do for you, see `http://developer.netscape.com/docs/technote/javascript/jsconsole.html`.

The "Something's Not Defined" Error

You'll see this written on a few JavaScript error boxes before too long. This is a runtime error that means something in the script doesn't jibe quite right. The text that is throwing the error has come out of the clear blue sky—to the computer anyway. When I get a "not defined" error, I always make sure the text wasn't created by a longer line being truncated. That's a fancy word for breaking one long line of text into two. If that's not the case, I try erasing the problem line. It can always be put back at another time. Typos occur. See whether this isn't one of those typos. It happens more times than you would believe.

There's not much more that can be said about error messages at this point. You now have enough knowledge to fix 99% of the problems that pop up. Just remember that getting error messages is actually a plus. If you didn't get them, all you would have is a blank page with no suggestion about what the problem might be.

Error messages are quite helpful if you think about them in the right light.

Your Assignment

 Go to your packet download and click on the link that reads Lesson Two Assignment. You can also go right to it online at `http://www.htmlgoodies.com/JSBook/assignment2.html`.

When you click on the link on that page, the script will throw two errors. Your assignment is to fix the two errors so that the script runs. Now, you probably won't recognize some of the commands in this script, but that doesn't matter. The error boxes that appear will give you enough information to make this script run.

Hint: You might only get one error when you run it. The second error might come after you fix the first.

If the JavaScript runs correctly, the current date will display on the page.

 After you get the script to run, or give up trying, you can look at the corrected script by going to `http://www.htmlgoodies.com/JSBook/assignment2_answer.html`.

You'll find a short explanation of what had to be fixed right on the page.

Lesson 3: Object Properties

You should be starting to get an understanding of the hierarchy of JavaScript. In fact, hierarchy is quite important in this language, so much so that we'll devote an entire lesson, Lesson 13, to it.

We know there are objects, like document, and methods, like write. We know that methods act upon objects. And we know how to write the document and method format in JavaScript:

```
document.write("This writes to the page";)
```

In this lesson, you're going to be introduced to a new part of the JavaScript hierarchy: object properties. A *property* is like a subsection of an object. It holds specific characteristics about the object. The object you're already familiar with, document, has a few properties such as its background color, its text color, and its location. The four scripts in the next section each cover one of the following objects and a great many of their properties:

- document
- navigator: This object represents the browser.
- history: This object represents the list the browser keeps of all the pages the user visited during the current online session.
- location: This represents the current URL of the page that is being displayed.

Figure 1.4 shows the results of running the four scripts we'll examine.

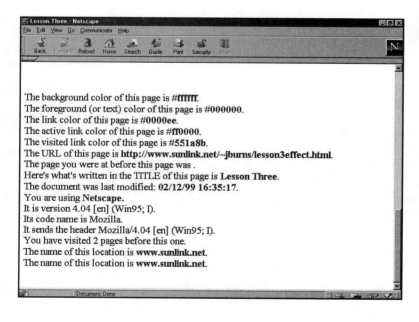

Figure 1.4
The property scripts.

You can see the effects of all the scripts by going to `http://www.htmlgoodes.com/JSBook/` `lesson3effect.html.`

The Property Scripts

There are actually four scripts below—but they all follow the same format: an `object.property` statement placed into a `document.write()` statement to be written to the page.

Writing **document** Object Properties

```
<SCRIPT LANGUAGE="javascript">
document.write("The background color of this page is <B>"
➥+document.bgColor+ "</B>.")
document.write("<BR>The foreground (or text) color
➥ of this page is <B>" +document.fgColor+ "</B>.")
document.write("<BR>The link color of this page is <B>"
➥ +document.linkColor+ "</B>.")
document.write("<BR>The active link color of this page is <B>"
➥ +document.alinkColor+ "</B>.")
document.write("<BR>The visited link color of this page is <B>"
➥ +document.vlinkColor+ "</B>.")
document.write("<BR>The URL of this page is <B>"
➥ +document.location+ "</B>.")
document.write("<BR>The page you were at before this page was <B>"
➥ +document.referrer+ "</B>.")
document.write("<BR>Here's what's written in the TITLE
➥ of this page is <B>" +document.title+ "</B>.")
document.write("<BR>The document was last modified: <B>"
➥ +document.lastModified+ "</B>.")
</SCRIPT>
```

Writing **navigator** Object Properties

```
<SCRIPT LANGUAGE="javascript">
document.write("You are using <B>" +navigator.appName+ ".</B><BR>")
document.write("It is version " +navigator.appVersion+ ".<BR>")
document.write("Its code name is " +navigator.appCodeName+ ".<BR>")
document.write("It sends the header " +navigator.userAgent+ "." );
</SCRIPT>
```

Writing **history** *Object Properties*

```
<SCRIPT LANGUAGE="javascript">
document.write("You have visited " +history.length+ "
➦ pages before this one.")
</SCRIPT>
```

Writing **location** *Object Properties*

```
<SCRIPT LANGUAGE="javascript">
document.write("The name of this location is <B>"
➦ + location.host + "</B>." )
</SCRIPT>
```

```
<SCRIPT LANGUAGE="javascript">
document.write("The name of this location is <B>"
➦ + location.hostname + "</B>." )
</SCRIPT>
```

Deconstructing the Scripts

Please notice that the format of calling a property is the same as attaching an object and a method. You write the object name, a dot, and then the property. The biggest difference in the appearance is there are no parentheses after the property. A method affects an object. A property already exists. You just want that property and nothing else, so there is no need for the parentheses instance. Plus, later in the book, we see that those parentheses are used to pass data around. The property already exists and thus has nothing that can be passed to it. Therefore, there's no need for the parentheses.

What Do Those Plus Signs Do?

Ah, you noticed that! You're very observant. Here's the first line of code from the first script:

```
document.write("The background color of this page is <B>"
➦ +document.bgColor+ "</B>.")
```

See the plus signs on either side of the code `document.bgColor`? Those plus signs are central to getting the results of the script.

You already know that whatever is within double quotation marks will be written to the page. This is a `document.write` statement, after all.

Those plus signs are used in JavaScript to set aside the *object.property* code as something that should be returned. You don't want the text `document.bgColor` to appear on the page, you want the property that line of text represents. In this case, it's the document's background color.

By enclosing the document.bgColor statement in plus signs, you tell the JavaScript to go find the property's value and write it in that space. Do you remember, from Figure 1.4, the text that one line of JavaScript wrote to the page? It was

```
The background color of this page is #FFFFFF.
```

The document.bgColor code was replaced by the property it represents.

Hey! The Text Is Bold in Some Places!

Yup. That's another extra little trick thrown in for fun. Look at the code for any of the items that appear in bold. All I did was add the <B> and </B> statements on either side of the object.property code—inside the double quotes. Because this is a document.write statement, the bold commands are written to the page and then act upon the property that was returned. I wanted you to see that you could also affect what is returned from the script, rather than just the text you write within the document.write statement.

Just make sure the HTML commands are inside the double quotes so they are seen as text rather than part of the script commands. If you don't—error.

Now let's find out what all of these properties mean.

Properties of the **document** Object

The HTML document object properties are very popular in JavaScript. The script displays nine. There are actually 19, but examples of the others would be above your heads at this point.

Pay close attention to the capitalization pattern of each property. Every time you write these properties, you must use that pattern. Why? Because that's the way JavaScript likes it:

- bgColor returns the background color in hexadecimal code.
- fgColor returns the foreground color in hexadecimal code.
- linkColor returns the link color in hexadecimal code.
- alinkColor returns the active link color in hexadecimal code.
- vlinkColor returns the visited link color in hexadecimal code.
- location returns the URL, or Web address, of the page. However, if you are not online, meaning no server is involved, this property will not return a value because it has nothing to return.
- referrer returns the page the user came from before the current page. If no page is available, this property returns a blank space. The one drawback to this command is that for a page to be recognized as a referring page, a click must have been made to get to the page containing the document.referrer code. If the page containing the document.referrer code was not arrived at by clicking, the property is returned as blank space.

- ● `title` returns the text between the HTML document's TITLE commands.
- ● `lastModified` returns the date the page was last modified (actually the date the page was uploaded to the server, or last saved on hard disk).

These `document` properties are not shown in the script:

- ● `cookie` returns the user's cookie text file.
- ● `anchors` returns the number of HREF anchors on the page.
- ● `forms` returns an array (listing) of the form items on a page.
- ● `links` returns a number for each individual link.

Properties of the `navigator` Object

People love these properties. The HTML Goodies email box always gets questions about how to display browser characteristics. This is it. The object is `navigator` and it has four properties (watch the capitalization!):

- ● `appName` returns the name of the browser, such as Netscape or Microsoft Internet Explorer.
- ● `appVersion` returns the version number of the browser and the platform it is created for.
- ● `appCodeName` returns the code name given to the browser. Netscape calls its browser Mozilla. Microsoft calls its browser Internet Explorer.
- ● `userAgent` returns the hypertext transfer protocol (HTTP) header used by the browser when working with servers so the server knows what it is dealing with. Web pages use HTTP protocol. You write that at the beginning of each Web page address.

Knowing all this information about the browser is important. Later on, we'll get into IF statements. Knowing the user's browser and version numbers allows you to say IF the browser is this, do this.

Properties of the `history` Object

This is a very popular object. Many readers want to be able to make links that take people back one or more pages, or forward one or more pages, with one click. The purpose is to recreate the Back and Forward buttons at the top of the browser window.

The `history` object has only one property that is supported by both Netscape Navigator and Microsoft's Internet Explorer: `length`. It represents the number of pages the user has visited during the current online session.

Properties of the `location` *Object*

Location is JavaScript for URL, or the address of the page. The `location` object has eight properties and we'll meet a few more later. However, these two properties are by far the most popular: `host` and `hostname`. The properties are equal in that they both do the same thing: return the URL in either IP number or text format depending on what format the server is using.

- `location.host` returns the URL plus the `port` the user is attached to.
- `location.hostname` returns only the URL.

If you are getting the same result with both commands, that means your server has not routed you to a specific port. In technical terms, the `port` property is null.

By the way, these two commands will not work if you are running the page from your hard drive. You must be running this from a server for there to be an address for the script to return.

Your Assignment

OK, smart person—do this: Using one of the `object.property` statements from above, write a JavaScript that creates a link to a page on your server on the HTML document. An example would be if you're on `www.you.com`, the JavaScript will create a link to the page `www.you.com/joe.html`.

 You can see a possible answer on your computer by opening Lesson Three Assignment in the download packet. But do yourself a favor. See it online at `http://www.htmlgoodies.com/JSBook/assignment3.html`*. The answer requires that the page be on a server to get the effect. That should be a pretty good hint right there.*

Lesson 4: Chapter Wrap Up and Review

We've reached the end of Chapter 1. The concept of this lesson is to stop, review the JavaScript commands you've learned to this point, and build something new.

The chapters are progressively longer and you'll be presented with this type of lesson at the end of each. Through years of teaching, Andree and I have learned that one of the hardest things for a student to do is to take what he or she has learned and apply it toward something outside of the realm of the class. In short—make something new. We're going to try to force you to think past just what we're showing you in this book.

Table 1.1 shows the JavaScript commands you've seen up to now.

Table 1.1   JavaScript Commands Demonstrated in Chapter 1

Object	Methods	Properties
document	write()	alinkColor, bgColor, fgColor, linkColor, lastModified, location, referrer, title, vlinkColor
history		length
location		host, hostname
navigator		appCodeName, appName, appVersion, userAgent

You know what each of these commands will do. Now we'll use the commands to create something functional that's different from what you have seen so far. Enter the following JavaScript:

```
<SCRIPT LANGUAGE="javascript">
document.write("Go <A HREF=" +document.referrer+ ">
➥back</A> one page.")
</SCRIPT>
```

Figure 1.5 shows the script's effect.

Figure 1.5
The script creates a link to the previous Web page.

 To see the script's effect on your own computer, open Lesson Four's Script Effect in the download packet or see it online at http://www.htmlgoodies.com/JSBook/previous.html.

23

Notice that this script uses the `document.referrer` object property. It's best to see that online. The page address above will provide a link to click to get to the page with the `document.referrer` code, so you'll see the code's effect correctly.

Deconstructing the Script

The purpose of the script is to create a link back one page. Here's the line of code that does the trick:

```
document.write("Go <A HREF=" +document.referrer+ ">
➥back</A> one page.")
```

It's a basic `document.write()` formula that posts the code of a hypertext link to the page. Note there are no spaces before or next to the double quotes. That means the text returned from the `document.referrer` command will butt right up against the hypertext link text.

The movement back one page through the user's history list is created by returning the `document's referrer` property to the browser to act as a hypertext link. It's simple and it's useful.

Your Assignment

Your final assignment in this chapter is to create something new and useful.

Take a moment and look back over the commands you've learned. What can you do with them? Remember that functionality does not always mean there has to be a flashy effect. You could use the commands to simply communicate with the user.

Here are a couple of suggestions:

- Create a page containing Internet Explorer–only commands and another containing Netscape Navigator-only commands. You could have the page read: `You're using a ***** browser. Please click on the ***** link below to go to a page made just for you.` The ***** would be filled in using some of the commands we've discussed.

- Use the commands to talk to the viewer about the page. The text could read: Thank you for coming in from **** to *****. I see you're using the ***** browser. Good choice.

 The code for both these examples is available for you to look at. Click on Lesson Four Assignment on your download packet or see it online at `http://www.htmlgoodies.com/JSBook/assignment4.html`.

I got the second suggested effect by using multiple `document.write` codes. Think about how you would get the effect and then go to the assignment page to see how I did it.

Chapter 2

Popping Up Text with Mouse Events

This chapter contains the following lessons and scripts:

- Lesson 5: JavaScript's `onMouseOver` Event Handler
- Lesson 6: More Event Handlers
- Lesson 7: `onUnLoad` and `onMouseOut`, the After-Effect Commands
- Lesson 8: HTML 4.0, the `SPAN` Flag, and Some New Event Handlers
- Lesson 9: Let's GO!
- Lesson 10: The Second End of Chapter Review

Lesson 5: JavaScript's `onMouseOver` Event Handler

We've discussed objects, methods, and properties. Now let's start playing with events. Think of events as things that happen. They add life and interest to your Web site. Events are things that make your viewers say "Ooooooo" without your having to create large JavaScripts. *Event Handlers* are the commands that make the events happen.

Now allow me to throw a curve into the process. Events, created using Event Handlers, are JavaScript, but unlike what you've seen so far, they are "built-in" to HTML code rather than standing alone. Event Handlers are meant to be embedded so they don't require the `<SCRIPT>` and `</SCRIPT>` commands. They themselves are not scripts, but are small interfaces allowing for interaction between your page and your reader.

There are multiple events and we'll get to them, but let's start with one of the most popular ones first: onMouseOver. Consider the following JavaScript:

```
<A HREF="http://www.htmlgoodies.com"
➥onMouseOver="window.status='Go to the Goodies Home Page';
➥   return true">Click Here</A>
```

The purpose of this script is to show text in the status bar, as shown in Figure 2.1, when your user rolls his or her mouse over the hypertext link.

Figure 2.1
The onMouseOver *event in our script makes text appear in the status bar.*

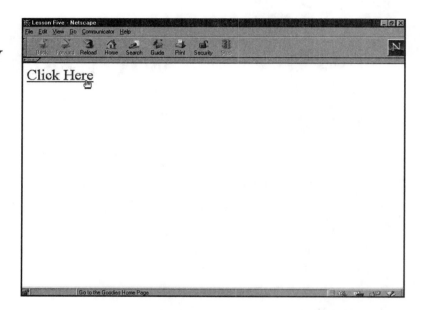

 To see the script working on your computer, click on Lesson Five Script Effect One in your download packet or see it online at http://www.htmlgoodies.com/JSBook/ lesson5effect1.html.

Deconstructing the Script

Knowing what you already know, this one just about explains itself. So let's look at it quickly, and then start to play around with it.

First off, onMouseOver (notice the capitalization pattern) is an Event Handler. It creates an event in conjunction with the hypertext link. Does that make sense? I'm using it *inside* the hypertext link.

The HTML format for the hypertext link remains the same. You use the same commands and the same double quotation marks. The Event Handler is stuck in right after the URL address, as you can see in the code. Now, just to be fair, the Event Handler doesn't have to be after the URL. It could go before, right after the A, but I like it sitting after the URL. It seems to be written in order when it's sitting after the URL. But, if you want it just after the A, go for it. To each their own.

The event is called for by writing `onMouseOver=`, and then telling the browser to do something when the mouse actually does pass over. In this case, `"window.status='Go to the Goodies Home Page'.`

The pattern should look somewhat familiar now: two items separated by a period. The `window` is an object; it exists. `status` is a property of `window`. It is the smaller section of the window where status messages go. You might be familiar with the traditional Document Done text that always appears in the status bar when an HTML page is finished loading. The `window.status` statement tells the browser where the following text should appear. It should appear in the status bar.

NOTE

Is it getting confusing, remembering which are properties and which are methods? I try to keep it straight by thinking that a method will usually be in the form of a verb, such as `write` or `go`. A property is a noun that exists as a smaller part of the item before the dot.

In the script, `window.status` is also followed by an equal sign (=) telling the browser that what follows is supposed to happen when the mouse actually does pass over. In this case, what follows is text *in single quotation marks*:

```
window.status='Go to the Goodies Home Page';
```

That text will show up in the status bar when you roll your mouse over the hypertext link.

Oh, Those Double and Single Quotation Marks

Match them up. When you use double quotation marks at the start of something, use double quotation marks at the end. If you use single quotation marks, use single quotation marks at the end.

The best method to keep the quotation marks straight in your own mind is to think that there is a hierarchy to them. I keep it all straight by thinking that double quotation marks always go on the outside. Single quotation marks sit inside double quotation marks. If there's something inside single quotation marks, such as an HTML attribute, I don't give it quotation marks. Here's an example:

```
OnClick="location.href='page.html'"
```

See how the double quotation marks surround the single quotation marks? If you follow that hierarchy thinking, you're more likely to make sure the quotation marks line up single with single, double with double.

But that is simply a suggestion. As long as you make the quotation marks equal, you're good to go.

That said, make a point of keeping an eye on the quotation marks pattern in each of your scripts. They are quote important.

The Semicolon

In JavaScript, the semicolon acts as a statement terminator. It basically says this code statement is done.

In our script, the semicolon is used because the effect we wanted to achieve through the Event Handler is finished:

```
onMouseOver="window.status='Go to the Goodies Home Page';
➥    return true">Click Here</A>
```

Now we want to do something new.

So why not write the code to a new line? We did just fine without a semicolon in Chapter 1, "The Basics," when we wrote document.write statements. Well, that was a different story. Each of those document.write statements sat on its own line and had only one function. This is different. Now there are two code statements. First there's onMouseOver, and then that return true statement.

That's why it's all on the same line separated by a semicolon. The JavaScript knows the two items are related, and now also understands where one stops and the other begins, thanks to the semicolon.

It should be said here that even though that semicolon is not needed, it is good practice to use one every time you end a line of code. It will help you quickly see where the lines end, and help you be a better JavaScript author. Really. I wouldn't lie to you.

Now, what about that return true code?

return true

Those extra two words have quite a bearing on what will happen when the mouse rolls over the link. If the words are present, the return true statement allows the script to overwrite whatever's there. Notice in the example that when you roll your mouse over the link, the text in the status bar is locked in. It doesn't change if you roll over the link again and again. If you refresh the page, you'll be able to see the effect a little better.

But what if we lose those two words? Well, let's think it out. If we do not have permission to overwrite what's in the status bar—well, we can't overwrite what is in the status bar. When your mouse moves away from the link, the event will only occur once.

If you remember your HTML, the default is to display the URL that the link is pointing to. Then, after the mouse is off the link, the onMouseOver event will take place. The event will occur every time you pass the mouse over the link. It's actually a better effect, in my opinion.

 To see what the effect would look like losing the return true *code, click on Lesson Five Script Effect Two in your download packet or see it online at* http://www.htmlgoodies.com/ JSBook/lesson5effect2.html.

Other Properties, Other Uses

You know other objects must have properties, too. How about a page's background color? In HTML code, the attribute to change the background color is BGCOLOR. Same here, except now we're concerned again with capitalization. In JavaScript, it's written bgColor (capital *C*). So let's think through creating a link that would change the window's background color using an onMouseOver event:

- First off, this will be a link, so it's a pretty good bet that the format is the same as the format in our earlier script. We'll keep it.
- Are we changing the window or are we changing our old standby, the document? Well, where does the BGCOLOR command go when you write a Web page? In the document. That must be the object we're concerned with. Let's change window in the earlier code to document.
- We want to change the document object's background, so let's change status to bgColor.
- We no longer want text to appear, so let's change that text to a color. We'll use pink.
- When we move the mouse over the link we probably want the color to stay whether the mouse runs over the links again or not, so we'll need to re-enter the return true after the semicolon.

Here's the resulting JavaScript:

```
<A HREF="http://www.htmlgoodies.com"
➥onMouseOver="document.bgColor='pink'; return true">Click Here</A>
```

 To see the background color effect, click on Lesson Five Script Effect Three in your download packet or see it online at http://www.htmlgoodies.com/JSBook/lesson5effect3.html.

But what if you want both effects, the background color change and the text in the status bar? OK, let's think it through:

☒ Common sense would suggest you write two onMouseOver commands. Let's try that.

The two commands are not separate from each other. We want them to occur at the same time, so we cannot separate them using a semicolon because we know a semicolon is a statement terminator.

☒ Here's a new rule: Use a comma when setting multiple JavaScript events.

And what about all those pesky quotation marks? Remember the double quotation marks go around the entire Event Handler statement and single quotation marks go around the effects, such as text to be printed or in the color to be used.

☒ Well, we want these two onMouseOver commands to happen as one, so we only need double quotation marks at the very beginning of the first Event Handler statement and at the very end of the second one. That way the quotation marks surround it all, showing it to the browser as if it were one event.

☒ The single quotation marks surround the color and the text.

Here's the resulting JavaScript:

```
<A HREF="http://www.htmlgoodies.com"
onMouseOver="document.bgColor='pink',
➥onMouseOver=window.status='Go to the Goodies Home Page';
➥return true">Click Here</A>
```

 See this double effect by clicking in Lesson Five Script Effect Four in your download packet or see it online at http://www.htmlgoodies.com/JSBook/lesson5effect4.html.

These Event Handlers are great and there are a slew of them. In the next lesson, we'll go over a whole handful.

NOTE

You might have noticed that the lessons are starting to "think things through" a bit. Remember that the JavaScript language is very logical. Later in this book, there will be a lesson just on the hierarchy of items because the language is so logical. Just for now, try taking a few minutes before you write and thinking out what must happen for your idea to come to life in script.

Your Assignment

Let's see whether I can't trip you up on this one. I'm going to give you a new method for this assignment: alert(). What it does is pop up a small dialog box with text written above an OK button. See whether you can get the alert box to pop up when your mouse rolls across a hypertext link. Here's the format:

```
alert('text that appears on the alert box')
```

Think it through, what must happen first, second, and so on. It's actually quite simple, not that that's a hint or anything.

 See a possible answer by clicking on Lesson Five Assignment in your packet download or see it online at `http://www.htmlgoodies.com/JSBook/assignment5.html`.

Lesson 6: More Event Handlers

Well, now you've got the basic hang of Event Handlers. So let's take a lesson and see a few more in action. Event Handlers all work basically the same way. As long as you know the format of the event, and then think through the logic of getting it to run, you'll be able to place these all over your pages.

The onClick *Command*

Think about onMouseOver. You already know onMouseOver causes an event when the mouse is passed over a link. It can be used other places, but to this point you've only seen it used in a link. Well, if passing over the link causes the event, clicking on the link should be just as successful when you use the onClick Event Handler. That seems logical, yes?

I'll use the alert method to show this one off. If you did the assignment from the last lesson, you know how it is used. But just for memory's sake, the alert format goes this way:

```
alert('Text that appears on the alert box')
```

So, following the same pattern as the onMouseOver, we get this JavaScript:

```
<A HREF="http://www.htmlgoodies.com"
➥onClick="alert('You are off!');">Click Here</A>
```

The result appears in Figure 2.2.

Figure 2.2
Using onClick *to display an alert box.*

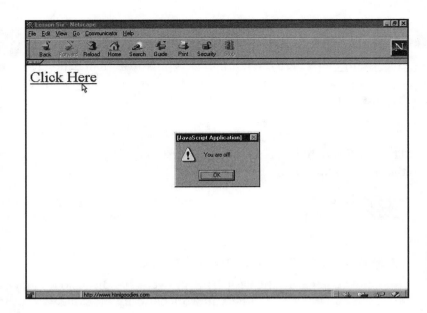

 See the effect on your computer by clicking on Lesson Six Script's Effect in your download packet or see it online at http://www.htmlgoodies.com/JSBook/lesson6effect.html.

> **TIP**
>
> Here's a good piece of knowledge to keep handy. In the previous example, I wrote *You are* instead of *You're*. There's a reason for that. If I had written *You're*, the apostrophe would have been seen by the browser as the end of the text, and not as a contraction as you intended it. Error.

The onFocus *Event Handler*

This is a great Event Handler that allows you to create action when your reader uses the mouse, tabs, or arrow keys to focus on one item on the page. This will work for FORM object drop-down boxes, text boxes, and textarea boxes.

Here's an example using a text box:

```
<FORM>
<INPUT TYPE="text" SIZE="30"
➥onFocus="window.status='Write your name in the box';">
</FORM>
```

Figure 2.3 shows the result of this JavaScript; as you can see, I followed the directions onscreen and entered my name.

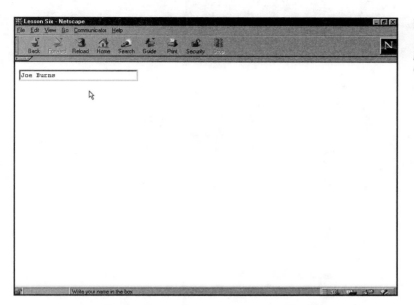

Figure 2.3
When the text box has focus, the status bar text appears.

TIP

Never make an alert box the event of an onFocus Event Handler. Here's why. Let's say you had the onFocus set up on a text box, just the same way I do in the preceding code. You click on the text box and the alert pops up. That causes focus to be lost from the text box. When you close the alert box, focus returns to the text box and the alert pops back up. It's a pretty nasty loop to get yourself caught in.

 See the effect on your computer by clicking on Lesson Six Script's Effect Two in your download packet or see it online at http://www.htmlgoodies.com/JSBook/lesson6effect2.html.

The onBlur *Event Handler*

If you can focus on an item, you can *blur*, or lose focus, on an item. The onBlur Event Handler allows you to alert a user to the fact that he has changed her input or answer.

You can pretty much guess at the code, but here it is anyway:

```
<FORM>
<INPUT TYPE="text" SIZE="40" onBlur="alert('You changed your answer -
➥ Is it still correct?');">
</FORM>
```

The resulting effect appears in Figure 2.4.

Figure 2.4
This alert box appears after clicking off the text box.

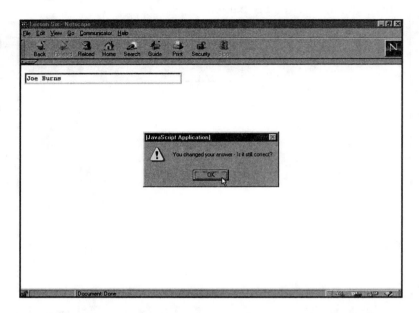

 See the effect on your computer by clicking on Lesson Six Script's Effect Three in your download packet or see it online at `http://www.htmlgoodies.com/JSBook/` `lesson6effect3.html.`

The onChange *Event Handler*

This command works much the same way as onBlur. Its main function is to work as a check mechanism. Think of this as an event that makes sure the user fills in what you are asking for:

```
<form>
<INPUT TYPE="text" SIZE="40"
➥onChange="alert('The text box has been changed')">
</form>
```

The result of this JavaScript appears in Figure 2.5.

onChange is a strange command in that even if the user doesn't change anything in the box, he or she can trigger the effect by revisiting the box. Maybe an onFocus might be a better choice for a text box? Try both and see what you think.

Figure 2.5
This alert box appears after the data in the text box is altered.

 See the effect on your computer by clicking on Lesson Six Script's Effect Four in your download packet or see it online at http://www.htmlgoodies.com/JSBook/lesson6effect4.html.

The onSubmit *Command*

This is the command everyone seems to want to lay his hands on. This command allows you to make the page change when the Submit button is clicked. People want this because they seem to require that wonderful effect when the user clicks on a form's Submit button, and the page changes to another page that says Thanks for writing!

Here's the format:

```
<FORM>
<INPUT TYPE="submit"  onSubmit="alert('thanksalot.html')";>
</FORM>
```

 This Event Handler is difficult to show you as a figure, so see the effect on your computer by clicking on Lesson Six Script's Effect Five in your download packet. Or see it online at http://www.htmlgoodies.com/JSBook/lesson6effect5.html.

location.href

You've noticed there are a few new commands in the previous script that responds to the Submit button. location.href is another command that causes a response—it is the basic format for setting up a link to another page. The href property might be new to you, but if you've programmed in HTML at all, you can guess what it means. HREF stands for *H*ypertext *REF*erence. It creates a link to another page. I use this format a great deal.

Just make a point of the single and double quotation mark configuration. Double quotation marks surround location through the end of the command. The page that the link will send the user to is surrounded in single quotation marks.

Remember, you have to surround the page location in quotation marks, but double quotation marks suggest to the browser that the command is over. So use single quotation marks.

The onLoad *Event Handler*

The onLoad Event Handler is a great, and extremely useful, command. Unlike the other Event Handers we've examined, onLoad sits within the HTML document's BODY flag. It's enacted when the page finishes loading into the browser window. The following example pops up a simple alert box to welcome the user to the page:

```
<BODY onLoad="alert('Thanks for coming to my page')">
```

Later in the book, you'll be using the onLoad command to trigger larger scripts to start working. It will become a real tool in your JavaScript toolbox.

Figure 2.6 shows the result of the onLoad JavaScript.

Figure 2.6
An alert box pops up when the page loads.

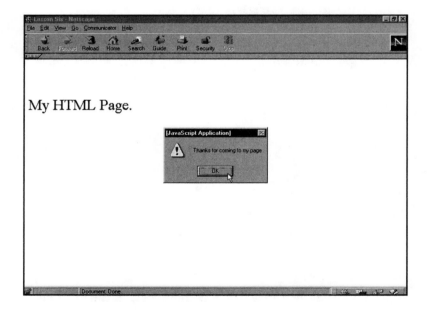

See the effect on your computer by clicking on Lesson Six Script's Effect Six in your download packet or see it online at http://www.htmlgoodies.com/JSBook/lesson6effect6.html.

Your Assignment

For this assignment, I want you to create a form that has some interaction with the user. I'm assuming you know how to create forms here. If forms are a bit foreign to you, see this HTML Goodies tutorial: http://www.htmlgoodies.com/tutors/forms.html.

The form should have four elements: a text box that asks for the person's name, two check boxes that ask whether the person prefers chocolate or vanilla, and a Submit button. Now, here's what I want to happen with each item:

- The text box should print Put your name in here in the status bar when the user fills it in.
- The two check boxes should write You have chosen --- in the status bar, indicating the user's choice.
- The Submit button should pop up an alert box thanking the user for filling out the form.

 See a possible answer on your own computer by clicking on Lesson Six Assignment in your download packet, or see it online at http://www.htmlgoodies.com/JSBook/assignment6.html.

Lesson 7: onUnload **and** onMouseOut, **the After-Effect Commands**

There are two great after-effect Event Handler commands you should have in your arsenal: onMouseOut and onUnload. Again, watch the capitalization pattern.

You already know the onMouseOver command makes things happen when the mouse passes over something on the HTML page. The onMouseOut command acts after the mouse leaves the link. You also know the onLoad command makes something happen when the HTML page fully loads. Well, the onUnload command makes something happen when the user unloads or leaves the page.

Both are quite useful, but try to keep the events that occur from your onUnload short. You don't want to slow the loading of the incoming page.

This script uses the onUnload Event Handler:

```
<BODY onUnload="alert('Leaving so soon?')">
```

This script uses the onMouseOut Event Handler:

```
<A HREF="thanksalot.html"
onMouseOver="window.status='Hey! Get off of me!'; return true
"onMouseOut="window.status='Much better - Thanks'; return true">
Place your mouse on and off of this</A>
```

The examples, shown in Figures 2.7a and 2.7b, actually use both scripts. In Figure 2.7a, there is a link on the HTML page that will produce text in the status bar both when the mouse passes over it and when the mouse leaves, thanks to the onMouseOver and onMouseOut Event Handlers. In Figure 2.7b, when you actually click on the link, the onUnload Event Handler pops up the alert window asking, Leaving so soon?

Figure 2.7a
onMouseOut *text appears in the status bar when the mouse leaves the link.*

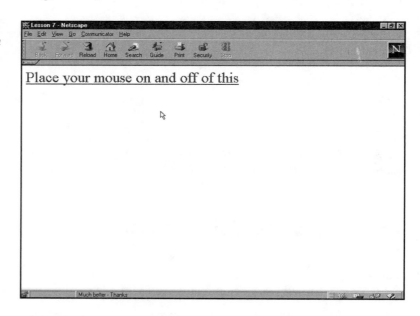

 See the effect on your computer by clicking on Lesson Seven's Script Effect in your download packet or see it online at http://www.htmlgoodies.com/JSBook/lesson7effect.html.

Deconstructing the Script

There's not a lot to tell that you probably haven't figured out for yourself at this point. The mouse-over effects are created by the onMouseOver and onMouseOut commands.

Please notice that unlike the simultaneous onMouseOver and bgColor effect from Lesson 5, the two commands here are quite separate from each other. You do not want these happening at the same time.

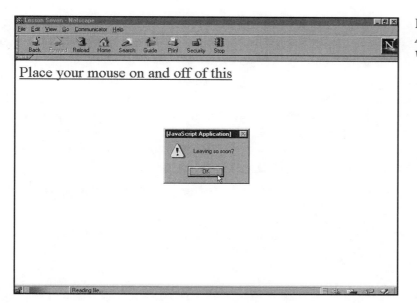

Figure 2.7b
An alert box is produced when the link is clicked.

You want one thing to happen when the mouse passes over the link and another to happen when the mouse moves off. So you write them as two totally separate commands, both containing their own return true statements, forcing the text to remain after the fact.

The effect when you're leaving the page was created by adding the onUnload="alert('Leaving so soon?')" command to the BODY flag of the HTML document.

Again, please notice the placements of the double and single quotation marks. You cannot use the double quotation marks surrounding the text because that would mean double quotation marks inside of double quotation marks. The browser would see it as the end of a line, and not understand what follows. Error.

You'll get lots o' use out of these Event Handlers.

Your Assignment

You're going to use an onUnload, an onMouseOver, and an onMouseOut in this assignment. Here's what I want to happen:

- Create a page with a hypertext link. The link should place the text Hello *browser name* user - Click here! in the status bar when the mouse passes over.
- The text You should leave *page URL* right away will then appear when the mouse moves off of the link.
- When the link is actually clicked, an alert should pop up that reads Leaving so soon? Do not use an onClick command to get the alert box. Use the onUnload command.

Think about it for a minute. You've been able to get `document.property` returns to appear on the page. Now, how do you get them to appear in the status bar? You need to combine the two formats you learned so far in this chapter with what you learned in Chapter 1. You can do it.

Hint: The problem you'll run into involves the double and single quotation marks. Remember that in a `document.write` command, the double quotation marks mean text to be printed to the page. Well, now you have double quotation marks around the entire text for the `window.status` command, so those double quotation marks around the text are out the window. Use single quotation marks instead.

But in case you don't hit it on the first try, read the error messages. They'll tell you where the problem is.

 See a possible answer to this assignment by clicking on Lesson Seven Assignment in your download packet or see it online at `http://www.htmlgoodies.com/JSBook/` `assignment7.html`.

Lesson 8: HTML 4.0, the SPAN Flag, and Some New Event Handlers

In late 1998, the World Wide Web Consortium (`http://www.w3c.org`) gave its thumbs-up to a new version of HTML, HTML 4.0. With the new version came new HTML flags, and with the new HTML flags, new JavaScript Event Handlers. As of the writing of this book, February 1999, a few of the new Event Handlers could be run using the Internet Explorer 4.0 and Netscape Navigator wouldn't run any of them. But time marches on, and soon these new Event Handlers will be in widespread use.

This lesson's example script will show three of those new Event Handlers in action. You'll also be introduced to a new HTML 4.0 delivery device flag, SPAN.

The SPAN Flag

First, let's look at the template for our example script. It looks like this:

```
<SPAN JavaScript Event Handlers>Text on HTML Page</SPAN>
```

If you haven't seen the SPAN HTML flag before, be prepared to become very familiar with it. As HTML 4.0 comes more and more into the mainstream, this flag will become the darling of Web artists everywhere.

"What does it do?" you ask? Nothing. Not a darn thing. The SPAN flag has no properties at all to affect or manipulate text or images in any way. In fact, if you take a piece of text and surround it with the `<SPAN>` and `</SPAN>` flags, you won't alter the text at all. The viewer wouldn't know it was there unless he looked at the source code.

But there has to be a reason this book is devoting page- space to the <SPAN> flag. There is and with good reason.

SPAN is a delivery device. The flag itself has no effect. But that's the point. SPAN's whole purpose is to act as a platform to carry other HTML attributes and JavaScript commands to text, images, tables, or whatever else you can think of to surround with <SPAN> and </SPAN>.

Look at the format again:

```
<SPAN JavaScript Event Handlers>Text on HTML Page</SPAN>
```

The text that is surrounded by the SPAN flags can include any Event Handler you've seen to this point. Once inside the SPAN flag, the Event Handler will be enacted when the user interacts with the text in some way.

Here's an example before we get into the specifics of this lesson's script. Let's say you wanted to create a piece of text that acted as a hypertext link, but didn't carry the blue coloring or the underline. You wanted it to look like any other text. Believe it or not, this is actually a fairly popular request. HTML Goodies receives a fair amount of mail asking how it's done.

Think it out. The link will occur when the text is clicked. That would suggest we use the onClick Event Handler. Then we need to set it so that when the user clicks, the page changes. You already know location.href as the code that creates a link. So let's build it.

The format would look like this:

```
<SPAN onClick="location.href='page.html'">Click to Go</SPAN>
```

 Now you have text that retains its color but carries with it the properties of a link, thanks to JavaScript. You can try out the link above by clicking on Lesson Eight Script's Effect Two in your download packet or see it online at http://www.htmlgoodies.com/JSBook/ lesson8effect2.html.

The Example Script

Now, let's look at this lesson's example script:

```
<SPAN onMouseDown="window.status='Mouse Is Down'";
onMouseUp="window.status='Mouse Is Up'";
➥onDblClick="location.href='thanksalot.html'";>
Click on this text
</SPAN>
```

The script's effect is shown in Figure 2.8. See the effect on your computer by clicking on Lesson Eight's Script Effect in your download packet or see it online at http://www.htmlgoodies.com/JSBook/lesson8effect.html.

Figure 2.8
Multiple event handlers are applied to this window.

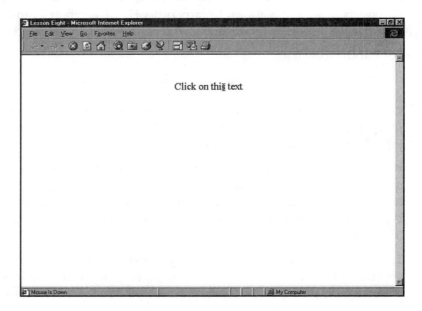

Make a point of looking at the example in an Internet Explorer browser, version 4.0 or higher. Those browsers will support the HTML flags and JavaScript commands. By the time you're reading this, other browsers might support the code too, but at the time of writing of this book, Internet Explorer 4.0 (and above) was the only available browser to display this script properly.

Deconstructing the Script

The script starts with the <SPAN> flag. There are three new JavaScript Event Handlers inside the flag.

The first Event Handler, onMouseDown, is enacted when the user has his or her pointer on the text and clicks down. Notice the Event Hander is set up to place text in the status bar.

Although the semicolon is not needed, I still use it to help me quickly see where each piece of code ends. It's my preference. You don't have to have it in your code.

The second Event Handler, onMouseUp, posts text to the status bar when the user lets the mouse click back up.

The third Event Handler, onDblClick, is put into use when the user double-clicks on the link. In this script, the double-click will send the user to a new page named thanksalot.html.

The text that will appear on the HTML document page is then written after the <SPAN> flag.

Finally, the </SPAN> flag ends the entire format.

The New Event Handlers

You've seen three of them in this lesson's script, onMouseDown, onMouseUp, and onDblClick. Note the capitalization pattern of each.

Now that I've whetted your appetite, here are a few other new Event Handlers and what they do.

- onKeyDown reacts when the user presses a key.
- onKeyUp reacts when the user lets the key back up.
- onKeyPress reacts when the user clicks a key up and down.
- onMouseMove reacts when the user moves the mouse.

Just remember that the Event Handlers in this lesson are not supported across the board yet, so use them sparingly, if at all. If you do use them, test them in a few different browsers on your own computer before posting the pages to the Web. If you can't run the command, the user probably can't either.

Your Assignment

Use the SPAN flag and a couple of Event Handlers on the text Green to Red so that when the mouse passes over it, the background turns green. When the mouse leaves the text, the background turns red. You'll get bonus points if you can get the page to change to purple when the user double-clicks.

Hint: Use Internet Explorer 4.0 or better to view your work.

 You can see a possible answer by clicking on Lesson Eight Assignment in your download packet or see it online at http://www.htmlgoodies.com/JSBook/assignment8.html.

Lesson 9: Let's GO!

So far, this chapter has dealt with user interaction through JavaScript Event Handlers. This particular lesson will deal with a new method, go(). Although putting a method in with a group of Event Handlers seems a bit odd, it isn't. The go() method often acts along with Event Handlers to move your user through his or her history object.

This lesson's JavaScript is as follows:

```
<FORM>
<INPUT TYPE="button" VALUE="BACK" onClick="history.go(-1)">
<INPUT TYPE="button" VALUE="FORWARD" onClick="history.go(1)">
</FORM>
```

This is a very popular use of the go() method. The code produces two buttons that act the same way as the Back and Forward buttons at the top of your browser window. Figure 2.9 shows these buttons in a browser.

Figure 2.9
Buttons that move users through their history *object.*

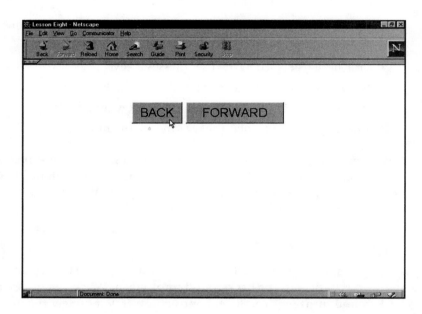

See the effect on your computer by clicking on Lesson Nine's Script Effect in your download packet or see it online at http://www.htmlgoodies.com/JSBook/lesson9effect.html.

Deconstructing the Script

The code for the two buttons is both HTML and JavaScript. The buttons are both FORM items created using this HTML code:

```
<FORM>
<INPUT TYPE="button" VALUE="BACK">
<INPUT TYPE="button" VALUE="FORWARD">
</FORM>
```

Using this format alone, the buttons will display, but they're little more than nice gray rectangles that don't actually do anything. It's the Event Handler and go() method that creates the effect.

The BACK Button

The code for the BACK button looks like this:

```
<INPUT TYPE="button" VALUE="BACK" onClick="history.go(-1)">
```

Let's read it from left to right.

- INPUT is HTML code for an input item.
- TYPE="button" tells the browser that the input item will be a button.
- VALUE="BACK" puts the text on the button.
- onClick= is the Event Handler that will trigger what follows it when the user clicks on the button.
- history.go is an object.method format JavaScript statement you should be pretty familiar with by now. history is the object. It represents the record the browser keeps of the user's current online session. Basically, it's a record of every page the user has been to, in order. The go method (parentheses left off on purpose) acts to move the user through that history object.
- (-1) is the instance of the method go. The -1 is telling the method to move one page back through the user's history object.

It would seem logical that if go(-1) is acceptable, go(-2) or go(-34) is also acceptable. They are. Just remember that the higher the number you put in that instance, the more pages the user will have had to have visited before coming to the current page. If the user is visiting the page containing this code first, the button is basically dead because there is no such thing as -1 in the history object.

However, there is one small exception to this rule. In Microsoft Internet Explorer 3.0, any negative value that is put into the go method parentheses will only send the user back one page. It's a known bug. You might want to keep that in mind when thinking about sending the user back multiple pages. Maybe one is enough.

The FORWARD Button

This code is similar to what you saw for the BACK button:

```
<INPUT TYPE="button" VALUE="FORWARD" onCLick="history.go(1)">
```

There are only two differences:

- VALUE= has been changed so that the button text will now read FORWARD, rather than BACK.

- go() has been changed to now read a positive number, rather than a negative one. It will move the user forward through the history object list.

The method is the same, except that now when the user clicks on the button, the next page up in the history object is loaded.

The FORWARD button is often dead because users might not have gone to another page and then returned to the page containing the code. However, I would still offer the button. Those who have gone to another page and returned can use it, and those who have not probably won't use it, knowing they didn't go anywhere. And if they do click the button, nothing will happen because there isn't a page to go to in the history object.

Your Assignment

The HTML Goodies site gets a great deal of mail asking how to set up guestbook, or form, pages so that when the user clicks to submit the page, either a thank-you page loads, or the user is taken back to the page where he or she came from before clicking to fill out the guestbook.

The second scenario is your assignment. Create a small guestbook, one text box will do, so that when the user clicks to submit the form, he or she is taken back to the page they came from to fill out the guestbook form.

 You can see one possible answer by clicking on Lesson Nine Assignment in your download packet or see it online at http://www.htmlgoodies.com/JSBook/assignment9.html.

The page that loads following this link will offer a link to the guestbook page. After you fill in the text box and submit, the original assignment page will reload.

Lesson 10: The Second End of Chapter Review

Once again, we're going to stop, look at the JavaScript commands you've learned up to this point, and build some new scripts. I'll offer one new script in this lesson, and then make a suggestion or two for some new scripts. But keep in mind the purpose of these reviews is for you to take what you've learned so far and create a new and functional script to use on your pages.

Table 2.1 contains the object-related JavaScript commands you've learned up to now. In addition, you've seen these other JavaScript elements:

- The alert() method
- These Event Handlers: onBlur, onChange, onClick, onDblClick, onFocus, onKeyDown, onKeyPress, onKeyUp, onLoad, onMouseDown, onMouseMove, onMouseOut, onMouseOver, onMouseUp, onSubmit
- The HTML 4.0 flag <SPAN>

Table 2.1 Object-Related JavaScript Commands Demonstrated in Chapters 1 and 2

Object	Methods	Properties
document	write()	alinkColor, bgColor, fgColor, linkColor, lastModified, location, referrer, title, vlinkColor
history	go()	length
location		host, hostname, href
navigator		appCodeName, appName, appVersion, userAgent
window		status

That's actually a pretty impressive list of commands. You can create some very nice JavaScripts out of just what I've listed, as you can see here:

```
<SPAN onClick="document.write('<FONT SIZE=+2>
➥To get to the other side.</FONT><FORM>
➥<INPUT TYPE=button VALUE=BACK onClick=history.go(-1)></FORM>')">
Why did the chicken cross the road?
</SPAN>
```

Allow me to explain a bit before you start copying the script. I am getting the before-and-after effect shown in Figures 2.10 and 2.11 by using only one <SPAN> flag. Remember that you cannot break document.write commands into multiple lines or the script will throw an error. So the entire preceding code should be kept on one long line. Also, because of the SPAN flag, you should look at this script's example in an Internet Explorer browser, version 4.0 or above.

Figure 2.10
The window before you click on the text.

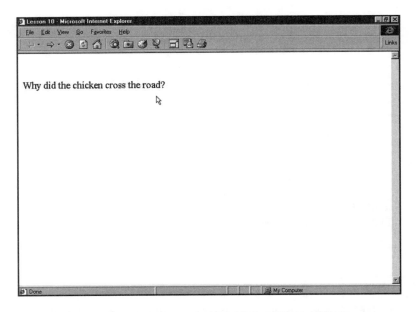

Figure 2.11
The window after you click on the text.

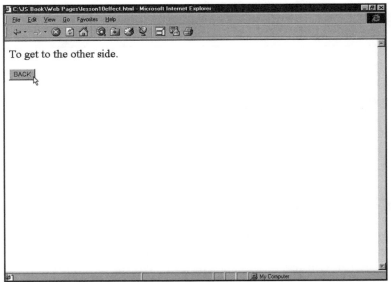

See the effect on your computer by clicking on Lesson Ten's Script Effect in your download packet or see it online at http://www.htmlgoodies.com/JSBook/lesson10effect.html.

Deconstructing the Script

When the script says `document.write`, it means `document.write`.

As you've been reading through this chapter, did you stop and wonder what would happen if you put a `document.write` statement after an Event Handler? Well, here's what happens: An entirely new document is written over the one currently in the browser window.

Look at the title bar on Figure 2.10: It says `Lesson Ten`. The title bar of Figure 2.11 says `JSBook\Web Pages\Lesson10effect.html`. The reason is that by putting the `document.write` command with an `onClick`, the browser did what you told it to. It wrote a brand-new page.

This is the code that did the trick:

```
<SPAN onClick="document.write('<FONT SIZE=+2>
➡To get to the other side.</FONT><FORM>
➡<INPUT TYPE=button VALUE=BACK onClick=history.go(-1)></FORM>')">
</SPAN>
```

I'll stress again that the code should all go on one line. The book page just isn't long enough to show it that way.

Let's take it piece by piece.

● `<SPAN>` is the HTML 4.0 code that acts as a delivery device so you can apply the `onClick` to an item, which in this case is text.

● `onClick=` is the Event Handler that will trigger what follows it when the user clicks.

● `document.write=` is the `object.method` statement used to write the text to the page. Please take note that there are double quotation marks before `document.write` and again at the very end of the SPAN flag, right before the >.

● There are single quotation marks around all of the text within the `document.write` instance.

● `<FONT SIZE=+2>To get to the other side.</FONT>` is basic HTML code that produces text at a font size of plus three.

● `<FORM><INPUT TYPE=button VALUE=BACK onClick=history.go(-1)></FORM>` is the HTML and JavaScript code that creates a BACK button. You just saw that in Lesson 9. The code will create a button that moves the user back one page on his or her `history` object. Notice there are no quotation marks around `button`, `BACK`, or `history.go(-1)`. You've already used double quotation marks around the `document.write` statement. Single quotation marks were used around the text in the instance. There's no quotation mark smaller than single quotation marks, so you don't use any.

● Finally, the text that will appear on the page is written in and the `</SPAN>` flag ends the code.

As I said earlier in this chapter, JavaScript is very logical. When you're creating a new script, stop and think about what you want to happen, what must come before what, and then write the code in a linear fashion. You should be able to break it down like I broke down the preceding lines of code.

Now take some time to think about what you can do with the commands you already know.

Your Assignment

Make something of your own. May I suggest using the `document.location` statement to create a reload button?

Or how about a line of hypertext that takes the user to a new page without having to click? A simple mouse pass would create the change of the page.

 I have both of those suggested scripts available for you to view if you click on Lesson Ten Assignment in your download packet. Or see it online at `http://www.htmlgoodies.com/ JSBook/assignment10.html`.

But first, go make your own!

Chapter 3

Manipulating Data and the Hierarchy of JavaScript

This chapter contains the following lessons and scripts:

- Lesson 11: Prompts and Variables
- Lesson 12: Dates and Times
- Lesson 13: Hierarchy of Objects
- Lesson 14: Creating a Function
- Lesson 15: An Introduction to Arrays
- Lesson 16: The Third End of Chapter Review—A `<BODY>` Flag Script

The JavaScript commands in this chapter were grouped together because they all deal with data in some way, shape, or form. That data can consist of dates, times, or input from the user. In addition, each of these lessons will introduce you to one of the most important topics in JavaScript, the hierarchy of objects.

You have already been introduced to JavaScript hierarchy in the `object.method` and `object.property` statements in the previous lesson. But now we get into creating hierarchy with variables and other types of JavaScript data.

As Lesson 13 states, "...after you understand the hierarchy of objects, you've conquered JavaScript."

Lesson 11: Prompts and Variables

I have two concepts in this lesson. One, the prompt box, you'll use when you want to prompt the user for information. The second, creating variables, you'll use throughout the remainder of your JavaScript life. Let's begin by examining these concepts.

Creating a Variable

The concept of variables is paramount in JavaScript. You must know how to create them. When you create a variable, you are denoting a one-word (or one-letter) representation for the output of a JavaScript command line. Remember when we were posting the name of the browser to the page using the method `appName`? When we placed the name into the `document.write` statement, we wrote out the entire `navigator.appName`. Because we only did it once, it wasn't so hard. But what if we wanted to write it ten times across the same page? Writing those nine characters again and again would get boring.

So we assign a variable to represent the output of the method. Let's say we choose the variable `NA`. That way, we would only have to write `navigator.appName` once and assign `NA` to it. The rest of the way through, we would only write `NA` when we wanted the `navigator.appName`. With me? Let's get back to this example.

This lesson's script will use the following line to denote a variable:

```
var username = prompt ("Write your name in the box below",
➥"Write it here")
```

We created the variable following this format:

- 🔵 `var` proclaims that the word immediately following will be the variable name.
- 🔵 `username` is the name of the variable. I made this up. It didn't have to be this long. In fact, I could have made it `N` if I wanted. It's always best to make the variable names so that you can easily remember what the variables represent. Just remember that JavaScript is case sensitive, so if you spell your code word *Dog*, the *D* has to remain capitalized every time you call for it, or the browser will see it as two separate names.
- 🔵 The equal sign (=) denotes that the variable name will equal the output of the commands that follow. In this case, the variable will represent the output of the prompt box.

One more thing: Variable names can be just about any word, or combination of letters and numbers you want; however, some variable names are off-limits.

For instance, you do not want to create a variable name that is the same word as a JavaScript command. You know you didn't mean for the word to be used as a command, but the computer doesn't.

In addition to not using JavaScript commands as variable names, Appendix C, "JavaScript Reserved Variable Words," has a list of other words you should avoid. Some of the words are already in use as JavaScript commands, and some are reserved words that will be used in upcoming JavaScript versions. You might want to take a quick look at the list before going further.

I've found that as long as you create a variable name that is representative of the data, you shouldn't run into any trouble. But just to be sure, take a look at Appendix C.

Please notice that there are no quotes surrounding either var or the variable name. Just follow one word with the next as shown in the code.

The `Prompt` Command

I use a new command in this example: `Prompt`. This method pops up a box prompting the user for a response.

Here's the basic format of the prompt:

```
var variable_name = prompt("Message on the gray box","Default Reply")
```

The default reply is the text that will appear in the user entry field on the prompt box. You should include text in case the user doesn't fill anything in. That way, you'll have something for the JavaScript to work with.

But if you like the look of an empty user entry field on the prompt box, that's fine. If the user doesn't enter any text, the text *null* will be returned for you.

In case you're wondering...

To get a blank white box in the user entry field, do not write any text between the second set of quotes. And yes, you need the quotes even if they're empty. If you do not put the second set of quotes in, the white box will read *undefined*.

The var and the variable name you assigned are included in the format. They have to be, otherwise you'll get the prompt, but nothing will be done with the data the user enters.

The Example Script

We're now back to creating full JavaScripts rather than just adding events to HTML, so we'll need to once again start using the full `<SCRIPT LANGUAGE="javascript">` to `</SCRIPT>` format.

Here's what we're going to do. We'll ask the user for his or her name, and assign a variable to that name. After the variable is assigned, we can enter it into a document.write line that will post the user's name to the page. The script is as follows:

```
<SCRIPT LANGUAGE="javascript">
/*This script is intended to take information from the user
and place it upon the page*/
var username = prompt ("Write your name in the box below",
➥"Write it here");
document.write("Hello " + username + ". Welcome to my page!");
</SCRIPT>
```

This script will bring up a prompt box to the page asking for the user's name, as shown in Figure 3.1. Figure 3.2 shows the result after the user enters his or her name and clicks OK.

Figure 3.1
The prompt box asks for the user's name.

To see this script's effect on your computer, click on Lesson 11 Effect in your download packet or see it online at http://www.htmlgoodies.com/JSBook/lesson11effect.html.

Wait! What Are Those /* and */ Things?

Yeah, I stuck in two extra commands that comment out text in the script. When you *comment out* something, the text will sit in the source code for you and anyone else who's interested to read, but it won't affect the script nor show up on the resulting page. It's a great way to add copyrights, tell what the script does, and generally help yourself along by adding text that's not part of the script.

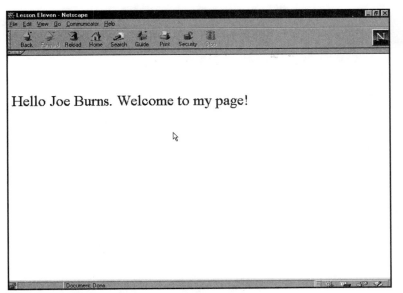

Figure 3.2
*The script responds appro-
priately to the user's input.*

These comment commands allow for multiple lines. Just have /* at the beginning and */ at the end, and everything in between will comment out. You can write a whole paragraph of commented text as long as it is between the two comment commands.

Deconstructing the Script

Now that you know all the parts of the prompt, let's examine the meat of the script:

```
var user_name = prompt ("Write your name in the box below",
➥"Write it here");
document.write("Hello " + user_name + ". Welcome to my page!");
```

- The variable name username is assigned to the output of the prompt.
- The prompt asks the user to write his name in the box. The white box reads "Write it here".
- A semicolon ends the line because I wanted it there. It is not needed.
- The document.write statement calls for the text "Hello " (space for continuity).
- The plus sign (+) denotes what follows will return a value.
- username is representative of the output of the prompt. No quotes—we don't want it printed.
- Another plus sign.
- ". Welcome to my page!" with a period and a space for continuity completes the text.
- The semicolon is placed on purpose to show me that the line has ended.

That's all.

Please make a point of truly understanding the concept of variables before you proceed. Variables are used extensively in this language. If you're lost at this point, reread the lesson.

Your Assignment

...is a review.

Let's combine a couple of the commands we've learned so far with the new variable and prompt commands we just learned.

Here's what I want you to do:

- Create two prompts. One will ask for the first name and one will ask for the last name. Don't let this throw you, just create two fully formed prompt lines line in the preceding script, and assign each one a different variable name. One will simply follow the other in the script.

- Using the prompts, create this line of text: Hello first-name last-name. I see you are using *browser-name*. Thanks for coming to *document-title*.

  BUT! Write the code so that the *browser-name* and *document title* items are called by the variables BN and PT, respectively.

- Think it through and then write the script. There's bonus points if you comment out a couple of lines.

 You can see a possible answer to this assignment on your own computer by clicking on Lesson Eleven Assignment in your download packet or see it online at http://www.htmlgoodies.com/JSBook/assignment11.html.

Lesson 12: Dates and Times

What's nice about writing JavaScript right to a Web page is all the stuff that already exists that you can grab and display.

In this lesson, we'll talk about how you can display existing information using a new object, Date, and seven new methods: getDay(), getDate(), getMonth(), getYear(), getHours(), getMinutes(), and getSeconds().

Date is an object that contains the current day of the week, month, day of the month, current hour, current minute, current second, and current year. All that and looks too, huh?

So, if `Date` has all that, why use any of the methods? Because you might not want all of that stuff every time. What if you only want the day of the week? Then you use `getDay()` to extract just that day of the week from the `Date` object.

The Date and Time Methods

Even before beginning to delve into the example script, let's explain each of `Date` object methods. They are quirky to say the least.

First off, all seven methods return numbers rather than text. It would be nice if `getDay()` would give you Monday, or Wednesday, or Saturday, but it doesn't. It gives you a number between 0 and 6.

Between 0 and 6?

Yup. Allow me to introduce you to one of the more frustrating aspects of JavaScript.

JavaScript counts starting at 0.

The common week starts on Sunday and ends on Saturday. You might see it differently, but JavaScript sees the 7-day week as Sunday through Saturday. Those seven days are in JavaScript's mind as being numbered from 0, Sunday, through 6, Saturday.

So, if you call for `getDay()` and it's Wednesday, you will actually only get the number 3 returned. Goofy, yes—but that's what happens.

But so what? The script above doesn't call for the day of the week. True. But it does call for the month. JavaScript counts that up from 0, too. Thus, the number returned for the month is always one less than you would expect.

The Methods and What They Return

Here's a quick rundown of each method and what it returns. It'll help you to understand what pops up on your page when using the variable as I'll show.

- `getDate()`: Believe it or not, this one acts normally. It will return the day of the month as the correct numbered day of the month.

- `getDay()`: Returns the numbers 0, Sunday, through 6, Saturday, depending on the day of the week.

- `getHours()`: Returns the hour of the day in a 24-hour format counting the hours up from 0. For example, 9 a.m. will be returned as the number 8. 10 p.m. will be returned as the number 19, one less than 20 hours.

- `getMinutes()`: Returns the minute of the hours counting up from 0 up through 59, but this one isn't bad. There actually is a zero at the top of the hour, so we're good to go with `getMinutes`.

- getMonth(): Returns the month of the year counting up from 0. The month of February will return the number 1.

- getSeconds(): Returns the second of the minute counting up from 0 to 59. This method, like getMinutes, is OK in that there is actually a zero at the top of the hour.

- getYear(): Returns the correct 2-digit year. The reason is that the number is figured by taking the current year and subtracting 1900. getYear() will cause problems in the year 2000, so to combat that concern, JavaScript was outfitted with a new Date object method getFullYear(), which will return a 4-digit year.

The Example Script

Take a look at this lesson's script:

```
<SCRIPT LANGUAGE="JavaScript">
//This script posts the exact day and time you arrived
RightNow = new Date();
document.write("Today's date is " + RightNow.getMonth()+ "-")
document.write("+ RightNow.getDate() + "-"
➥+ RightNow.getYear() + ".")
document.write("You entered this Web Page at exactly: "
➥ + RightNow.getHours() + "hours")
document.write("+ RightNow.getMinutes() + " minutes and "
➥ + RightNow.getSeconds() + " seconds")
</SCRIPT>
```

The script displays the date and time the page was loaded with this script, as shown in Figure 3.3.

 To see this script's effect on your computer, click on Lesson 11 Effect in your download packet or see it online at http://www.htmlgoodies.com/JSBook/lesson11effect.html.

Wait! What's That // Thing?

You are an observant one, aren't you? That double slash denotes a single comment line inside the script. It means that the text that follows will not be used in the process, but will rather just be reprinted as is. It works just like the multiline comment you saw in Lesson 11. You can add as many of them as you would like, as long as each line starts with the double slash.

You can also use the double slashes at the end of a line of JavaScript to remind yourself, or tell your users, what the line of JavaScript does. For example:

```
document.write("text")  //This writes text to the page
```

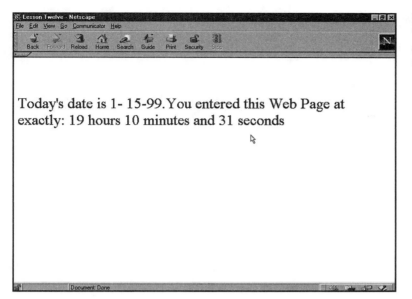

Deconstructing the Script

If you look at the example script, you'll see that the effect is created by asking the script to write the month, date, year, hour, minute, and second to the page. The extra verbiage stuck in there just makes it obvious what you're looking at.

Let's start with the first one called for in the preceding script, the month, and then we can start to break down how this pup works. As stated before, getMonth() is a method. That said, we now must concern ourselves with what object getMonth() is a method of.

It might appear from the script that get*Something*() is a method of document. Not so. The method of document is write. getMonth() is actually a method of the object Date. Look at the script. Date is set aside in the command

```
RightNow = new Date();
```

What is happening here is we are setting aside the object for the method getMonth() to work on. Actually, we're creating a new Date object to work with in the script.

Date, remember, contains all the date and time information you'll need. In fact, when you use one of the get*Something()* methods, you're simply extracting one section of what Date possesses.

I'll prove that to you. Here's code that uses only the Date object without any method.

```
<SCRIPT LANGUAGE="javascript">
document.write("Here's some information: " +Date()+ ".")
</SCRIPT>
```

With just that, look at Figure 3.4 to see all the good stuff you get.

Figure 3.4
Using the Date *object yields lots of information.*

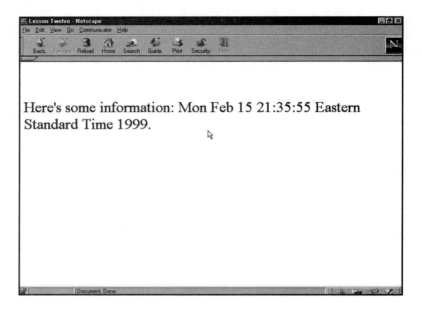

Defining a Variable for the **Date** Object

The variable name given to the Date object in the example script is RightNow. Now, I could have called it Zork or Fred, for all the browser cares. It doesn't matter as long as the object is given an original name that isn't found in JavaScript. See Appendix C, "JavaScript Reserved Variable Words," for a list of unusable words.

If that seems backward to you, it does to me, too. It seems like it should be new Date = RightNow, but it isn't. You're learning a new language and you have to play by its rules.

The earlier command is saying: RightNow is the variable that represents a new Date();.

But why new Date? The date has to be new. That way you get a new date every time the page is entered or reloaded. Without the new command, the date would remain static. You reinforce the fact that the date has to be new by giving it a variable name, too.

Hooray! We have our object variable name set so that our getMonth() method can act upon it. We want this month to be printed on the page, so we need to have a document.write() statement in there somewhere. We also know that what appears in the parentheses is printed on the page, so let's put together a smaller version of the big script in this lesson by following a logical process:

- We need to place the <SCRIPT LANGUAGE="javascript"> first.
- Then we'll put in a comment line that tells what this thing does.

- We'll need to create a new Date object before we can call on the getMonth() portion, so we'll put that in. Make sure the call ends with a semicolon.
- Now we can place the document.write() statement.
- Inside the document.write's incidence, we follow the same format as in Lesson 1.
- Text that is to be printed must be inside of double quotation marks (single quotation marks on any HTML inside).
- Finish up with </SCRIPT>.

Here's what we get:

```
<SCRIPT LANGUAGE="javascript">
//This script will post the month of the month
RightNow = new Date();
document.write("This is the month " + RightNow.getMonth() + ".")
</SCRIPT>
```

Look at the full script again. That long line of text doesn't look so tough now. It's simply the RightNow object variable name followed by the next getSomething() method. I separated each with a hyphen. Remember the hyphen is to be printed so it must be in quotes. Each of the RightNow.getSomething statements is contained in plus signs in order to return a value rather than print the text to the page.

Building the Lines of document.write Code

I won't go through it all because you probably have the swing of it by now, so I'll do just the date portion of the script. It looks like this:

```
document.write("Today's date is " + RightNow.getMonth()+ "-")
document.write(+ RightNow.getDate() + "-" + RightNow.getYear() + ".")
```

- Start with "Today's date is ", adding a space at the end for continuity.
- The plus sign is next.
- RightNow.getMonth() is added without quotes because we do not want that printed, we want the number returned.
- Another plus sign.
- Now, a hyphen in quotation marks to separate it from the next number. No space because I want the next number to butt right up against it.
- A plus sign.
- On to the next document.write statement.
- Start with a plus sign because the first item in this statement is a return.

● Now add `RightNow.getDate` because I want the number of the day. No quotation marks.
● A plus sign.
● Another hyphen in quotes so it is printed right to the page.
● A plus sign.
● Another new method, `RightNow.getYear`, will return the number of the year.

Just continue to follow this same format and the script will print out what you tell it to. So now you can tell everyone what time it is. But as Chicago sang, "Does anybody really know what time it is? Does anybody really care?"

Wait! What About Some of the Numbers Being One Off?

It's actually pretty easy to fix. So far, you've seen the plus sign used to surround text so that it acts as a return rather than printing to the page.

That plus sign can also act as a, well, as a plus sign intended to add things together. We'll get more into the mathematics of JavaScript in Chapter 5, "Forms: A Great Way to Interact with Your Users," but for now, we'll do some simple addition.

To get the returns from `getDay()`, `getHours()`, `getMonth()`, `getSeconds()`, and `getYear()` to display the correct year, you must add a couple of steps to the process.

To return the correct number, you need to return each of the `method.objects` (listed earlier) and assign it a variable name.

Also, when you assign a variable name, you must add 1. Here's an example of a script that will return the date in ##/##/#### format:

```
<SCRIPT LANGUAGE="javascript">
RightNow = new Date();
var dy = RightNow.getDate() + 1
var mth = RightNow.getMonth() + 1
var yr = RightNow.getYear() + 1900
document.write(+ dy + "/" + mth + "/" + yr + ".")
</SCRIPT>
```

See the format? I assigned the variable name `dy` to the code that would return the number representing the day of the week and added 1. Then in the `document.write` statement, I called only for the variable name `dy`. That returns the number returned by `RightNow.getDay()` plus 1.

Now it's correct.

I did the same for `RightNow.getMonth()`.

For `RightNow.getYear()`, I added 1900 to get a full four-digit year date returned.

And Speaking of a Four-Digit Year...

I didn't put this method in the main text of the lesson because it is one of the newer commands to JavaScript.

```
getFullYear()
```

The method `getFullYear()` was created in response to the need for a four-digit year. If you use that method in place of the `getYear()` used in the preceding section, you won't need to add 1900 to get the four digits. This will do it for you. But remember, this is a newer command to JavaScript and might not be supported on the browser your user is running.

Your Assignment

This one isn't so tough.

- Write a script that asks for the user's name through a prompt.
- Use that name to write a piece of text that reads: `Welcome` *`user-name`*`. It is` *`minutes`* `past` *`hour`*`. Thanks for coming.`
- Now, here's the kicker. Make that text appear in an alert that pops up when the page loads.
- Bonus points are available if you call for the minutes and hours by using variable names.

 You can see a possible answer on your own computer by clicking on Lesson 12 Assignment in your download packet to see it online at `http://www.htmlgoodies.com/JSBook/` `assignment12.html`*.*

Lesson 13: Hierarchy of Objects

WHOA! Let's pause and get familiar with the concept of hierarchy. And what better time to stop than lucky Lesson 13?

We know that JavaScript has objects, which are like nouns. We also know that objects have properties that describe how objects look, just as adjectives describe nouns.

We also know that objects have methods, or actions, that can be performed to the object. Different objects have access to different properties and methods. But what follows what, and which of these is most important? How do I write the code to the page so that the JavaScript understands that this is a property of that, and this method is to act upon that object? By writing objects, methods, and properties in a hierarchical fashion.

Now we'll learn THE secret to understanding JavaScript, the hierarchy of objects, illustrated in Figure 3.5. Don't tell a soul, but after you understand the hierarchy of objects, you've conquered JavaScript!

Figure 3.5
The concept of an object hierarchy.

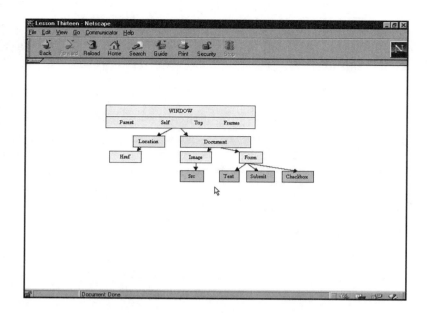

Click Here You can see this diagram up close by clicking on *Lesson Thirteen Script's Effect* or see it online at http://www.htmlgoodies.com/JSBook/lesson13effect.html.

Please understand that the image is not a complete representation of the hierarchy of JavaScript; it represents only what you've learned up to this point.

Terms, Terms, Terms: DOM

The purpose of this book is to teach you JavaScript in the friendliest and most easy-to-understand method possible.

Figure 3.5 shows the hierarchy of JavaScript. That hierarchy actually has a term. It's called a *Document Object Model*, or DOM for short.

I don't use the term because it really doesn't tell you, the reader, anything. In fact, at the level you're at, it might actually be confusing.

I use the term *hierarchy statement* because it is a better representation of the code.

But just keep in mind at your next party full of technical people, the true term is DOM, or Document Object Model.

The Hierarchy of Objects' Effect

All references begin with the top object, the window (the browser screen), and go down. window is the highest level object in JavaScript. So much so that JavaScript doesn't even require that you use it in your code. JavaScript just understands that, unless told otherwise, everything happens within the browser window.

That means that everything we've shown you so far actually should be written with the object window at the beginning:

```
window.document.write
window.RightNow.getDay()
window.default.status
```

If you would like to write your code this way, great. But it's not required, obviously, because the top-level object, window, is understood to be the overriding object.

Here are some examples. Notice they follow the hierarchy pattern from Figure 3.5, from top to bottom.

```
document.mypic.src = "pic1.gif"
```

Again, window is not needed at the very beginning. It is assumed all this is inside the window. This references an image named mypic, changing its contents to pic1.gif. Did you follow that? document is the page the item is on, mypic is the item's name, and SRC is the item's source.

It is getting smaller going left to right, one inside the other like a page contains a sentence, a sentence contains a word, and a word contains a letter.

```
document.write(location.href)
```

write() is a method of the document object. location.href returns the full URL of the window. Notice that location and document are at the same level. They are written to the left of the only dot. One has a method following it, write, and the other has a property following it, href.

That means you get the location of that same-level document denoted by document.write, even though one hierarchy statement is sitting in the instance, the parentheses, of the other. Both document.write and location.href will act within the same document window. They are at the same level. Still with me?

Deconstructing the Hierarchy of Objects

What's most confusing about this is that some objects are also properties. I'm referencing Figure 3.5 again here.

- ⬤ window is just an object.
- ⬤ document is an object inside the window.
- ⬤ form is a property of document, but it is also an object with its own properties!
- ⬤ Note that value and src are just properties!

Not all objects and properties are displayed here. However, this should be enough to help you understand this format. All references start at the top with window and go down writing them left to right, separated by dots.

You cannot write document.mytext.myform or mypic.src.document. They are not in the correct order. The order must go biggest to smallest from left to right.

A Very Important Concept

This is paramount in hierarchy. It will come into play when we start to talk about forms in Chapter 6, "Mathematics, Random Things, and Loops."

Let's say you have an HTML text box on your page. The user writes something in the text box. To return the contents of that text box using JavaScript, you must use the property value; for example, document.myform.mytext.value. Just writing document.myform.mytext will give information about the form field, but not its contents. The value command will return what is written inside the text box.

Just know that an HTML form field, like a text box or a radio button, is given a name. In the preceding example, it's myform. If you call for that alone, you'll get information about the form item itself, just like getDay() returns the day number. But if you want what is written in the form itself, add value to the end of the hierarchy statement. Now you're one level below the form field itself. You're at the level of what the user wrote.

Think of value as a reading of what something is or is not at a specific time. A check box can have a value of on or off depending on whether it's been clicked. A text box field can have a value of hidden if you don't want the user to see it. And, as noted above, a TEXT field can have input written to it. That's that field's value. Get it?

Maybe not yet, but you will. Hierarchy is at the very heart of JavaScript. We will begin to talk about hierarchy a great deal throughout the rest of the book.

Your Assignment

Here's a little bit of code for you to look at:

```
<FORM>
<INPUT TYPE="button" Value="Click Here"
onClick="parent.frames[1].location='zippy5.html';
parent.frames[2].location='zippy6.html';
parent.frames[3].location='zippy7.html';">
</FORM>
```

You can see the basic format as a FORM button. But what does all that stuff after the onClick stand for?

Follow the thought process from the preceding lesson and without looking at the answer, make a point of writing down what you think this script does.

Also—think about how it does it.

 You can see a full tutorial on what that link does by clicking on Lesson 13 Assignment in your download packet or see it online at http://www.htmlgoodies.com/JSBook/ assignment13.html.

Lesson 14: Creating a Function

In creating a variable, you assign a one-word title to the output of a JavaScript command or event. Creating a function is doing the same thing, except you are assigning a title to an entire series of commands. You are combining many JavaScript commands into one.

Here's an example. Let's say you have some JavaScript code that grabs the hour, minute, and second. Then you have some code that writes that code to the page. You want the return from that code to appear on the page four times. There's no reason why you couldn't write the code again and again. It will work just fine. But wouldn't it be easier to assign a one-word title to both pieces of code? Then you could call for the two pieces of code by just calling on that one word.

It's good programming, too, because you only need to call on one name to get an effect. Your page isn't full of extra, and probably confusing, code.

To illustrate, we'll use a script that's actually in two parts: the script itself, which contains the function; and the onLoad Event Handler, which triggers the function to work.

Here are both parts:

```
<SCRIPT LANGUAGE="javascript">
<!-- Hide from browsers that do not understand JavaScript
function dateinbar()
{
var d = new Date();
var y = d.getYear() + 1900;
var m = d.getMonth() + 1;
var d = d.getDate();
var t = m + '/' + d + '/' + y + ' ';
defaultStatus = "You arrived at the page on " + t + ".";
}
// end hiding -->
</SCRIPT>
```

...and the onLoad command in the <BODY>:

```
<BODY BGCOLOR="FFFFcc" onLoad="dateinbar()">
```

The script's effect will display in the status bar, as shown in Figure 3.6.

We kept basically the same kind of date script we've been using in past lessons so it would all look somewhat familiar to you. See how we assigned the getSomething() methods variable names and added 1?

Figure 3.6
The function displays the date in the status bar.

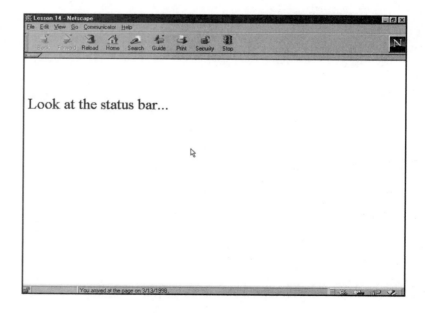

You can see this effect on your computer by clicking on *Lesson Fourteen Script's Effect* or see it online at `http://www.htmlgoodies.com/JSBook/lesson14effect.html`.

Hey! What Are Those <!-- and --> Things?

They're yet another extra command stuck in for good measure. Those probably look familiar to you. They're the two comment flags you use to comment out text in an HTML document. It looks like this:

```
<!-- The text in here would comment out -->
```

I am using them here because, believe it or not, there are still browsers out there that do not read JavaScript. By using these comment commands, the text of the JavaScript is commented out so that it isn't printed on the page. You see, if the browser doesn't understand JavaScript, it sees that text as something to be printed on the page, and it looks bad. But if you use the comment flags, the browser that can't read JavaScript happily ignores the text and displays the page.

If you use these comment flags, there are a few very important rules to follow.

The commands go inside the `<SCRIPT>` and `</SCRIPT>` flags. If you put them outside of those commands you would comment out the entire JavaScript on all browsers and nothing would run. The `<!--` flag can be followed by a line of text as long as the text is all on the same line. The `-->` flag must be commented out using the double slashes or the JavaScript thinks the command is part of the script. Error.

Notice you can also put some text before it because it is commented out. No, you do not have to use text along with these commands. I put the text in because it made it easier to explain the purpose of the flags. Follow the format and placement style discussed earlier, and you'll have no trouble.

Deconstructing the Script

Two things are happening here. The first is the script section that creates the function. The second is the command found in the HTML `<BODY>` flag that triggers the function to work. Let's look at the concept of the function first:

```
function dateinbar()
{
var d = new Date();
var y = d.getYear() + 1900;
var m = d.getMonth() + 1;
var d = d.getDate();
var t = m + '/' + d + '/' + y + ' ';
defaultStatus = "You arrived at the page on " + t + ".";
}
```

The format is straightforward.

- The function is given a name by writing `function` and then the name you want to assign to the function. It's very similar to the way you create a variable name.

  But please note that the function name has the parentheses following it the same way that method commands do. I always keep it straight by thinking that in creating a function, I am actually creating a new method for performing a task.

- A variable is made for the year. Another variable is assigned to the month, and another for the day.

- A fourth variable, `t`, is created to represent the entire date format. It should look familiar. It was done so that now you can call for the full date anywhere in the HTML document by just calling for `t`.

- The last command is new to you:

  ```
  defaultStatus = "You arrived at the page on " + t + ".";
  ```

  `defaultStatus` is a property of the object `window`. Its purpose is to place text into the status bar at the bottom of the browser window.

There's only one status bar. That has to be the default.

The `onLoad=` *Command*

The command `onLoad` tells the browser that upon loading the page, do what follows. In this case, what follows is the function `dateinbar()`.

This `onLoad=`*functionname*`()` command format is almost always is found in the BODY portion of the HTML document.

Placement of These Items

Where you put the two sections, the function and the `onLoad` command, is important. You know the `onLoad` command goes in the BODY portion. The script that contains the function should be placed between the <HEAD> and </HEAD> commands in the HTML document. You can actually stick it anywhere on the page and it'll run, but placing it after the `onLoad` command will cause it to start after the entire page has been loaded. Putting it before the `onLoad` command places it into the computer's memory first, so it's there ready to go when the `onLoad` calls for it.

An Exception to That Rule

75% of all the functions you'll create will sit within the <HEAD> and </HEAD> flags. An exception would be when you want the function to place text in a specific part of the page.

If that's the case, place the function in the BODY of the HTML document and load the page into the browser window without using an onLoad command. In the BODY of the HTML document, it'll probably run by itself. If it doesn't, add the onLoad to trigger the function.

A Word About Global and Local Variables

OK, now you understand how to assign a variable name and how to create a function. What you might not know is that variables are seen by JavaScript as different depending on whether they are inside the function or outside the function.

JavaScript allows for two levels of variables, local and global.

Local variables are variables that are only viable within a function. JavaScript understands that whenever a variable is encased within a function, that variable name is viable only inside that function. That way, if you copy and paste a script onto a page that already has a script on it, any existing variables that are equally named will not clash as long as that variable name is found within a function.

Global variables are variables that are not found within functions, and thus *can* clash with the existing variables on the same page.

Here's an example:

```
<SCRIPT LANGUAGE="javascript">
var joe = 12
function writeit()
{
var joe = "Joe Burns"
document.write(joe)
}
</SCRIPT>
```

The variable joe is used twice, but because one is found outside the function, the global variable, and one is found inside of the function, the local variable, the two will not clash.

Now, with all that said, it is not a good idea to follow the preceding format and use like variable names within your scripts. The purpose of the local variables being hidden is far more for protection against clashes with other scripts on the same page than clashes with variables names within the same script.

Name all of your variables descriptively and differently, and you'll run into very few, if any, problems.

Your Assignment

Just about any group of JavaScript commands that produce an effect can be set into a function format. In fact, your assignment today is to try to prove that theory.

This one's a little involved.

- Create a function that calls for two prompts. The first asks for the person's first name. The second prompt asks for the person's second name.

- Then, in the same function, have an alert box pop up with the text Hello *first name last name*, Welcome to *page address*, My Great Page!

- Make sure you make a variable for the page address.

- If you would like to make this assignment a little more fun, present My Great Page to the viewer some other way than simply writing it in text in the alert command. Make a variable for that, too.

You can see a possible answer by clicking on Lesson 14 Assignment in your download packet or see it online at http://www.htmlgoodies.com/JSBook/assignment14.html.

Lesson 15: An Introduction to Arrays

Let's return to Lesson 12. When you used any one of the get*Something*() date or time methods, a number representing the Date object property was returned. In some cases, such as the hour and day of the month, that's fine, but for other Date returns it isn't so good. Take getDay(), for example. As you probably thought, it's not very helpful to have the days of the week returned as 0, 1, 2, 3, 4, 5, or 6.

The best approach would be to take the number that's returned and change it into text. That would make more sense. It would also be easier to read.

Here's how:

```
<SCRIPT LANGUAGE="JavaScript">
var dayName=new Array("Sunday","Monday","Tuesday",
➥"Wednesday","Thursday","Friday","Saturday")
var y=new Date();
document.write("Today is "+dayName[y.getDay()] + ".");
</SCRIPT>
```

Figure 3.7 shows the result of this script. You can also see this effect on your computer by clicking on Lesson Fifteen Script's Effect or see it online at http://www.htmlgoodies.com/ JSBook/lesson15effect.html.

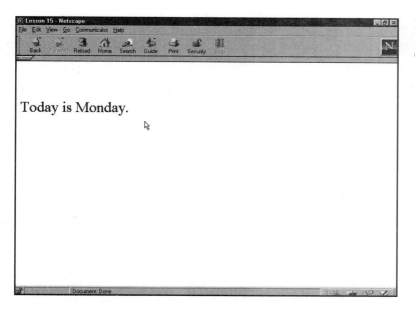

Figure 3.7
The function displays the day of the week.

Deconstructing the Script

Let's start with the same rule that started out Lesson 12:

JavaScript starts counting at 0.

That's why the month number is always returned one less than what the month actual is. JavaScript started counting January at 0.

For this lesson, we'll add to the preceding rule:

JavaScript counts everything you give it and always starts counting at 0.

If we offer JavaScript a list of simple text items, like a number of names or words, known in JavaScript as *literals*, the script will assign numbers to the items in that list. Guess what number it assigns to the first item? That's right: 0.

So let's give JavaScript a long list of things. We'll give it the days of the week. But like everything else, we can't just throw a bunch of words in a script and hope the browser picks up what we mean. There is a method to offering a long list of items, such as the days of the week.

It's called creating an *array*.

Setting Up the Array

Here's the array line from the example script:

```
var dayName=new Array("Sunday","Monday","Tuesday",
➥"Wednesday","Thursday","Friday","Saturday")
```

The format for creating an array is pretty simple:

- You assign the array of literals a variable name. In this case, I called the array dayName.

- You tell the browser that this is a new array by writing new Array. That makes sense. Note the capitalization pattern.

- The array of literals will go within parentheses.

- Each new array item will be surrounded with double quotation marks. Remember that each array item is text, and that requires double quotation marks.

- Each array item is separated from the next by a comma, no spaces. You can have spaces if you would like, but I feel this format looks a little cleaner.

- The big question is in what order to put the array items. Here the answer is easy. We know that the days of the week are represented Sunday through to Saturday, 0 to 6. We list Sunday first because we know it will receive the 0 both from the getDay() method and from the JavaScript assigning numbers to the array. That makes it a pretty sure bet that a 0 will return Sunday to the page.

Later in the book, we'll discuss arrays that do not come with a 0 through whatever pattern is already set. That gets a little more complicated. For now, we'll stay with the rather easy-to-create arrays because JavaScript has set the order for us already.

Grab a Piece of the Array

Now that we've set up the seven day text array, we need to create a method to return the numeric day of the week through the getDay() method, and then turn that number into the correct day from the array.

Here's the code that does it:

```
var y=new Date();
document.write("Today is "+dayName[y.getDay()] + ".");
```

The first line should be familiar by now. We are setting up a variable, y, that represents the new Date().

The document.write statement should also look familiar. The text within the double quotation marks will write to the page, whereas the text within the plus signs will return something to the page in its place.

Here's the magic in the script:

```
dayName[y.getDay()]
```

The code turns the attention of the return to the array, dayName.

The code in the brackets is the same format used to return the numeric day of the week number: *variablename*.getDay().

The y.getDay() will be replaced by a number representing the day of the week like it always is.

So what the command is actually saying is *Go to this array*[*find this number*].

If we were running this script on a Monday, the y.getDay() would return the number 1. The browser would see the command dayName[y.getDay()] as dayName[1], and would return the text in the array associated with the number 1. The number 1 is Monday because JavaScript counts up from 0.

Get it? Good.

Your Assignment

Use the instructions and array above to create a script that will print this line to the page Today is *Day-Of-The-Week* in the month of *Month-Name*.

You already know the format for the day of the week. Now create an array that returns the name of the month. Just follow the pattern shown earlier to create the array. Just remember to give the new array a new variable name. You can't have two variable in the same script with the same name.

Remember, even in months, JavaScript starts counting at 0.

 You can see a possible answer by clicking on Lesson 15 Assignment in your download packet or see it online at http://www.htmlgoodies.com/JSBook/assignment15.html.

Lesson 16: The Third End of Chapter Review—A <BODY> Flag Script

If you stopped at this point, you would do just fine. What you have is sufficient to create some wonderful scripts.

But why stop now? Let's review!

Table 3.1 contains the object-related JavaScript commands you've learned up to now. In addition, you've been introduced to these JavaScript concepts:

- The `alert()` method and the `prompt()` method
- These Event Handlers: onBlur, onChange, onClick, onDblClick, onFocus, onKeyDown, onKeyPress, onKeyUp, onLoad, onMouseDown, onMouseMove, onMouseOut, onMouseOver, onMouseUp, onSubmit
- The HTML 4.0 flag <SPAN>
- Creating variable names
- Creating a function

Table 3.1 Object-Related JavaScript Commands Demonstrated in Chapters 1 Through 3

Object	Methods	Properties
date	getDate() getDay() getHours() getMinutes() getMonth() getSeconds() getYear()	
document	write()	alinkColor, bgColor, fgColor, linkColor, lastModified, location, referrer, title, vlinkColor
history	go()	length
location		host, hostname, href
navigator		appCodeName, appName, appVersion, userAgent
window		defaultstatus, status

We're going to use some of these commands to create a script that allows the viewer help to create the page. The script will ask the viewer what background and text colors he or she would like. Then the page will display with those colors. Finally, the viewer will be told, in the status bar, Here's your *color* background and *color* text.

The script is as follows:

```
<SCRIPT LANGUAGE="javascript">
var color = prompt("What color would you like
➥the page's background to be","")
var txtcolor = prompt("What color would you like the text to be?","")
```

```
document.write("<BODY BGCOLOR=" +color+ " TEXT=" +txtcolor+ ">")
defaultStatus="Here's your " +color+ " background and "
➥ +txtcolor+ " text"
</SCRIPT>
```

Figure 3.8 shows the script's effect.

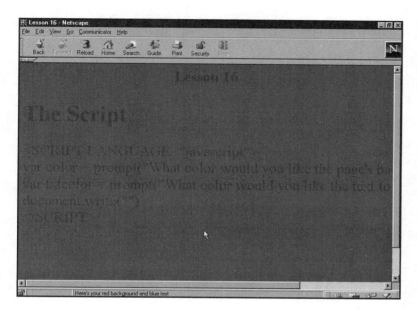

Figure 3.8
The script creates a page with the user's desired background color and text color.

 You can see this effect on your computer by clicking on Lesson Sixteen Script's Effect or see it online at http://www.htmlgoodies.com/JSBook/lesson16effect.html.

Deconstructing the Script

The script starts off by setting a couple of variables using prompts. We need to get the user's input on what background and text color he or she would like, so this seems as good a way as any.

The variables are color and txtcolor, respectively. The code looks like this:

```
var color = prompt("What color would you like
➥the page's background to be","")
var txtcolor = prompt("What color would you like the text to be?","")
```

Now that we have the input from the user, we'll need to use that data to alter the page. The real beauty of this script is its placement on the page.

Up until now, each of the scripts in this book had no real placement concerns. The script could pretty much sit anywhere in an HTML document and the results would display. Now we are concerned with where this script will place its output.

The script must write its line of text so that that line of text becomes the HTML document's BODY flag.

The quickest way to implement the user's background and text color requests would be to write them to the <BODY> flag. So we did. This script's main purpose is to write the HTML document's <BODY> flag to the page, so we have to make sure that the entire script sits right where the body command needs to sit on the HTML page. And of course, we need to make sure we don't write a <BODY> into the HTML document ourselves. We need to let the script do that for us.

Here's the code that writes the <BODY> flag:

```
document.write("<BODY BGCOLOR=" +color+ " TEXT=" +txtcolor+ ">")
```

The colors are entered as return variables inside the two plus signs. That way, what the user wrote in the prompt is what will be returned.

Status Bar Too?

But the script goes a little farther than just writing a <BODY> flag. It also places the viewer's data to the status bar, almost as if the page were served to him or her.

Here's the line of that does it:

```
defaultStatus="Here's your " +color+ " background and "
➡+txtcolor+ " text"
```

It follows the same format as the document.write statement, with text surrounded by double quotation marks and return variables surrounded by plus signs, except in this case the text is sent to the status bar.

Your Assignment

OK, your turn. Make a new script. Make it something that adds to your page. I stuck with prompts and variables for my example.

If you want to, may I suggest making a Mad-Lib party game? It's that game where you're asked for a noun, a verb, a state, and things like that. Then you read the sentence you created using those words. And you know from playing it that the sentence never makes any sense.

It would be your first JavaScript game.

For my brand-new script, I created a button that, when you click on it, displays the current date and time. It's rather simple. (You should try the Mad-Lib game or something even more helpful.)

 You can see a possible answer to making the button that shows the time by clicking on Lesson 16 Assignment in your download packet or see it online at http://www.htmlgoodies.com/JSBook/assignment16.html.

Chapter 4

Flipping Images and Opening Windows with Mouse Events

This chapter contains the following lessons and scripts:

- Lesson 17: An Image Flip Using `onMouseOver` and Pre-Loading Images
- Lesson 18: An Image Flip with a Function
- Lesson 19: Opening New Windows
- Lesson 20: Opening a Window with a Function
- Lesson 21: The `Confirm` Method, with an Introduction to `If` and `Else`
- Lesson 22: The Fourth End of Chapter Review—Some Jumping Jacks

Up to this point, each of the JavaScripts we've built has dealt with altering, changing, or writing text to the page. Sure, there's been some color, but there has to be more than text to JavaScript. In this chapter, we'll start to look at manipulating images, opening new windows, and offering users a choice, rather than simply taking information from them.

Lesson 17: An Image Flip Using `onMouseOver` and Pre-Loading Images

An image flip is a great effect. Some people call it a mouse rollover or an image rollover. The user rolls his or her mouse pointer over an image and it changes to a new image. When the mouse leaves the image, it changes back. It's a very popular event on the Web.

This example goes back to the use of onMouseOver and onMouseOut Event Handlers. We're going to use the Event Handler to affect not only text, but also the space the image is sitting in. Here's the script:

```
<A HREF="http://www.cnn.com"
onMouseOver="document.pic1.src='menu1on.gif'"
onMouseOut="document.pic1.src='menu1off.gif'">
<IMG SRC="menu1off.gif" BORDER=0 NAME="pic1"></a>
```

It'll take two figures to show you this one. Take a look at Figures 4.1 and 4.2.

Figure 4.1
The page looks like this when the mouse is off the image.

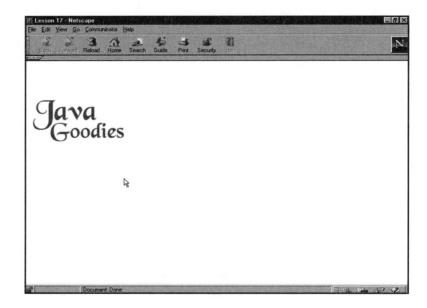

 You can see the effect on your own computer by clicking on Lesson 17 Example in your download packet or see it online at http://www.htmlgoodies.com/JSBook/ lesson17example.html.

In this example, and the ones that follow for that matter, the images are all the same size. You don't need to use same-size images for your image flips, but it's a good idea. It really heightens the look.

Notice again that there is no need for the <SCRIPT> and </SCRIPT> tags. We're using Event Handlers again. The JavaScript onMouseOver and onMouseOut events are built into an <A HREF> HTML flag, so not only is this an image flip, it's also a hypertext link.

Also notice that by including BORDER="0" in the <IMG SRC> tag, no link box appears around the image.

Figure 4.2
When the mouse is on the image, the message changes.

Deconstructing the Script

From what you already know about Event Handlers, you should be able to go a long way toward picking this one apart by yourself. When the mouse is off the image space, the image menu1off.gif is displayed. That's the image displayed when the page first loads. It's the image called for in the <IMG SRC> flag. When the mouse is on the image, the menu1on.gif image is shown.

The NAME Attribute

Notice the <IMG SRC> flag has been given a NAME= attribute. In this example, the name given to the image—or more correctly, the space the image is occupying—is pic1.

That NAME= attribute becomes quite important if you want to put multiple image flips on the same page. For every new image flip you put on the page, you must choose a different name for the new image space. Here an example of three image flips in a row:

```
<A HREF="http://www.htmlgoodies.com"
onMouseOver="document.pic1.src='menu1on.gif'"
onMouseOut="document.pic1.src='menu1off.gif'">
<IMG SRC="menu1off.gif" BORDER=0 NAME="pic1"> </A>

<A HREF="http://www.developer.com"
onMouseOver="document.pic2.src='menu1on.gif'"
onMouseOut="document.pic2.src='menu1off.gif'">
<IMG SRC="menu1off.gif" BORDER=0 NAME="pic2"> </A>
```

```
<A HREF="http://www.javagoodies.com"
onMouseOver="document.pic3.src='menu1on.gif'"
onMouseOut="document.pic3.src='menu1off.gif'">
<IMG SRC="menu1off.gif" BORDER=0 NAME="pic3"> </A>
```

Not only were the links changed to new locations, but notice also that all the names were changed, both in the <IMG SRC> and in the hierarchy statements.

The Hierarchy Statement

The name of the space the image is sitting in, pic1 in this case, is referenced in the hierarchy statement referenced by the onMouseOver and onMouseOut statements. The hierarchy statement, document.pic1.src, reads this way:

- window is implied. You could have written this with the object window at the beginning, but as you read in Lesson 13, it is not needed. JavaScript simply assumes all that is going on is going on inside a browser window.
- document refers to the current HTML document object.
- pic1 is the name of this image object. We made up that NAME and stuck it in the <IMG SRC> flag.
- src is a property of the image object that allows you to load a new image into the current image's space.

When the mouse passes over the space occupied by the image, the onMouseOver Event Handler springs into action, replacing the menu1off.gif image with the menu1on.gif image.

The process might take a second or two to allow the image that will display to be loaded into the browser. But you cut down on that time by pre-loading the image.

Pre-Loading Images

Through JavaScript, you can set up code that will download images into the user's browser cache for later use. Using the image flip code above, the menu1off.gif image will load to the cache because it is being called for by the HTML document in the <IMG SRC>.

If the term *cache* is new to you, here's what's so great about it. The cache is a section of your hard drive, set aside by your browser, so it can store files after it has displayed them for you. Have you noticed how much faster a page loads after you've seen it? That's because the browser is not reading the images and text from the server anymore. It is reading from your hard drive.

By pre-caching, or pre-loading, images for your viewer, you make it so that when he or she starts to use the image flip, the browser works quickly the first time without having to contact the server again for the image that it wants to display. It's a very clever way of doing things.

What we want to do here is call for the menu1on.gif to load into the cache with the rest of the page. Then, when the image flip is called for, the menu1on.gif is there ready and waiting to be posted. The flips will go much faster the first time around because the browser isn't waiting for the server to be contacted and the new image to be loaded.

Here's the code that performs the pre-load:

```
<SCRIPT LANGUAGE="javascript">


Image1= new Image(200,200)

Image1.src = "menu1on.gif"

</SCRIPT>
```

The pre-load will occur thanks to a completely different script than the image flip. The format follows this pattern:

- `Image1 = new Image(200,200)` assigns a variable name to a new image that is 200 pixels wide by 200 high. The script doesn't know what the image is yet, it just knows that now the image will be brought into the cache under that variable name.
- `Image1.src = "menu1on.gif"` tells the JavaScript the source, or path, to find the image.

The preceding JavaScript will load the image into the browser cache under the variable name Image1. But the name used to pull the image into the cache becomes immaterial because we never call for the image by that variable name. We only call for it by its true, or literal name: menu1on.gif.

The purpose of the preceding JavaScript is to load the image to the browser cache, period. The variable names assigned mean nothing past a format you must use to get that behind-the-scenes download to occur.

Let's say you had multiple images to download. Again, the variable names don't matter, so you might as well just keeping adding one to the variable name Image1. Pre-loading three images might look like this:

```
<SCRIPT LANGUAGE="javascript">

Image1= new Image(200,200)
Image1.src = "menu1on.gif"

Image2= new Image(125,15)
Image2.src = "line.gif"
```

```
Image3= new Image(20,10)
Image3.src = "button.gif"
</SCRIPT>
```

Notice each new two-line command group is given a new variable name and a new image to pre-load. The height and width parameters have also changed to fit the image.

Put this script in between the <HEAD> flags in your script and the pre-loaded images should be there waiting when your user tries the image flips for the first time.

Your Assignment

Take our example code and add a few comments so that when the mouse is on the image, the status bar reads Oh, Click it!. Then when the mouse is off the image, the status bar should read Click to go!.

Here's a hint: return true.

 To see a possible answer on your own computer, click on Lesson 17 Assignment in your download packet or see it online at http://www.htmlgoodies.com/JSBook/ assignment17.html.

Lesson 18: An Image Flip with a Function

Here is another example of onMouseOver and onMouseOut Event Handlers being used to create an image flip effect. But this time, instead of including the JavaScript statements to swap pictures in the <A HREF> tag, the event is called for in a function.

To show you where each of the parts should be placed on your page, this display includes the entire HTML document format:

```
<HTML>
<HEAD>
<TITLE>Javascript Example 18</TITLE>
<SCRIPT LANGUAGE="JavaScript">
function up()
{
document.mypic.src="up.gif"
}
function down()
{
document.mypic.src="down.gif"
}
</SCRIPT>
</HEAD>
```

```
<BODY>
<CENTER>
<h2>Sample Animation</h2>
<A HREF=http://www.htmlgoodies.com onMouseOver="up()"
➥ onMouseOut="down()"; return true>
<IMG SRC="down.gif" NAME="mypic" BORDER=0></A>
</BODY>
</HTML>
```

It's a simple image flip animation with onMouseOver and onMouseOut in a function. In the example, if you mouse over and out quickly, this looks like a animation of a stick figure doing jumping jacks.

Andree did the artwork shown in Figures 4.3 and 4.4. I take no responsibility for that.

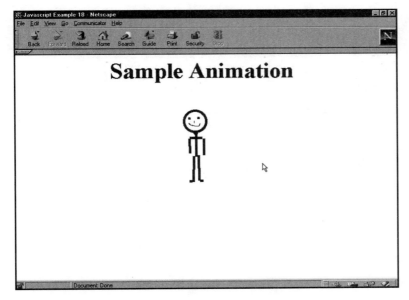

Figure 4.3
The stick figure stands up straight when the mouse is off the image.

 You can see the man (we think it's a man), doing jumping jacks on your own computer by clicking on Lesson 18 Example in your download packet or see it online at http://www.htmlgoodies.com/JSBook/lesson18example.html.

There aren't a whole lot of external words on the page. I just took the preceding code and pasted it into an HTML document.

Figure 4.4
The figure does a jumping jack when the mouse is on the image.

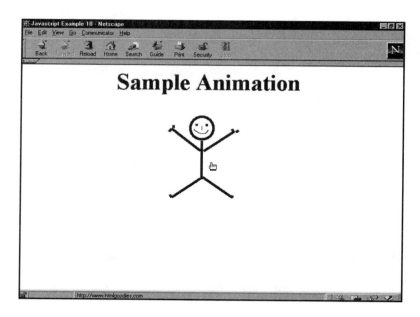

Deconstructing the Script

In this example you are calling for two different images, so you will need two separate functions. Here's what they look like:

```
<SCRIPT LANGUAGE="JavaScript">
function up()
{
document.mypic.src="up.gif"
}
function down()
{
document.mypic.src="down.gif"
}
</SCRIPT>
```

Look again at the format for creating a function.

The command function is followed immediately by the name of the function followed by the two parentheses. In this case, the parentheses are empty because we are passing nothing to the function. Later in the book, we'll discuss putting parameters into the parentheses so that information can be passed to the function. The commands that make up the function are housed within left and right braces {}.

The functions are equal to the statements used in the previous JavaScript lesson on image flips. Remember the hierarchy statements? Here the function contains the statements, rather than adding them into the <A HREF> flag.

The format for the hierarchy statement is document, and then comes the NAME assigned to the image space, and finally the SRC path to the image.

The two functions were named up() and down(). The names could have been just about anything, but we went with these two because of the actual position of the man doing jumping jacks.

Calling for the Function

Now let's look at the call for the function:

```
<A HREF="http://www.htmlgoodies.com" onMouseOver="up()"
➥ onMouseOut="down()"; return true>
<IMG SRC="down.gif" NAME="mypic"  BORDER=0></A>
```

The format is close to that used in Lesson 15, but we are calling on a function here, rather than including the hierarchy statement in the HREF command itself.

By calling for the function name following onMouseOver and onMouseOff we are, in effect, replacing what is included in the function statements with the function name.

The code onMouseOver="up()" basically means this:

```
onMouseOver="document.mypic.src='up.gif'"
```

More Than One Image Flip

Remember from Lesson 17 that if you wanted to create multiple image flips on a page, you had to continue using new NAME= attributes to separate each image space in the browser's mind? It's the same thing here, except now you'll have to create whole new function names in addition to new NAME= attributes.

For example, suppose we want to place on the page another JavaScript image flip like our first example. You would create two new functions by copying and pasting the same functions shown earlier and altering the function name. The easiest and quickest method is to add the number 2.

Then you'll also have to change the NAME=. So we'll change the name to mypic2. Make sure to change the name of the image space every time it appears.

Now we get code that looks like this in the HEAD commands:

```
<SCRIPT LANGUAGE="JavaScript">
function up()
{
document.mypic.src="up.gif"
}
function down()
{
document.mypic.src="down.gif"
}
function up2()
{
document.mypic2.src="upagain.gif"
}
function down2()
{
document.mypic2.src="downagain.gif"
}
</SCRIPT>
```

And code like the following to call for the two different images:

```
<A HREF="http://www.htmlgoodies.com" onMouseOver="up()"
➥ onMouseOut="down()"; return true>
<IMG SRC="down.gif" NAME="mypic"  BORDER=0></A>

<a href="http://www.htmlgoodies.com" onMouseOver="up2()"
➥ onMouseOut="down2()"; return true>
<IMG SRC="downagain.gif" NAME="mypic2"  BORDER=0></A>
```

See how the new functions are linked to a specific image space through the NAME=, and all the image space names were changed? Follow that process every time you add a new image flip and you can put hundreds on the same page. Well, maybe not hundreds. Just about 100 will probably do the trick.

Pre-Load Those Images

Keep in mind that you can help your viewer along by pre-loading the images that will be called for in the flip.

Here again is the format:

```
<SCRIPT LANGUAGE="javascript">

Image1= new Image(200,200)
```

```
Image1.src = "menu1on.gif"

</SCRIPT>
```

It'll help your user greatly. He or she won't be sitting around waiting.

Your Assignment

First, you need to get four images. If you can supply them, great. If not, I have four for you at

http://www.htmlgoodies.com/JSBook/img1.html

http://www.htmlgoodies.com/JSBook/img2.html

http://www.htmlgoodies.com/JSBook/img3.html

http://www.htmlgoodies.com/JSBook/img4.html

Download them into your computer. Use the function and code shown earlier to get `img1.gif` and `img2.gif` to create an image flip, and then get `img3.gif` and `img4.gif` to do an image flip. You will create two image flips from the preceding code.

Hint: Watch the order in which you put the images in the function. You'll know you have it right when you roll your pointer over the image and it flips correctly. If it stays flipped, you're out of order.

 To see a possible answer on your own computer, click on Lesson 18 Assignment in your download packet or see it online at http://www.htmlgoodies.com/JSBook/ assignment18.html.

Lesson 19: Opening New Windows

This is the first of two lessons on opening a new window through JavaScript. This first new-window lesson will deal with the JavaScript commands you would use to open a new window that will display a second HTML document.

Let's get started with a basic script:

```
<SCRIPT LANGUAGE="javascript">
window.open('opened.html','joe',config='height=300,width=300')
</SCRIPT>
```

The script's effect appears in Figure 4.5.

Figure 4.5
Our script opens a new window.

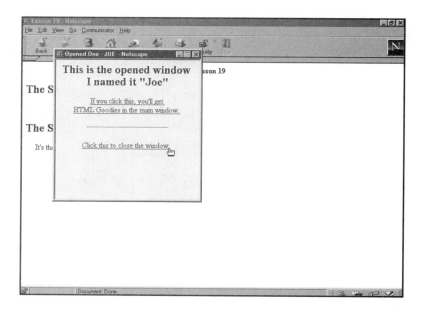

You can try the script out or yourself by clicking on Lesson 19 Script's Effect in your download packet or see it online at http://www.htmlgoodies.com/JSBook/lesson19example.html.

Please note: This script only opens the window. The links that appear in the new window were written on the HTML page that filled the new window. But what about those links in the new window? They're functional, too.

If you look at this example in your download packet or online, you'll see a link in the little window load a new page in the big window, and then you'll see a link close the little window. It's like fireworks at a fairground. You can even say "Oooo" and "Ahhh," if the mood strikes you.

I'll get to those links in the little window and how they are written to control the main window, as well as how to close the window itself, later in this chapter.

Deconstructing the Script

Let's start by talking about the placement of this script in your HTML document. Until now, I have always said it's good to place scripts up high in the document so they can run early in the page load. When you're dealing with a function, the script goes up in the head commands. Here, I would like to make a different suggestion.

If you're going to open a second window, put the commands that do it down pretty low in the HTML document. In fact, make them last. The reasoning is simple: The page loads—then the new window pops up. If you have the commands first, the new window pops up before the viewer gets to see what's there in the big window. There's also a greater chance that the user will close the little window before it can be used.

That's just my opinion, of course. You can actually place this script anywhere in the document you want. It'll run from wherever it sits. I just think the order of the window popping last is more beneficial to your viewers.

Let's look at the basic window-opening code again:

```
<SCRIPT LANGUAGE="javascript">
window.open('opened.html','joe',config='height=300,width=300')
</SCRIPT>
```

The code window.open couldn't be more blatant. window is the object and open is the method that acts upon it. That's the easy part. Now we get to configuring the window.

Configuring the Window

This is all that good stuff in the instance of the command (that's the parentheses, remember?). Here's the format you need to follow:

```
('URL of document in window', 'New Window Name',
➥ config='New Window Parameters')
```

Here's the command from our script with the current elements:

```
('opened.html', 'joe', config='height=300,width=300')
```

- opened.html is the URL of the page that will appear in the new window. If the page is from your server, or in a different directory, you'll need to add the http:// stuff or a directory path so the browser can find it.
- joe is the name of the new window. This will be important in a moment.
- config= reads that what follows will configure the window. Currently there are only a couple of configuration settings—the height and the width of the window—but there are many more window parameters you can set.

The Config Commands

You might be pleased to hear that config is pretty much a dead command. You do not have to use it if you don't want to. But the teacher in me suggests you should continue with it. It's good coding and helps you to understand what is happening. I still use it every time I write code for a new window.

The config commands in our script will open a new window that is 300 pixels wide by 300 pixels high.

NOTE

By the way—always make your window a little larger than you need. Many people have screens set at smaller resolutions than you do and the window that fits perfectly for you will not for them. Be kind. Go big.

You may be wondering if these config= subcommands are properties. No. But if thinking of them as properties helps you remember them, great. In reality, these little gems are called "features." A feature is something that acts as a parameter of a JavaScript event. These little pups are features of the new window that the script opened up.

There are numerous features that work under the config= command. Height and width you already know. They work by adding the number wide by number high in pixels. The remainder of these commands all work using yes or no, depending on whether or not you want to include the element in your page. Remember, even if you use every one of these attributes, be sure to run them all together just as we did the height and width in the example script. A space equals an error. Here are the Config commands and what they do:

- toolbar= The toolbar is the line of buttons at the top of the browser window that contains Back, Forward, Stop, Reload, and other buttons.
- menubar= The menu bar is the line of items labeled File, Edit, View, Go, and so on, which gives the user access to menus of options.
- scrollbars= I wouldn't make a new window that would need scrollbars. I think it kills the effect.
- resizable= Denotes whether the user can change the size of the window by dragging the window's resize area.
- location= The location bar is the space at the top of the browser window where the page URL is displayed.
- directories= This is the bar at the top of the Netscape browser window that has the bookmarks and such.
- status= Denotes whether the window will contain a status bar.

Here's an example of what code would look like using some of these commands:

```
('opened.html', 'joe', config='height=300,width=300,
➥toolbar=no,menubar=0,status=1')
```

You should notice that for the toolbar, we used no because we didn't want one. For the menu bar and status bars, we used 0 and 1. Which is right?

Well, you can use both. Remember that JavaScript counts everything…and…it starts counting from zero. To JavaScript, zero means *no*. One means *yes*.

But use the words *yes* and *no*. We just wanted to make you aware that, once again, JavaScript was counting and it was counting up from zero.

What About the Title Bar?

In case you're wondering whether you can lose the title bar, and apparently you are, the answer is no. That's a given. You get it, like it or not.

Tags in the New Window

The new window that pops up can be more than a frame for the HTML document that is posted inside. As you can see from the new window in this lesson's example, I made the background a nice greenish-blue. Also, there were two links.

The first link opened the HTML Goodies site in the main window. This is the code that made it happen:

```
<A HREF="http://www.htmlgoodies.com" TARGET="main"></A>
```

Whether you knew it or not, the big window has a name, main. There's no need for you to name it main; it's already done from the start for you. It's the default name of the big window. In fact, it has three names: main, parent, and opener. Use any one of those as the target and the output of the hypertext link will display in the big window. It's another little extra from the friendly folks at JavaScript, Inc. (Netscape, actually. It invented JavaScript.)

All I did was add the command TARGET="--" to the <A HREF> flag, and enter main to indicate where the page should load.

But what if you wanted the page to load in the small window? In that case, you would add nothing. You should know from basic HTML that any hypertext link, by default, loads into its own window. Just make a link to appear in the little window and when you click, the page will display in the little window.

Multiple Windows

You can actually have multiple windows by adding multiple window.open commands. Just make sure to give each window a different name. Then you can have links from window to window, as long as you continue to target the links correctly.

Suppose you have this code on your main window page:

```
<SCRIPT LANGUAGE="javascript">
window.open('opened.html','joe',config='height=300,width=300')
</SCRIPT>

<SCRIPT LANGUAGE="javascript">
window.open('nextopened.html','andree',
➥config='height=300,width=300')
</SCRIPT>
```

Two windows will pop up. Then, as long as you set the target correctly, you could target links from one window to the next. This HTML code, which showed up in the small window named joe, would target a link to open in the second small window named andree:

```
<A HREF="page.html" TARGET="andree">Click</A>
```

As long as you keep the names straight, you can target your links to the main window or any one of the smaller windows that have opened.

Closing the Window

In the original example for this lesson, the second link on the new window closed it. Here's the format to do that:

```
<A HREF="" onClick="self.close()">Click To Close</A>
```

It's a basic <A HREF> link that points to nothing. See the empty quotation marks following the HREF=? Setting the link to point to nothing disallows another page to load. The command that actually closes the window is onClick="self.close()".

self is a property of window. The command close is a method that does the dirty work.

Some people would rather their window not be closed by a simple link. They believe a button looks much more official. There's some merit in that. If you would rather use a button to close your window, here's the code:

```
<FORM>
<INPUT TYPE="button" VALUE="Click to Close the Window"
➥ onClick="self.close()">
</FORM>
```

One More Thing—Opening the Window on Call

Let's say you wanted to open a window on command rather than just having it occur when the person logs in. Try this.

```
<A HREF="curretpage.html" onClick="window.open('opened.html', 'joe',
config='height=300,width=300')">Click To Open 'joe'</A>
```

The format is a HREF link pointed towards itself. You see, this main window will stay open. It must have a page to load, so make it reload itself. The onClick command does the work and the instance contains the parameters.

If you would like the effect in button form, the code is even a little bit cleaner. You don't need to point an <A HREF> link anywhere.

```
<FORM>
<INPUT TYPE="button" VALUE="Click to Open a New Window"
➥ onClick="window.open('opened.html', 'joe',
➥config='height=300,width=300')">
</FORM>
```

And you never thought there was so much to getting a new window to open.

Your Assignment

I didn't get a chance to show you all the extra little functions that are available in action. So, your assignment is to write a script that opens a new window incorporating every one of those features:

- Make the window 300 pixels tall by 500 pixels wide.
- Include a location bar and a status bar.
- Don't include a toolbar, menu bar, scrollbar, or directories.
- Make the new window resizable.

There should be two links:

- One opens a new page in the main window.
- The second page opens a new page in the same window.
- The second page that opens in the small window should have the links to close the window.

Oh, and make the background yellow (ffff00).

To see a possible answer on your own computer, click on Lesson 19 Assignment in your download packet or see it online at http://www.htmlgoodies.com/JSBook/ assignment19.html.

Lesson 20: Opening a Window with a Function

In Lesson 19, we opened a new window using the `window.open` command. That window was then filled with a different HTML document we named in the instance.

Here we're going to create a new window function where the new window, and all of its contents, will be carried along in the same HTML document. It is literally the equivalent of two pages in one.

Remember in Lessons 17 and 18 we talked about pre-loading images for your image flips? Think of this as pre-loading a second page. Here's our example script:

```
<SCRIPT LANGUAGE="javascript">
function openindex()
{
var OpenWindow=window.open("", "newwin", "height=300,width=300");
OpenWindow.document.write("<HTML>")
OpenWindow.document.write("<TITLE>New Window</TITLE>")
OpenWindow.document.write("<BODY BGCOLOR='00ffff'>")
OpenWindow.document.write("<CENTER>")
OpenWindow.document.write("<font size=+1> New Window</font><P>")
OpenWindow.document.write("<a href= 'http://www.htmlgoodies.com'
➡ target='main'>")
OpenWindow.document.write("This will open<BR>
➡ in the main window</a><p>")
OpenWindow.document.write("<P><HR WIDTH='60%'><P>")
OpenWindow.document.write("<a href='' onClick='self.close()'>
➡ This closes the window</a><p>")
OpenWindow.document.write("</CENTER>")
OpenWindow.document.write("</HTML>")
}
</SCRIPT>
```

...and in the BODY command:

```
onLoad="openindex()"
```

The script's effect is exactly the same as in Lesson 19, as you can see in Figure 4.6. The same size window opens and contains the same two links. The difference is that it was all done with one page.

 You can try the script out for yourself by clicking on Lesson 20 Script's Effect in your download packet or see it online at `http://www.htmlgoodies.com/JSBook/lesson20example.html`*.*

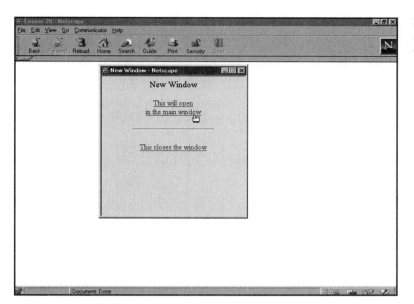

Figure 4.6
Our script opens a new window.

Deconstructing the Script

The main script, the code between the <SCRIPT> and </SCRIPT> that contains the function, is placed between the <HEAD> and </HEAD>, as are most functions.

The function is named openindex(), in the normal fashion.

Then the braces go in to surround what the function will do when called upon.

We now get to the meat of the script. The variable OpenWindow is created to represent the window.open("instance") command. It looks like this:

```
var OpenWindow=window.open("", "newwin", "height=300,width=300');
```

The format is familiar. The only real difference is that there is no URL writing the first set of quotation marks. See the empty double quotation marks? They tell the browser to look to the script to find the new window information, rather than looking for a another page somewhere on the server.

It's very similar to not placing a URL in the command that closed the window. It wouldn't close if it had something to load. Same here. It wouldn't look to the script if it had something else to load.

Now we start to build the HTML page that will go inside the new window. Here's the first line of text:

```
OpenWindow.document.write("<HTML>")
```

This format should also look somewhat familiar. The command is saying that on the variable OpenWindow (the new window) this line of text should be written.

Look back at the full script. That format is followed again and again, writing line after line of text. There's no reason why there cannot be hundreds on lines of text creating a fully functioning HTML document.

I would suggest again that you pay close attention to the double and single quotation mark patterns.

Finally, the function is triggered in the BODY command through an onLoad Event Handler.

Getting the Window on Call

Maybe you don't want this window to open when the page loads. The effect might be better if the page opened when the user clicked on a link or a button.

You would follow the same patterns outlined in Lesson 19, except here the user's click would activate the function rather than call for a new window.

Here's the format for a hypertext link that opens the window:

```
<A HREF="curretpage.html" onClick="openindex()">
➥Click To Open 'joe'</A>
```

And here's the code for the button:

```
<FORM>
<INPUT TYPE="button" VALUE="Click to Open a New Window"
➥ onClick="openindex()">
</FORM>
```

Your Assignment

For today's assignment, you'll create a window that opens using a function. Please make the document that appears in the window have a green background.

In addition, make the TITLE command read Hello *user name* - Here is your window! You can gather the user's name through a prompt. Of course, make a link that closes the window.

The big concern now is where to put the prompt. Think about when you want it to appear. If you want the prompt to appear when the user first enters the page, put it in the document outside of the function. If you want the prompt to appear when the new window is called for, put it in the function. Put it first in the function.

To see a possible answer on your own computer, click on Lesson 20 Assignment in your download packet or see it online at http://www.htmlgoodies.com/JSBook/ assignment20.html.

Lesson 21: The Confirm Method, with an Introduction to If and Else

The confirm() method acts very much like the alert() method, except confirm() adds a Cancel button to the dialog box. You should use alert to simply pass along information to the user. confirm is best for when you want some feedback.

If you use the confirm() method by itself, it doesn't do much except post the OK and Cancel buttons. No matter which button you choose, you go in.

But add the if and else commands, and you start to get some neat effects.

First, we'll look at the basic format. This script doesn't do much:

```
<SCRIPT LANGUAGE="javascript">
confirm("Are you sure you want to enter?")
</SCRIPT>
```

Look familiar? It should. It's the same format as an alert(), except the word *confirm* is used instead of *alert*. Figure 4.7 shows an example of what this little script does.

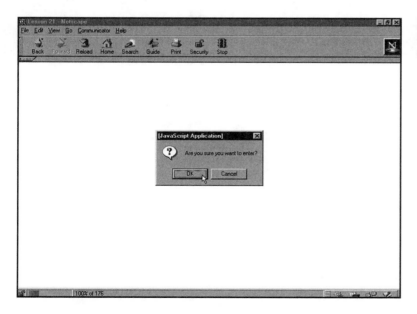

Figure 4.7
The script displays a confirm box.

You can try the confirm box yourself by clicking on Lesson 21 Script's Effect One in your download packet or see it online at http://www.htmlgoodies.com/JSBook/ lesson21example.html.

As you saw, if you looked, no matter which button you chose, you got to see the page load.

Now here's the same script with some new additions:

```
<SCRIPT LANGUAGE="javascript">
if (confirm("Are you sure you want to enter Effect Two?") )
{
location.href='lesson21effect2c.html'
alert("Good choice")
}
else
{
alert("Then you'll stay right here")
}
</SCRIPT>
```

You can see what you get in Figure 4.8. The effect works best if you are coming from another page to see it. When you open the page listed above, you'll get a link. Click on the link, and then you'll see the effect.

Figure 4.8
The confirm box after clicking OK.

You can try the second confirm box yourself by clicking on Lesson 21 Script's Effect Two in your download packet or see it online at `http://www.htmlgoodies.com/JSBook/` `lesson21example2.html`*.*

Now we're getting somewhere. Here's a link that will ask you if you want to enter. Only this time—if you say OK, you'll go in. If you say Cancel, you don't.

There are actually three pages involved in the effect:

- The page with the Click To Go! Link.
- The page that contains the `confirm` script. This page displays if the user clicks Cancel. In the preceding example, if this page loads, the word *Chicken!* shows up.
- The page that displays whether the user clicks OK. This is the page URL in the `confirm` script.

Try the script again. See whether you can pick out the three pages.

Deconstructing the Script

The process of the script is quite logical, as is all JavaScript. First, the script makes the statement:

```
if (confirm("Are you sure you want to enter HTML Goodies?") )
```

The `if` means, "Here is your chance to make a choice."

Before going on, look at the multiple use of parentheses. The `if` statement always has an instance, and that means parentheses. But you also know that `confirm()`, too, has parentheses. That's fine. Just use the parentheses like you normally would, and you'll get the look above. Notice how the parentheses from the `if` command simply surround the entire `confirm` method, including its parentheses. Back to the script.

Because this is a choice, there are options. In this case, we're using a `confirm()` method to offer two choices, OK and Cancel. I think of them as yes and no.

Immediately following the `if` statement are the commands to be carried out for each choice. Please notice the commands are encased inside those lovely little {braces}. Because {} are involved, you might think that what is encased is a function. I guess if you want to think of it that way, that is fine, but technically it isn't. That's just the format of an `if` statement. The commands in the first set of {braces} are what should happen if the user chooses OK:

```
{
location.href='lesson21effect2c.html'
alert("Good choice")
}
```

The line `location.href` creates a link. If that's the choice the user makes, we have a basic alert proclaiming `Good Choice`.

But what if you choose Cancel? We already know that the commands that immediately follows the `if` statement is what will happen if you choose OK.

Notice that right after the first set of braces ends, the word `else` pops up.

Think of the command `else` as meaning *if not*. So, the code

```
else
{
alert("Then you'll stay right here")
}
```

means, "if not, post the alert message and do not change the page."

Put it all together, and you get the effect of giving the user a choice—go in or don't go in. And you've also set up an event to occur either way.

Your Assignment

Don't get nervous! You can do this. Your assignment is to turn the commands we've discussed into a function. Oh, and make it so that when the person chooses not to go in, not only does the alert pop up, but the status bar of the window reads `Chicken!`.

If you really want to be fancy, if the person chooses OK, make the page come up on a new window.

 To see a possible answer on your own computer, click on Lesson 21 Assignment in your download packet or see it online at `http://www.htmlgoodies.com/JSBook/` `assignment21.html`.

By the way, to see the answer, you actually have to hit the Cancel button. Sorry about the `Chicken!` in the status bar. I mean it in the nicest way.

Lesson 22: The Fourth End of Chapter Review—Some Jumping Jacks

The scripts and commands in this chapter are real crowd pleasers, so this should be a pretty good end of chapter wrap up.

I'm going to list the commands you've learned so far. Read them over and start thinking how you could use them to create something new and functional to use on your pages.

Table 4.1 contains the object-related JavaScript commands we've discussed. In addition, you've been introduced to these other JavaScript concepts:

- The alert(), confirm(), and prompt() methods
- The If/Else conditional statement
- These Event Handlers: onBlur, onChange, onClick, onDblClick, onFocus, onKeyDown, onKeyPress, onKeyUp, onLoad, onMouseDown, onMouseMove, onMouseOut, onMouseOver, onMouseUp, onSubmit
- The HTML 4.0 flag <SPAN>
- Creating variable names
- Creating a function

Table 4.1   Object-Related JavaScript Commands Demonstrated in Chapters 1 Through 4

Object	Methods	Properties
date	getDate() getDay() getHours() getMinutes() getMonth() getSeconds() getYear()	
document	write()	alinkColor, bgColor, fgColor, linkColor, lastModified, location, referrer, title, vlinkColor
history	go()	length
location		host, hostname, href
navigator userAgent		appCodeName, appName, appVersion,
window	close()	defaultstatus, directories, location, menubar, resizable, self, scrollbars, status, toolbar

Here's a script that puts some of the JavaScript commands to work:

```
<FORM>
<INPUT TYPE="button" VALUE="Jump!"
onClick="document.jj.src='up.gif',
➥ window.status='Put me down!'; return true">
<INPUT TYPE="button" VALUE="Stop"
➥ onClick="document.jj.src='down.gif', window.status='Thank you!'">?
</FORM>
<IMG SRC="up.gif" NAME="jj">
```

We're using Andree's wonderful artwork again for this one. You already know how to make the jumping jack images work as an image flip. This script will allow your user to decide when the person jumps by clicking form buttons, as you can see in Figure 4.9. Better yet, the little image yells at the person clicking the buttons in the status bar.

Figure 4.9
Manual jumping jacks.

 You can try the manual jumping jacks yourself by clicking on Lesson 22 Script's Effect One in your download packet or see it online at `http://www.htmlgoodies.com/JSBook/` `lesson22example.html`.

Deconstructing the Script

What we've got here is basically something that's fun. But stop and think of the uses for changing an image when a click occurs. You could make one of the images a solid color, the same color as the background so that when the user clicks, it appears as if the image comes up out of nowhere.

You could use one of the buttons as a link and have the image change when the user clicks. It would be great for clicks where the user stays at the same page. A link to a file to be downloaded is a good example.

The concept we want to get across here is that images and the items that control them do not have to be in the same HTML flag like the image flips.

As long as you keep the names equal in the hierarchy statements, you can separate the buttons and the images completely, as we've done here.

Let's break it down.

The Form Buttons

The code for the form buttons looks like this:

```
<FORM>
<INPUT TYPE="button" VALUE="Jump!"
onClick="document.jj.src='up.gif',
➥ window.status='Put me down!'; return true">
<INPUT TYPE="button" VALUE="Stop"
➥onClick="document.jj.src='down.gif'; window.status='Thank you!'">?
</FORM>
```

The only reason we have one `<FORM>` and one `</FORM>` flag to make the two buttons is because that allows the buttons to sit on the same line. If we used separate `<FORM>` and `</FORM>` flags for each button, they would have stacked on top of each other.

Changing the Image

Here's the code that creates the image flip:

```
onClick="document.jj.src='up.gif'
```

You should recognize the `onClick` Event Handler by now. The hierarchy statement might still be a little new. We'll take it piece by piece, biggest to smallest, left to right:

- document is the HTML document the buttons and images will sit upon.
- jj is the name we have assigned to the image command.
- src stands for the source of the image.
- After an equal sign, the image name, or URL if needed, is written in.

The Text in the Status Bar

The text in the status bar is produced at the same time as the click, so we get that `window.status` command right next to the `onClick` Event Handler, separated by a comma. It looks like this:

```
, window.status='Put me down!'; return true"
```

The `return true` statement ensures the text will act only when the click comes.

The second button is put together the same way, but is calling for the original image. Thus, it appears you are putting the jumping jacks man down.

The Image

The image code should look pretty familiar:

```
<IMG SRC="up.gif" NAME="jj">
```

The NAME attribute is used to connect this image with the buttons that sit just above it. Remember in the hierarchy statement in the buttons that we used the name jj? Here you can see how we connected jj to the image.

Now, see whether you can think of a few more interesting ways to use the button to image link. There have to be a hundred good things that can come out of my giggling at the little stick figure screaming for me to stop.

Your Assignment

As always, your assignment is to look over the commands you've learned and create something new, interesting, and functional to put on your Web page. But as always, I make a suggestion.

Can you alter the confirm() script in Lesson 21 so that when the user clicks Cancel, he or she is taken back one page?

That way, the user would go back to where he or she came from, rather than to the page that contains the script loading. Try it.

 To see a possible answer on your own computer, click on Lesson 22 Assignment in your download packet or see it online at http://www.htmlgoodies.com/JSBook/ assignment22.html.

Chapter 5

Forms: A Great Way to Interact with Your Users

This chapter contains the following lessons and scripts:

Until this point, we have gathered information from the user mostly through a prompt. In this chapter, we're going to look at using JavaScript commands along with HTML form flags. Users will be able to enter their data into form fields, and send the results along to you or use the form elements as new methods of choosing links.

We should state here that the forms below are all simply mailto: format scripts. We have not gone as far as attaching the output of the script to a CGI, as is commonplace today.

The possibilities of what you can do with JavaScript and HTML forms are endless.

Lesson 23: What Is Written in the Text Box?

When you are dealing with form elements, there are three basic JavaScript events you want to be able to perform.

- Extract the information from the fields so that you can use it for other purposes
- Display information in a form element
- Send the information to yourself over email

This lesson will deal with the first event. Someone has written something into a form field on your HTML document. Now you want to extract and display back to that person what she wrote in the field.

In this lesson, pay close attention to how the form elements are named and the format of the JavaScript hierarchy statement. Those two elements are, by far, the most important concepts in this lesson, and possibly this chapter.

The sample script is being displayed in full HTML format to show the placement of the elements:

```
<HTML>
<HEAD>
<TITLE>Lesson 23</TITLE>
<SCRIPT LANGUAGE="JavaScript">
function readit()
{
alert("You wrote " + document.myform.thebox.value + " in the box.")
}
</SCRIPT>
</HEAD>
<BODY>
<FORM NAME="myform">
Write something in the box. <INPUT TYPE="text" NAME="thebox"><p>
<INPUT TYPE="button" VALUE="Then Click Here" onClick="readit()">
</FORM>

</BODY>
</HTML>
```

In Figure 5.1, I've entered my name into the box and pressed the button.

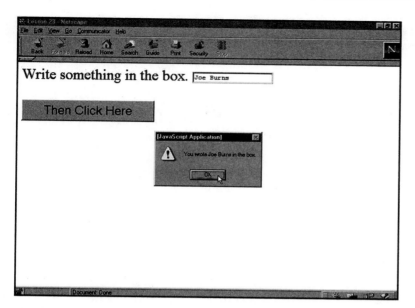

Figure 5.1
Displaying text box data.

Click Here To see the effect on your own computer click on Lesson 23 Script's Effect in your download packet or see it online at http://www.htmlgoodies.com/JSBook/lesson23example.html.

Deconstructing the Script

When you start working with forms, the uses of hierarchy statement and NAME attributes become very important. We will move through this script from top to bottom, often referencing from the function to the form elements.

The Function

The function's purpose in this script is to take the information that was written to the text box and display it as part of an alert() box. It looks like this:

```
<SCRIPT LANGUAGE="JavaScript">
function readit()
{
alert("You wrote " + document.myform.thebox.value + " in the box.")
}
</SCRIPT>
```

The alert() format should be familiar. The new coding is the longer, more specific hierarchy statement representing what is written in the box. The hierarchy statement reads like this:

```
document.myform.thebox.value
```

111

Without a more in-depth explanation, now we'll stop and look at the HTML form elements. You need to become familiar with them in order to understand the hierarchy statement when we do return to it. The FORM code is as follows:

```
<FORM NAME="myform">
Write something in the box. <INPUT TYPE="text" NAME="thebox"><p>
<INPUT TYPE="button" VALUE="Then Click Here" onClick="readit()">
</FORM>
```

Here is each line of the form and what it means.

- <FORM NAME="myform"> is the overriding form command that starts the entire form process. The NAME= attribute gives the entire form a name. You must do this even if there is only one form on the page. Every form must have an overriding name.

- <INPUT TYPE="text" NAME="thebox"> is the name of the form element we are most concerned with. This is the element where I wrote my name. The NAME= attribute in this case gives a name to the form element.

  Now the form itself has a name and the form element has a name. It is important that you make that separation in your mind. The form is now named myform and the specific form element is named thebox.

- <INPUT TYPE="button" VALUE="Then Click Here" onClick="readit()"> is the button you clicked to get the alert. The JavaScript in this button is an Event Handler that calls upon the function above, onClick="readit()".

- </FORM> ends the HTML form section of the script.

Back to the Hierarchy Statement

Here is the hierarchy statement from the function, one more time:

```
document.myform.thebox.value
```

Remember that in hierarchy statements, things go from biggest to smallest, left to right. In this case, the hierarchy statement is narrowing down the items on the page until we get to the specific text I wrote in the box:

- document refers to the HTML document sitting inside the browser window.

- myform is the name of the form on the page. Again, because there is only one form on the page, this seems unneeded, but you're speaking JavaScript. You have to follow the syntax.

- thebox is the name of the text box form element where I wrote my name.

- value is the JavaScript representation of what I wrote in the box.

Now here's the entire `alert()` command from the function above:

```
alert("You wrote " + document.myform.thebox.value + " in the box.")
```

The format is very similar to what we did in earlier lessons. We gathered information from the user, usually in the form of a prompt, and then returned that value to the page through an `alert()` or a `document.write`.

This is exactly the same method, except we are gathering the text written into a text box through a hierarchy statement pointed right at the value.

The more things change, the more they stay the same.

The Entire Process

So what is happening in this JavaScript?

The function is loaded into the browser's memory, but nothing is actually done with it. It isn't needed until the form button is clicked.

After something is written into the form box, the user then clicks the button.

The button click triggers the function. It starts to post an alert box. However, if the button isn't clicked, nothing happens. But let's assume the user clicks the button. The text of the alert box calls for the value of a form element, `thebox`, inside a form, `myform`, on the current document.

After that data is retrieved, the alert box is posted. End of JavaScript.

Your Assignment

Your assignment should take you a little bit of brainpower. Take the preceding script and add a second text box to it. You'll have to assign it a NAME, of course.

Then get the alert button to pop up and read Hello *firstname lastname*!

You'll get extra points if you can turn the long hierarchy statements into variable names.

 You can see a possible answer to this assignment on your own computer by clicking on Lesson 23 Assignment in your download packet or see it online at `http://www.htmlgoodies.com/ JSBook/assignment23.html`.

Lesson 24: Passing Information to the Function

Now that we understand the concept of how to extract the value from a form item, let's play with it a bit. This lesson's script will post a series of alert boxes that tell you the values in the boxes, change the text to all uppercase, and then to all lowercase.

After all the alert boxes have finished, text will show up in a third text box thanking you for watching the show.

The concept is this: If you can take information out of a form element, you can certainly put it back.

```
<SCRIPT LANGUAGE="JavaScript">
function readitagain()
{
var greeting="Hello "

alert(greeting + document.myform.fname.value + " "
➥ + document.myform.lname.value)

alert("length of first name " + document.myform.fname.value.length)

alert("First name in ALL CAPS: "
➥ + document.myform.fname.value.toUpperCase())

alert("Full name in all lowercase letters: "
➥ + document.myform.fname.value.toLowerCase() + " "
➥ + document.myform.lname.value.toLowerCase())

document.myform.receiver.value= ("Thanks "
➥ + document.myform.fname.value + ".")

}
</SCRIPT>
<FORM NAME="myform">
What is your First Name? <INPUT TYPE="text" NAME="fname"><p>
What is your Last Name? <INPUT TYPE="text" NAME="lname"><p>
<INPUT TYPE="button" VALUE="Submit" onClick="readitagain()"><P>
Look Here after Alert Boxes: <INPUT TYPE="text" NAME="receiver"><P>
</FORM>
```

Figure 5.2 shows the script's effect.

 You can try the script out for yourself by clicking on Lesson 24 Script's Effect in your download packet or see it online at http://www.htmlgoodies.com/JSBook/lesson24effect.html.

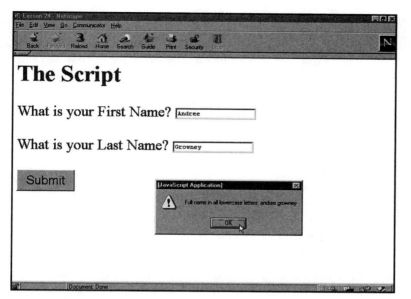

Figure 5.2
This alert box changes a name to lowercase letters.

Deconstructing the Script

Let's start at the bottom and work our way back up the scale of the script. Here are the four form elements first:

```
<FORM NAME="myform">
What is your First Name? <INPUT TYPE="text" NAME="fname"><p>
What is your Last Name? <INPUT TYPE="text" NAME="lname"><p>
<INPUT TYPE="button" VALUE="Submit" onClick="readitagain()"><P>
Look Here after Alert Boxes: <INPUT TYPE="text" NAME="receiver"><P>
</FORM>
```

- The entire form has been named myform. That will go first, immediately following document in the hierarchy statement.
- The first text box is named fname. It will contain the first name. That makes sense.
- The second text box is named lname. It will contain the last name. Again, that's logical.
- The input button is the familiar format. It is used to trigger the earlier function we called readitagain().
- The third text box is named receiver because it will receive something from the function.

OK, now you know the players, let's get to the plays found in the function.

The Alert Boxes

Probably the easiest way to break down this script is to look at each element in the function. You might have already quickly noticed that the function is a long list of alerts that will run one right after the other.

Finally, there's a hierarchy statement pointing at something. We'll look at that last. But first, the alerts:

```
var greeting="Hello "

alert(greeting + document.myform.fname.value + " "
➥ + document.myform.lname.value)
```

The first alert shown in the preceding code uses a variable greeting to place the word *Hello*. Do you find it funny that our variable name is longer than the actual word and space it's representing? Me too, but all this is to teach, so we did it.

We then called for the first and last name from the text boxes using the full hierarchy statements.

No surprises here.

```
alert("length of first name " + document.myform.fname.value.length)
```

Here's something new. The alert posts the length, in letters, or whatever you put into the first text box.

You might have taken it from the earlier lesson that value was at the end of the hierarchy food chain when it came to forms. It was for that lesson, but not for all of JavaScript. value has a couple of properties, actually. Its length is just one of them. The JavaScript counts the letters, spaces, and any symbols in the value and posts the number it comes up with.

Luckily, in this case, JavaScript does not start counting at zero.

Once again, we see a familiar hierarchy statement with something stuck on the end of it:

```
alert("First name in ALL CAPS: "
➥ + document.myform.fname.value.toUpperCase())
```

This statement takes the information from the first name box and changes all the letters to uppercase.

It's done by attaching the toUpperCase() method on the very end. Please note that toUpperCase() is a method and you need those parentheses at the end.

Now be careful; it might appear that toUpperCase() is part of the hierarchy. It is not. toUpperCase() is there to act upon the text string returned from the hierarchy statement, the value inside the text box. Don't let that confuse you. toUpperCase() is not part of the hierarchy.

If you can change letters to uppercase, it follows logically that you can change them to lowercase:

```
alert("Full name in all lowercase letters: "
➡ + document.myform.fname.value.toLowerCase() + " "
➡ + document.myform.lname.value.toLowerCase())
```

It's done by following the same formula shown earlier, but changing the method at the end to toLowerCase(). Again, note the parentheses. toLowerCase() is a method.

Writing to the Text Box

Now we get to the most interesting part of this script. How did we get that text to show up in the text box? Here's the line of code that did it:

```
document.myform.receiver.value= ("Thanks "
➡ + document.myform.fname.value + ".")
```

The concept is fairly straightforward. When you use the hierarchy statement document.myform.receiver.value as a return, you get the value of the text box returned.

But if you turn the process around and use the hierarchy statement as a target, as is being done above, the statement places the value rather than returning it.

That's why the text in the instance pops into the box.

Your Assignment

OK, smart person! Try to do this one:

- Create a script that has two prompts. The first prompt asks for a name, the second one asks for a home state.
- After the two prompts have been filled in, two text boxes and a button should appear.
- When you click the button, the first text box should read: Your name is *name*.
- The second box should read: You are from *state*.
- Both effects should occur with one click of the button.

 You can see a possible answer to this assignment on your own computer by clicking on Lesson 24 Assignment in your download packet or see it online at http://www.htmlgoodies.com/ JSBook/assignment24.html.

Lesson 25: Calling Functions with Forms

At face value, this lesson's script might seem rather simple, but its workings are quite new and rather important. Up until now, the functions that we created have been stable in that they couldn't be altered by the user.

This script will allow your users to pass information from form elements to the function itself before the function runs.

The following script will again show the full HTML document. (Forms always begin with <FORM> and end with </FORM>. No surprises here yet, just good old HTML!)

```
<HTML>
<HEAD>
<SCRIPT LANGUAGE="JavaScript">
function newcolor(color)
{
alert("You Chose " + color)
document.bgColor=color
}
</SCRIPT>
</HEAD>
<BODY>
<h3>Select a Background Color</h3>
<FORM>
<INPUT TYPE="button" VALUE="Blue" onClick="newcolor('lightblue')">
<INPUT TYPE="button" VALUE="Pink" onClick="newcolor('pink')">
</FORM>
</BODY>
</HTML>
```

As you can see in Figure 5.3, this script uses form buttons to allow you to choose a background color, either blue or pink.

 You can try the script out for yourself by clicking on Lesson 25 Script's Effect in your download packet or see it online at http://www.htmlgoodies.com/JSBook/lesson25effect.html.

Literals

We mentioned this term in passing before, but now you can add it to your JavaScript vocabulary. A *literal* is a data value that appears directly in a program, and can be a string in double or single quotation marks, a value, or numbers. Even NULL is considered to be a literal. Just remember that a literal is solid. It cannot be altered.

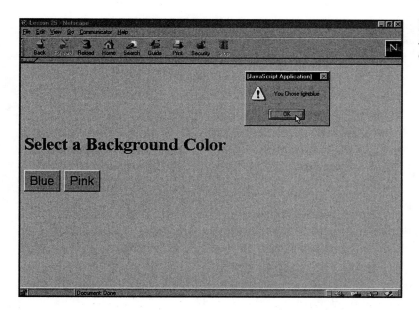

Figure 5.3
*Describing the change in
color in a message box.*

String

A *string* is any run of letters or numbers within single or double quotation marks. Therefore, the following section from the sample script

```
onClick="newcolor('lightblue')
```

defines the literal string lightblue.

You might now ask, so what? Well, the *so what* is this: When you place text into a format like this, it becomes a literal, and you cannot then use the text for something else.

Let's say you set up this script with literals like document.title and Date(). You know that you want the page title and the full date returned, but JavaScript doesn't see it like that. It sees those commands only as text and displays them as such.

Go ahead—try it. Drive yourself nuts.

Deconstructing the Script

Here are the script's input items again:

```
function newcolor(color)
{
alert("You chose " + color)
document.bgColor=color
}
<form>
```

119

```
<INPUT TYPE="button" VALUE="blue" onClick="newcolor('lightblue')">
<INPUT TYPE="button" VALUE="Pink" onClick="newcolor('pink')">
</form>
```

Here's the basic concept: We are passing a literal string, `'lightblue'` or `'pink'`, to the function `newcolor(color)`.

Basically, the function is waiting until it is called on and given the information it needs to perform.

Remember that in all functions up until this point, the parentheses were empty. The function had all the parts it needed. Here it does not have the required parts, and it won't until someone clicks on a button.

Look again at the form button code. The buttons contain the function format in their `onClick=`, only this time the function has the data it needs: a color command.

Think of it this way: The function line at the top of the script is sitting there with a variable name inside the function instance. Here, it's `color`. When you trigger the `onClick` in the button, the same function name is used. But this time, there is a real color name in the instance, and it is assigned the variable name it replaced, `color`.

So how does the JavaScript know that the word *color* in the original function is only a variable name? It doesn't. In fact, the JavaScript never looked at it. The function text was loaded into memory, but until it's triggered by the button, the function never runs.

That's good to know because what happens is we've set up a basic template, `function()`. Every time the user clicks, the function is given a new `function()` header, but the `function()` is run with the new value in the parentheses, `lightblue` or `pink`.

If you set up your `onClicks` to include the same text as the function, when the click is made, the `onClick function()` statement replaces the old function line, and assigns the variable name to the new string brought up from the button.

Until now, functions were static. They did what they were written to do. Now you can write functions with a dummy `function()` header, and let the user pass along what he wants to happen.

This is a fairly difficult concept to grasp, but look over the script again, and follow its path from the button back up to the top of the function and then runs.

Your Assignment

Alter the script in this lesson so that you now have three buttons: blue, yellow, and green. Make the same background effect occur, but lose the alert button and post a text box.

When you click on one of the color buttons, the background color should change right away and the text box should read `You Chose color`.

120

You'll get bonus points if you change all the variable names to new words.

 You can see a possible answer to this assignment on your own computer by clicking on Lesson 25 Assignment in your download packet or see it online at `http://www.htmlgoodies.com/ JSBook/assignment25.html`.

Lesson 26: Form Fields and the Value Property

This lesson takes the last one a little farther. You'll transfer information into the function again, but this time you'll transfer a string the user enters into a field. The string will then be used to create a hypertext link and send a search to Yahoo!:

```
<SCRIPT LANGUAGE="JavaScript">
function Gofindit()
{
var searchfor = document.formsearch.findthis.value;
var FullSearchUrl =  "http://av.yahoo.com/bin/query?p=" + searchfor ;
location.href = FullSearchUrl;
}
</SCRIPT>
<FORM NAME="formsearch">
Search Yahoo for: <INPUT NAME="findthis" SIZE="40" TYPE="text">
<INPUT TYPE="button" VALUE="Go Find It" onClick="Gofindit()">
</FORM>
```

Figure 5.4 shows the script in action.

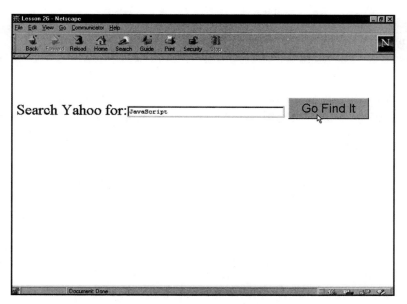

Figure 5.4
Our form is ready to search Yahoo!.

You can try the script out for yourself by clicking on Lesson 26 Script's Effect in your download packet or see it online at `http://www.htmlgoodies.com/JSBook/lesson26effect.html`.

Deconstructing the Script

Do you remember that at the very beginning of this chapter I said there were two main reasons for using forms?

The first reason was to accept and manipulate input from your users. The second was to allow information to be sent back to you or around the Internet.

We have arrived at reason number two.

The Function

The function `Gofindit()` is created in the normal fashion:

```
function Gofindit()
{
var searchfor = document.formsearch.findthis.value;
var FullSearchUrl =  "http://av.yahoo.com/bin/query?p=" + searchfor ;
location.href = FullSearchUrl;
}
```

That's a good title for this one, don't you think?

Three variables are set up. This is a wonderful example of one variable building from the one before it.

The first assigns `searchfor` to a hierarchy statement representing the text box where the user will enter his or her keyword. At this point, assuming everything is correct, you should be able to pick out that the name of the form must be `formsearch` and the name of the text box must be `findthis`.

Another variable is created: `FullSearchUrl`. `FullSearchUrl` is the address to Yahoo's search engine, plus the variable we just created representing the value of the text box.

Finally, `location.href` is assigned `FullSearchUrl`, which represents the entire URL and input, a string literal, from the user.

By going to all this trouble, you get the entire URL, plus the text input down to one word that you can easily put with `location.href`. It's a very clean form of coding.

The HTML Form Code

Now we move on to the FORM flags. There are two flags this time around. One is a text box that receives a string from the user, and the other is a button that enacts the function.

It looks like this:

```
<FORM NAME="formsearch">
Search Yahoo for: <INPUT NAME="findthis" SIZE="40" TYPE="text">
<INPUT TYPE="button" VALUE="Go Find It" onClick="Gofindit()">
</FORM>
```

The entire form is named `formsearch`. The TEXT box has been named `findthis`. But we knew that without looking.

The form button has the `onClick="Gofindit()"` command that triggers the function. Finally, make sure you have a `</FORM>` command to kill the form. Mission accomplished.

What Happens

The user enters a literal string into the box and clicks the button to begin the search. The function is triggered and the value is taken from the text box. The value is attached to the Yahoo! URL for its search engine. The full URL is assigned a variable name and given to a `location.href` command. The information is sent on its way.

Your Assignment

Alter the script so that it uses a search engine other than Yahoo. Also, change the script so that when the user clicks, an alert pops up that reads `Going to Search....`

You might have to go to a different search engine and look at its code to be able to do this assignment.

 You can see a possible answer to this assignment on your own computer by clicking on Lesson 26 Assignment in your download packet or see it online at `http://www.htmlgoodies.com/JSBook/assignment26.html`.

Lesson 27: Pull-Down Menu of Links

Ever since the JavaGoodies Web site first went up, this has been one of the most requested scripts. People just seem to love the look of it. It is nice.

This is a simple drop-down box made with form commands. You choose the link you want and click the button to complete the link, as you can see in Figure 5.5:

```
<SCRIPT LANGUAGE="javascript">
function LinkUp()
{
var number = document.DropDown.DDlinks.selectedIndex;
location.href = document.DropDown.DDlinks.options[number].value;
}
```

```
</SCRIPT>

<FORM NAME="DropDown">
<SELECT NAME="DDlinks">
<OPTION SELECTED>Choose a Link
<OPTION VALUE="page.html"> Page One
<OPTION VALUE="page2.html"> Page Two
<OPTION VALUE="page3.html"> Page Three
</SELECT>

<INPUT TYPE="BUTTON" VALUE="Click to Go!" onClick="LinkUp()">
</FORM>
```

Figure 5.5
Choosing a link from a drop-down list.

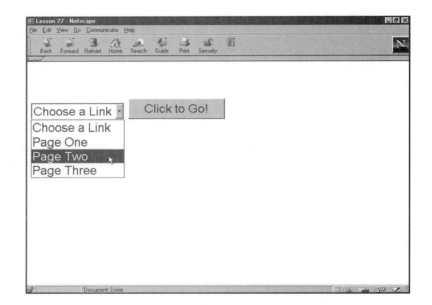

Click Here *You can try the script out for yourself by clicking on Lesson 27 Script's Effect in your download packet or see it online at* http://www.htmlgoodies.com/JSBook/lesson27effect.html.

Deconstructing the Script

Keep two concepts in mind as we go through this deconstruction:

- JavaScript counts everything starting at zero.
- If the HTML form element can't accept a value, you assign it one.

The HTML Form Code

We'll start this from the ground up. Here is the HTML form code:

```
<FORM NAME="DropDown">
<SELECT NAME="DDlinks">
<OPTION SELECTED>Choose a Link
<OPTION VALUE="page.html"> Page One
<OPTION VALUE="page2.html"> Page Two
<OPTION VALUE="page3.html"> Page Three
</SELECT>

<INPUT TYPE="BUTTON" VALUE="Click to Go!" onClick="LinkUp()">
</FORM>
```

Let's get the vitals out of the way first:

- The name of the entire form is DropDown. It is a name I assigned.
- The name of this SELECT form element is DDlinks. It stands for *drop-down links*. It is a name I assigned.
- The first OPTION flag is not part of the links menu simply because I chose to not make it part of the links menu. The code <OPTION SELECTED>Choose a Link displays the text *Choose a Link* on the drop-down box before it's been clicked.
- The next three OPTION statements are links. They have been given VALUEs of page.html, page2.html, and page3.html, respectively. Those are the three links you will get to choose from.

   It is important that you see the VALUE is the actual link, and not the text that follows. Because the drop-down link format is not something that will accept data from a viewer, it cannot accept a literal string. But it can have one assigned to it. That's what we did.
- </SELECT> ends the SELECT drop-down menu box.
- The button code should be familiar by now. It is set with an onClick trigger to activate the function, which we'll get to next.
- </FORM> ends the code.

The Function

This is where the magic happens. It might look complicated at first, but if you've read up to this point, you should have no trouble understanding what's here. Except for two commands, you've actually seen it all before. The function is enacted after a choice is made and the user clicks the button triggering it to start. Here's the function:

```
function LinkUp()
{
var number = document.DropDown.DDlinks.selectedIndex;
location.href = document.DropDown.DDlinks.options[number].value;
}
```

The function is called `LinkUp()`. It's a name we made up.

First, a variable, `number`, is created that represents the number of a link in the drop-down menu.

If you follow along in the hierarchy statement from left to right, `document` is first. Then comes the name of the form itself, `DropDown`, followed by the name of the form element, `DDlinks`. Last in the statement is that new thing, `selectedIndex`.

selectedIndex

This is the command that makes it possible to turn this drop-down menu into a series of links.

Remember that JavaScript counts everything and starts at zero. That means the four items in this list have all been assigned a number, zero through three, starting with the first OPTION SELECTED item, even though it will never come into play.

The `selectedIndex` command allows us to choose one of the items on the list and grab its number. We make it a *selected Index*. Get it?

Setting Up Link Properties

Now that we have a variable set up that will represent the number of the item in the drop-down box, we can start setting up the link properties of the JavaScript.

Here's the code that does that:

```
location.href = document.DropDown.DDlinks.options[number].value;
```

You know that `location.href` means a link. But a link to what? A link to a specific value from the drop-down menu. We know the values are all URLs, so the purpose of this line is to grab a specific value chosen by the user.

It's done with another hierarchy statement. `document` leads it off, and it is followed by the name of the form itself, the name of the form element, and then the option.

In this case, think of the user's option as a property of an array of strings. This drop-down box is as good an array as any other, so we want an option. But which one? The one the user chooses. We know which one he or she chooses because the option is given the number of the choice through the `number` variable in brackets.

So, if I choose the last option in the drop-down menu, I get the number three returned to the `options` property. JavaScript counts everything and it starts at zero.

Then the hierarchy gets going and asks for the `value` of the number returned.

The value is a URL, and the process is complete. The hierarchy link returns a specific value and the link is performed.

It's a very clever method of drawing a link out of the drop-down menu and using it to make a connection.

Your Assignment

This is mostly an assignment to see whether you have the ability to keep everything straight.

Using the script above, copy and paste it a second time on the page. When your page displays, there should be two drop-down boxes: one of them going to links on your site, and one of them going to links off your site.

You know you're obviously going to need to change out the values to change the links, but be careful. There are a few other things you'll need to change as well.

 You can see a possible answer to this assignment on your own computer by clicking on Lesson 27 Assignment in your download packet or see it online at `http://www.htmlgoodies.com/ JSBook/assignment27.html`.

Lesson 28: A Guestbook with All the Bells and Whistles

Whenever you hear someone talking about forms, it's a good bet he wants to use the forms to act as a guestbook for his site.

Most people can get the mail to send to them just fine through basic HTML form code, but then they want more, and the guestbook in this lesson carries every one of the bells and whistles. Once you understand it, apply only the parts you like to your own site's guestbook, or use the whole thing.

This guestbook is a JavaScript driven event that will open with two prompts. One will ask for the person's name and the second, their email address.

The guestbook page will then display. After the user writes in the text box and clicks submit, a second window will pop up thanking them for their email, which is written there for them to see.

When the email arrives in your mailbox, the subject line will read *Mail from user's name at user's email address.*

You'll be the envy of Web designers everywhere.

It actually takes three different scripts and then some HTML form code to make this technique work:

```
<SCRIPT LANGUAGE="javascript">
var name = prompt("What is your name?","Write It Here")
var email = prompt("What is your email address", "Write It Here")
</SCRIPT>


<SCRIPT LANGUAGE="javascript">
function verify()
{
var OpenWindow=window.open("", "newwin", "height=300,width=300");
OpenWindow.document.write("<HTML>")
OpenWindow.document.write("<TITLE>Thanks for Writing</TITLE>")
OpenWindow.document.write("<BODY BGCOLOR='ffffcc'>")
OpenWindow.document.write("<CENTER>")
OpenWindow.document.write("Thank you <B>" + name +
➥ "</B> from <B>" +email+ "</B><P>")
OpenWindow.document.write("Your message <P><I>"
➥ + document.gbookForm.maintext.value + "</I><P>")
OpenWindow.document.write("from " + name + " / " +email+ "<P>")
OpenWindow.document.write("will be sent along
➥ when you close this window.<p>")
OpenWindow.document.write("<CENTER>")
OpenWindow.document.write("<FORM><INPUT TYPE='button'
➥ VALUE='Close Window'  onClick='self.close()'></FORM>")
OpenWindow.document.write("</CENTER>")
OpenWindow.document.write("</HTML>")
}
</SCRIPT>


<SCRIPT LANGUAGE='javascript'>
document.write("<FORM METHOD='post'
➥ ACTION='mailto:jburns@sunlink.net?Subject=Mail from "
➥ +name+ " at " +email+ "'
➥ ENCTYPE='text/plain' NAME='gbookForm'>")
</SCRIPT>


<b>What would you like to tell me?<BR></b>
<TEXTAREA COLS="40"  ROWS="20" NAME="maintext"></TEXTAREA><P>
<INPUT TYPE="submit" VALUE="Send It"  onClick="verify()">
</FORM>
```

As you can see in Figure 5.6, the guestbook is set up to send the output to Joe Burns. So if you want to write me, this is the place to do it. It's coming to a mailbox set up just for this guestbook.

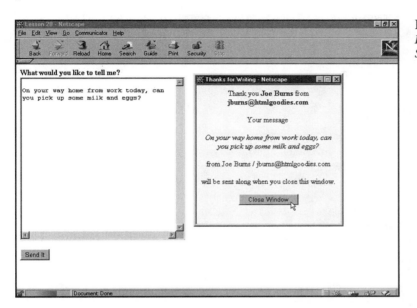

Figure 5.6
Results of the pushing the Send It button.

You can try the script out for yourself by clicking on *Lesson 28 Script's Effect* in your download packet or see it online at `http://www.htmlgoodies.com/JSBook/lesson28effect.html`.

Deconstructing the Script

There is a lot to this script so we're going to talk about it script by script and then at the end, put it all together into one working guestbook package.

The Prompt Script

We'll start where the guestbook event starts. The first thing that happens when the page loads is a couple of prompts pop up asking for your name and email address:

```
<SCRIPT LANGUAGE="javascript">
var name = prompt("What is your name?","Write It Here")
var email = prompt("What is your email address", "Write It Here")
</SCRIPT>
```

There shouldn't be any surprises here. The prompts are in the traditional format. Just remember that the prompt that asked for the name was assigned the variable `name` and the prompt that asked for the email was given the variable `email`.

Those variable names will become quite important later.

The Verification Window Script

This is the script that creates the smaller window that pops up when the user clicks to submit the guestbook data:

```
<SCRIPT LANGUAGE="javascript">
function verify()
{
var OpenWindow=window.open("", "newwin", "height=300,width=300");
OpenWindow.document.write("<HTML>")
OpenWindow.document.write("<TITLE>Thanks for Writing</TITLE>")
OpenWindow.document.write("<BODY BGCOLOR='ffffcc'>")
OpenWindow.document.write("<CENTER>")
OpenWindow.document.write("Thank you <B>" + name + "</B> from <B>"
➥ +email+ "</B><P>")
OpenWindow.document.write("Your message <P><I>"
➥ + document.gbookForm.maintext.value + "</I><P>")
OpenWindow.document.write("from " + name + " / " +email+ "<P>")
OpenWindow.document.write("will be sent along
➥ when you close this window.<p>")
OpenWindow.document.write("<CENTER>")
OpenWindow.document.write("<FORM><INPUT TYPE='button'
➥ VALUE='Close Window' onClick='self.close()'></FORM>")
OpenWindow.document.write("</CENTER>")
OpenWindow.document.write("</HTML>")
}
</SCRIPT>
```

We used the format from Lesson 20, opening a new window with a function. We named the function verify().

The window will open 300 pixels wide and 300 pixels tall. The background will be an off-yellow represented by the hex code ffffcc, and the text in the new window will be centered.

Now we get into how all the relevant text was entered into the window. Remember that we assigned the variables name and email to the information from the two prompts in the first script. Here those returned literal strings come into play. The line

```
OpenWindow.document.write("Thank you <B>" + name + "</B> from <B>"
➥ +email+ "</B><P>")
```

will write the text *Thank you name from email@address.com* to the news window. It's a nice personal touch. Pay close attention to where the double quotes fell as well as where the <B> and </B> flags come into play.

In the next line, we make the connection with the HTML form items that are yet to come in this deconstruction:

```
OpenWindow.document.write("Your message <P><I>"
➥ + document.gbookForm.maintext.value + "</I><P>")
```

Notice first the hierarchy statement that will take the information from the <TEXTAREA> box.

It starts with document, and then calls for a form named gbookForm, then a form element named maintext, and finally that form element's value.

When the HTML in the instance is written to the page, you get the text *Your Message* followed by what the user wrote to the <TEXTAREA> box. It's a very clean effect.

The next lines of code again list the user's name and email address using the name and email returns from the prompts. That might look like overkill since those two pieces of information were already posted; we put them in because it gave the appearance that the information was posted as a signature.

The next code creates a traditional button that will close the window and the last two document.write lines close the HTML document that is being written to the new window's page.

The <FORM> *Flag Script*

In Lesson 16, we talked about using the input from a user to build a line of HTML. The big concern was that the script must be sitting right where the line of HTML code itself will sit.

That's what we're doing here. We are using a simple document.write line to create the main HTML FORM flag:

```
<SCRIPT LANGUAGE='javascript'>
document.write("<FORM METHOD='post'
➥ ACTION='mailto:jburns@sunlink.net?Subject=Mail from "
➥ +name+ " at " +email+ "'
➥ ENCTYPE='text/plain' NAME='gbookForm'>")
</SCRIPT>
```

By doing this, we can use the literal returns from prompts to make the ACTION text actually write the user's name and email address.

NOTE

Please note that the line above is truncated into a couple of lines. That's bad, but the book page just isn't wide enough. When you get this to your page, make sure it all goes on one line.

This was the line in the code that took us the longest time to build. Look at all of the double and single quotes. It gets rather hairy, be we stuck to it, error after error, and got the effect.

As you might have guessed from the hierarchy statement above, the name of this entire form will be gbookForm.

The Rest of the FORM Items

It's not written here because the main FORM flag is in a script by itself, but this is the remainder of the FORM gbookForm:

```
<b>What would you like to tell me?<BR></b>
<TEXTAREA COLS="40"  ROWS="20" NAME="maintext"></TEXTAREA><P>
<INPUT TYPE="submit" VALUE="Send It"  onClick="verify()">
</FORM>
```

The <TEXTAREA> element is named maintext. This is an HTML tip, but remember that when you use a <TEXTAREA> box, it requires an end flag.

Look at the button code. This is quite important. Notice the TYPE is set to submit. Remember, you are submitting this form. If you just wrote in that the type was equal to button, the format would not work. This button not only activates the function verify()—note the onClick=—but it also sends the form.

Wait!

The little window says the button on it sends the mail. I know, but it's part of the illusion of the guestbook. It was done on purpose. The actual mail-sending dirty work was accomplished by the TYPE="submit" button.

It's done so that the user stops for a moment to read the window. That way the browser is given a spot of downtime with which to send the mail.

Clever, no?

What Is Happening?

The process of the guestbook is pretty straightforward:

- The user enters the page and is asked for his or her name and email address.
- Those two literal strings are assigned the variables name and email, respectively.
- The rest of the page loads. The new FORM flag, with the user's name and email address, is written to the page.
- The user writes in the <TEXTAREA> box and presses the submit button.
- The function is triggered and a new page is displayed showing the user what he or she wrote.
- In the background, the mail is being sent while the user reads the mail and thinks what a fantastic guestbook you have.
- The mail arrives in your box with a subject line that tells you have mail from a specific person with a specific email address.

Your Assignment

This was quite a large, multiscript event, but can you add one more touch to it?

When the user clicks on the Send It button, can you make a page that reads Thanks A Lot load into the mail window and still get that new little window?

 You can see a possible answer to this assignment on your own computer by clicking on Lesson 28 Assignment in your download packet or see it online at http://www.htmlgoodies.com/ JSBook/assignment28.html.

Lesson 29: The Fifth End of Chapter Review—Posting Link Descriptions While Users Pass Over

I'm going to list the commands you've learned so far again. Read them over, and start thinking how you could use them to create something new and functional to use on your pages.

Table 5.1 contains the object-related JavaScript commands we've discussed. In addition, you've been introduced to these other JavaScript concepts:

- The alert(), confirm(), and prompt() methods
- The If/Else conditional statement
- These Event Handlers: onBlur, onChange, onClick, onDblClick, onFocus, onKeyDown, onKeyPress, onKeyUp, onLoad, onMouseDown, onMouseMove, onMouseOut, onMouseOver, onMouseUp, onSubmit

- The HTML 4.0 flag `<SPAN>`
- Creating variable names
- Creating a function
- HTML form items
- Form item attribute `NAME=`
- Form item properties: `length, value, selectedIndex`
- Form item methods: `toLowerCase, toUpperCase()`

Table 5.1   Object-Related JavaScript Commands Demonstrated in Chapters 1 Through 5

Object	Methods	Properties
date	getDate() getDay() getHours() getMinutes() getMonth() getSeconds() getYear()	
document	write()	alinkColor, bgColor, fgColor, linkColor, lastModified, location, referrer, title, vlinkColor
history	go()	length
location		host, hostname, href
navigator userAgent		appCodeName, appName, appVersion,
window	close()	defaultstatus, directories, location, menubar, resizable, self, scrollbars, status, toolbar

Here's a script that puts some of the JavaScript commands to work:

```
<TABLE BORDER="0"><TD>

<A HREF="http://www.htmlgoodies.com"
onMouseOver="document.pic1.src='flip1b.gif',
document.PostText.Receive.value='This link points toward the
➡ HTML Goodies Home Page'"
onMouseOut="document.pic1.src='flip1.gif'"><img src="flip1.gif"
➡ NAME="pic1" border="0"></a>
```

```
<A HREF="http://www.JavaGoodies.com"
onMouseOver="document.pic2.src='flip1b.gif',
document.PostText.Receive.value='Click here to go to JavaGoodies'"
onMouseOut="document.pic2.src='flip1.gif'"><img src="flip1.gif"
➥ NAME="pic2" border="0"></a>

<A HREF="http://www.Developer.com"
onMouseOver="document.pic3.src='flip1b.gif',
document.PostText.Receive.value='This is HTML Goodies parent company.
➥   Go see what they are all about.'"
➥ onMouseOut="document.pic3.src='flip1.gif'">
<img src="flip1.gif" NAME="pic3" border="0"></a>

</TD>
<TD>

<FORM NAME="PostText">
<TEXTAREA COLS="20" ROWS="20" they go."
➥   NAME="Receive" wrap="virtual"></TEXTAREA>
</FORM>

</TD>
</TABLE>
```

We're going to combine some image flips with form items in this example. There will be three image flip mystery links sitting to the left of a <TEXTAREA> box. When you pass your mouse over the top of each link, a description of where that link points will pop up in the <TEXTAREA> box, as shown in Figure 5.7.

Think about how you would do it, and then read how we did it.

 You can try the script out for yourself by clicking on Lesson 29 Script's Effect in your download packet or see it online at http://www.htmlgoodies.com/JSBook/lesson29effect.html.

Deconstructing the Script

Let's take this script apart piece by piece. We'll start with its layout and design. Until now, the layout of the scripts didn't much matter. The output was posted somewhere and the look didn't come into play.

Figure 5.7
Image flips posting text to a form item.

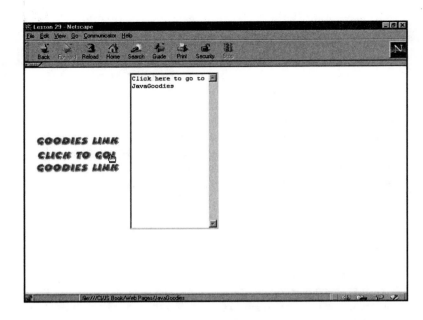

Well, now the layout does matter. The layout is set so that the buttons are all on the left of the <TEXTAREA> box. We got that look through a simple two-celled TABLE layout:

```
<TABLE BORDER="0">
<TD>
The image flips went in here
</TD><TD>
The <TEXTAREA> box went in here
</TD>
</TABLE>
```

However, let me offer a word of caution. When you use tables and JavaScript, you can run into trouble. It's not enough trouble for me to say never use tables and JavaScript together. But be aware that placing HTML elements and JavaScript into table formats, especially if you put different code sections into different table cells, can cause trouble and throw errors.

If you are trying to combine tables and JavaScript and are getting errors, try eliminating the tables. If the script runs, that was your problem. Find a different layout and design format.

The Form

Let's go a little backward. We're going to start with the form and the <TEXTAREA> box first. It looks like this:

```
<FORM NAME="PostText">
<TEXTAREA COLS="20" ROWS="20" NAME="Receive" wrap="virtual"></TEXTAREA>
</FORM>
```

The form itself is named `PostText` and the `<TEXTAREA>` box is named `Receive`.

What I wanted to show was a new HTML attribute that will help with script: `WRAP="virtual"`. The code makes the text that will fall into this box wrap at the end, rather than just running off the right. It's really needed to get the effect we're shooting for.

Now that we know the elements required to create a hierarchy statement, we can get to the image flips.

The Image Flips

This is where all the magic occurs. Here's the first image flip:

```
<A HREF="http://www.htmlgoodies.com"
onMouseOver="document.pic1.src='flip1b.gif',
document.PostText.Receive.value='This link points toward the
➥ HTML Goodies Home Page'"
onMouseOut="document.pic1.src='flip1.gif'"><img src="flip1.gif"
➥ NAME="pic1" border="0"></a>
```

If you learn this one, the others will fall right into place. They follow the same pattern.

This is a lot of text, but the script will work best if everything that is above is allowed to stay on one line, one very long line.

The format for the image flips is pretty basic. The `onMouseOver` points to the document, and then the name of the image space, `pic1`, and finally the `src`, `flip1b.gif`.

But notice that immediately following that, we've placed a comma and then a hierarchy statement pointing at the `<TEXTAREA>` box. It reads:

```
,document.PostText.Receive.value='This link points toward the
➥ HTML Goodies Home Page'"
```

That is what places the text into the box. The hierarchy statement refers to the document, the form we named `PostText`, and the form element we named `Receive`, and then sets its value to `'This link points toward the HTML Goodies Home Page'`.

Because the two hierarchy statements were separated by a comma, the `onMouseOver` triggers them both. The image flips and the text pops up in the box.

A neat effect indeed.

Image Flips

Just remember that when you are doing multiple image flips on the same page, you must always give each image space a new name and change that name in each image flip's hierarchy statements.

Your Assignment

At the end of the chapters, your assignment is always to create a new and functional script from what you know to this point. But I always make a suggestion.

Can you create a drop-down box that will answer people's questions? For example, create a drop-down box that people can use to find out what HTML code they should use to get an effect. Make the box read What is the code for?, and when the user opens the box, she can choose from bold, italic, and underline.

After the user has made her choice, she will click on a button and a text box will show her the code.

 You can see a possible answer to this assignment on your own computer by clicking on Lesson 29 Assignment in your download packet or see it online at http://www.htmlgoodies.com/ JSBook/assignment29.html.

Chapter 6

Mathematics, Random Things, and Loops

This chapter contains the following lessons and scripts:

- Lesson 30: Math Operators
- Lesson 31: Mathematics and Forms
- Lesson 32: Creating Random Numbers with a Date
- Lesson 33: Creating Random Numbers Through Mathematics
- Lesson 34: Producing Random Statements and Images
- Lesson 35: Introduction to `for` Loops
- Lesson 36: Introduction to `while` Loops
- Lesson 37: End of Chapter Review—A Browser Detect Script

From Joe Burns: One of the first things I ever saw done with JavaScript involved entering numbers on a page and having that page perform a mathematical computation using those numbers. The actual example was to figure a 15% tip. I thought that was the greatest thing I had ever seen. In fact, I wrote a script that does the same thing in Lesson 31.

The purpose of this chapter is to take you back to math class, teach you how to make random events occur, and how to use math to create JavaScript loops. All these events are seldom standalone items. Math is normally used to create a greater event. Case in point: Generating random numbers is nice, but what good is it unless the numbers help you to win the lottery?

Hey! That's a great idea for a script.

But you have to walk before you can run. We start with the basics of JavaScript mathematics.

Lesson 30: Math Operators

This page will not only show you how to use numeric values to perform computation with JavaScript, but it will also test your basic math skills. There might be a test later. Its purpose is to introduce you to mathematical operators, something you'll use often. If you have done any type of computer programming before, you should be experiencing déjà vu! If not, don't panic. Using this script, I'll give you an easy introduction:

```
<SCRIPT LANGUAGE="javascript">

var result = 10 * 2 + 1 / 3 - 7
alert ("the answer to 10 * 2 + 1 / 3 - 7  is " +result + ".")

var numsums = 10 + 2
alert("10 + 2 is " + numsums)

var x = 10
alert("ten is " + x)

var y = x * 2
alert("10 * 2 = " + y)

var z = "Hello " + "Good Bye"
alert(z)

</SCRIPT>
```

The script's effect appears in Figure 6.1.

 To see the effect on your own computer click on Lesson 30 Script's Effect in your download packet or see it online at http://www.htmlgoodies.com/JSBook/lesson30example.html.

The Arithmetic Operators

I think it would hard to get to this point in the book and not be able to figure this one out pretty quickly. But it's not the makeup of the script that's important. The purpose here is to show you the JavaScript binary operators.

That's a fancy way to refer to the addition (+), subtraction (-), multiplication (*), and division (/) symbols.

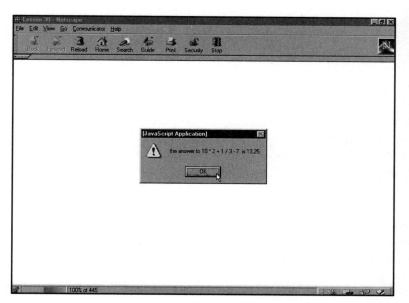

Figure 6.1
Alert box displaying math answers.

Percent (%) is also a binary operator. Its technical name is a *modulus operator*. However, it doesn't create percentages. You actually have to create the percentages by hand, dividing one number into the other. The percent sign only returns any number left over, a remainder, in a division equation.

For example, the code 10 % 2 would return 0 because 2 divides into 10 evenly. But 10 % 3 would return the number 1. That's what's left over.

Deconstructing the Super Math Script

Well, maybe it's not super, but it makes its point.

Each two-line piece of code sets up a mathematical equation or number usage and then uses an alert method to display the answers. Here's the quick rundown:

```
var result = 10 * 2 + 1 / 3 - 7
alert ("the answer to 10 * 2 + 1 / 3 - 7  is " +result + ".")
```

We tried to create an equation that would use all the traditional binary operators. This is what came out. The answer is 13.333333333.

Now, when you look at the equation it might seem that the JavaScript is doing the wrong calculation. If you pull out a calculator and follow the format, you might come up with this:

10*2+1 (that equals 21) / 3-7 (that equals -4)

Right? Well, JavaScript doesn't see it that way. Remember, we're dealing with a computer here. That computer just bulls through left to right without stopping to see this as a division problem. If you simply read the equation straight through, you'll get the answer the computer did:

`10*2` (equals 20) + `1/3` (a third) `-7` = `13.333333`

So how do you get around the computer bulling through? Parentheses, my friend. Remember that from high school algebra? In math, the stuff in the parentheses is evaluated first. Same here. If I wanted to turn this into a division problem with an equation on either side of the slash, it would look like this:

```
var result = (10 * 2 + 1) / (3 - 7)
```

Be careful when you put together mathematical equations in your JavaScript. Make sure the computer is figuring out what you want it to figure out. Always check the math against a calculator before offering your work to the public.

```
var numsums = 10 + 2
alert("10 + 2 is " + numsums)
```

The script sets a `numsums` variable. Can you see that it's equal to 12 (10+2)? The script transfers that variable to an `alert` box and displays that 10 + 2 = the variable, or 12.

```
var x = 10
alert("ten is " + x)
```

Another variable, x, is set to equal 10. The `alert` box then displays that value.

```
var y = x * 2
alert("10 X 2 = " + y)
```

Another variable, y, is set to equal the x variable multiplied by 2. That should be 20, right? It is. The answer is displayed in the `alert` method.

```
var z = "Hello " + "Good Bye"
alert(z)
```

Finally, the variable z is created, showing you can connect text using the computation symbols. That variable is then displayed using the `alert` boxes. That will become very important later on.

The nice thing about the binary operator (+) is that it fulfils two duties. If it is placed between two numbers, it adds them. If it is placed between two strings, it puts them together into a single string, a process known as *concatenation*.

In Terms of Numbers and Binary Operators

Never put quotation marks around numbers. If you do put quotation marks around a number, it becomes a string. That's bad. For example, if you run the equation "3"+4, you will get 34 because the quotation marks made the "3" a string, and the plus sign simply put the two items together rather than adding them. If you want 7 to be the result, don't use any quotation marks so the plus sign sees both the 3 and the 4 as numbers.

Your Assignment

Write a script in which a prompt is used to ask the user for a number between 2 and 10. Then have that number's square display on the page.

You do know what a square is, right? The number times itself.

 You can see a possible answer to this assignment on your own computer by clicking on Lesson 30 Assignment in your download packet or see it online at http://www.htmlgoodies.com/ JSBook/assignment30.html.

Lesson 31: Mathematics and Forms

After Chapter 5, "Forms: A Great Way to Interact with Your Users," you should be pretty familiar with entering data into form fields and then getting values to show up.

Here we're going to take a look at that tip script that impressed Joe so much. It's basic, but it does the trick:

```
<SCRIPT LANGUAGE="javascript">
function figureItOut()
{
var dinCost = document.meal.dinner.value
var tipCost = dinCost * .15
var bigtipCost = dinCost * .25
document.meal.tip.value = tipCost
document.meal.bigtip.value = bigtipCost
}
</SCRIPT>

<FORM NAME="meal">

How much was dinner? $<INPUT TYPE="text" NAME="dinner"><BR>

<INPUT TYPE="button" VALUE = "OK, Hit Me!" onClick="figureItOut()"><P>

You should tip: $<INPUT TYPE="text" NAME="tip"><BR>
```

```
A big tipper would leave 25% $<INPUT TYPE="text" NAME="bigtip"><BR>

</FORM>
```

This script accepts input from the user, manipulates the data, and then posts an answer. Very clever. You can see the script's effect in Figure 6.2.

Figure 6.2
How much should you tip?

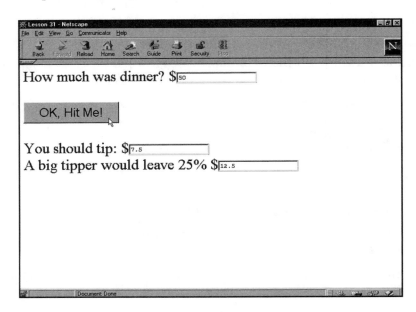

 To see the effect on your own computer click on Lesson 31 Script's Effect in your download packet or see it online at `http://www.htmlgoodies.com/JSBook/lesson31example.html`.

Deconstructing the Script

We'll start with the form elements this time around because they are probably still somewhat fresh in your mind:

```
<FORM NAME="meal">
How much was dinner? $<INPUT TYPE="text" NAME="dinner"><BR>
<INPUT TYPE="button" VALUE = "OK, Hit Me!" onClick="figureItOut()"><P>
You should tip: $<INPUT TYPE="text" NAME="tip"><BR>
A big tipper would leave 25% $<INPUT TYPE="text" NAME="bigtip"><BR>
</FORM>
```

First, note the formal names. The entire form is called meal. The first input text box is called dinner. The button is set up to trigger a function called, smartly enough, figureItOut().

144

The results of the normal 15% tip will show up in a text box called `tip` and the larger 25% tip result will display in a text box called `bigtip`.

Okay, now you know the players, let's get to the plays of the script:

```
function figureItOut()
{
var dinCost = document.meal.dinner.value
var tipCost = dinCost * .15
var bigtipCost = dinCost * .25
document.meal.tip.value = tipCost
document.meal.bigtip.value = bigtipCost
}
</SCRIPT>
```

We could have written out the hierarchy statement for the text box that accepted the user's data, but because it was going to be used at least twice, we decided to assign a variable to it. `document.meal.dinner.value` was assigned the variable `dinCost`.

Now that we have that variable, we can start to create some mathematical equations with it.

The variable `tipCost` was assigned to the cost of dinner multiplied by the tradition 15% or .15 tip. Remember that the `%` sign does not mean percentage. It means the remainder of a multiplication. That's why we use the .15 and .25 rather that 15% and 25%.

The variable `bigtipCost` was assigned to the cost of dinner and multiplied by the better tip amount 25% or .25.

Now we need to get those values into the correct form items when we click the button. That is done by these lines of code:

```
document.meal.tip.value = tipCost
document.meal.bigtip.value = bigtipCost
```

Notice the hierarchy statement points at the two form elements set up to receive the data. The values assigned to each box are the variable names that represent the equations set up a moment ago.

When you put the whole process together, the function figures the tip amounts, assigns variable names to them, and writes them to the form element.

Nothing to it.

Your Assignment

Until now, you have had it easy with the math. Now let's try something a little harder. Can you create a two–text box form with a button in the middle that changes Celsius degrees to Fahrenheit degrees?

Here's the equation:

```
Fahrenheit = (Celsius X 9/5)+32
```

In case you want to get clever, Fahrenheit to Celsius is done using the formula

```
(Fahrenheit - 32) X 5/9
```

Hint: You'll do best by taking each section of the equation and making it its own variable. You can then do the equation with text, and you're sure the numbers within the parentheses are being figured by themselves.

 You can see a possible answer to this assignment on your own computer by clicking on Lesson 31 Assignment in your download packet or see it online at http://www.htmlgoodies.com/JSBook/assignment31.html.

Lesson 32: Creating Random Numbers with a Date

This example introduces you to random numbers. People love random numbers for some reason. Here's our example:

```
<SCRIPT LANGUAGE="JavaScript">
function rand()
{
var now=new Date()
var num=(now.getSeconds())%9
var numEnd=num+1
alert(numEnd)
}
</SCRIPT>
<FORM>
<INPUT TYPE="button" VALUE="Random Number from 1 to 10" onClick="rand()">
</FORM>
```

You can see the script's effect in Figure 6.3.

 To see the effect on your own computer, click on Lesson 32 Script's Effect in your download packet or see it online at http://www.htmlgoodies.com/JSBook/lesson32example.html.

Notice this in the script: the number after the % is the ending number. The following example picks a random number between 1 and 10.

But wait! The number after the % is 9! And there's that % sign we keep mentioning for some reason. Keep reading to find out why.

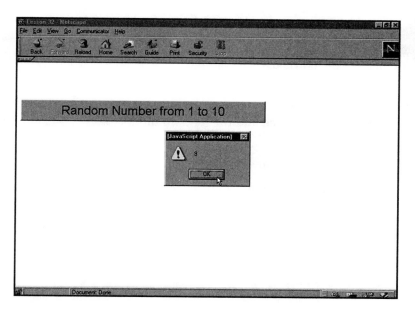

Figure 6.3
Generating a random number.

Deconstructing the Script

We'll start with the function this time:

```
function rand()
{
var now=new Date()
var num=(now.getSeconds())%9
var numEnd=num+1
alert(numEnd)
}
```

It will take a few steps to get the random number.

First, set aside a function. We called ours rand().

Next, we set aside a variable that will act as a method called new Date().

Another variable, called num, is set aside. It contains the method getSeconds() in order to grab a number between 0 and 59.

JavaScript counts everything and starts counting from zero. The number returned from getSeconds() is divided by 9, and a remainder is returned. Remember that the % sign returns only the remainder of a division.

The remainder has one number added to it. That number is assigned the variable name numEnd.

The alert() method then displays the number.

How Does That Give a Random Number?

Here's the concept. 9 divides into 0 through 60 approximately 6.7 times. So, every six and a half seconds or so, a new number can be returned.

Let's say the second returned is 54. 9 divides into 54 with a result of 6. That's a perfect number. There is no remainder. Therefore, the remainder is 0. Remember that the % sign returns only the remainder of a division. 1 is added and the random number is 1.

Here's another example. The second returned is 22. 9 divides into it 2.4 times. 4 is the remainder. 1 is added to it, you get a random number of 5.

You'll never get a zero returned as the random number because 1 is always added to the mix.

It's hard to believe it works, but it does.

The Form Items

```
<FORM>
<INPUT TYPE="button" VALUE="Random Number from 1 to 10" onClick="rand()">
</FORM>
```

There's no real need to name the form or the form items in this case. None of the elements comes into play. The button is simply there to act as a trigger to produce the number through the rand() function.

It's a neat trick.

Your Assignment

Do you play the lottery? Let's create a JavaScript that picks the three-digit daily lotto drawing numbers. You have to return three random numbers, 0 through 9.

Make the numbers appear on an alert box. For good measure, put the text Good Luck! in the status bar.

Hint: If you use getSeconds() for all three number generators, you're always going to get all three numbers the same.

 You can see a possible answer to this assignment on your own computer by clicking on Lesson 32 Assignment in your download packet or see it online at http://www.htmlgoodies.com/ JSBook/assignment32.html.

Lesson 33: Creating Random Numbers Through Mathematics

This script will allow us to create a random number using new JavaScript mathematics statements rather than relying on a date return:

```
<SCRIPT LANGUAGE="javascript">
var num = Math.round(35 * Math.random());
document.write("Random number between 0 and 35: <B>" + num + "</B>.")
</SCRIPT>
```

The script's effect appears in Figure 6.4.

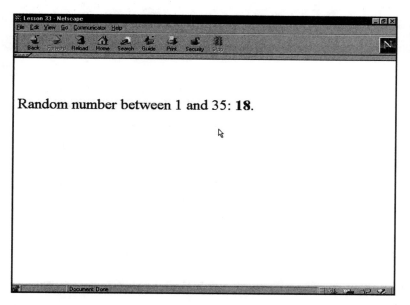

Figure 6.4
Generating a random number through math.

 To see the effect on your own computer, click on Lesson 33 Script's Effect in your download packet or see it online at http://www.htmlgoodies.com/JSBook/lesson33example.html.

Deconstructing the Script

It might not seem at first that there is a lot to this script, but it is quite useful. First, it's compact, and always returns a positive integer starting at zero.

In addition, the fact that it runs without a function is also helpful.

Here's the line of code that does the trick:

```
var num = Math.round(35 * Math.random());
```

The line is set up as a variable assigned the name num. That way we can post the result anywhere on the page.

The mathematics are done through two object.method statements.

Math is an object that alerts the browser that the methods that follow are to be used specifically to produce mathematical results. The Math object itself carries no value. It simply sets the course of the methods that follow to do math.

Math.round() is an object.method statement that will take whatever is in its instance and round it to the nearest integer.

Math.random() is an object method that returns a number between 0 and 1. Now, that might sound silly right off, but here's another thing about how JavaScript counts. It starts at 0 and goes up, yes. But better than that, JavaScript has the ability to count in milliseconds.

There are actually a thousand different responses this Math.random can return, from .000 up to .999.

The number 35 is in there because we put it there. It is known as the upper limit. The answer will return between 0 and 35 because it is mathematically impossible to go higher than what you're multiplying.

The random number is produced by rounding off the results of 35, our upper limit, multiplied by a random number between .000 and .999.

For example, Math.random() returns .234. 35 times .234 is 8.19. That rounds down because it's closer to 8 than it is to 9. The random number produced is 8.

The line

```
document.write("Random number between 0 and 35: <B>" + num + "</B>.")
```

writes the random number to the document surrounded by text that explains to the user what the number represents.

But what if you do not want 0 as one of the random numbers? Well, you'll have to do two things:

- Add 1 to the output of the random number equation. Remember how we did that in the last lesson.
- Make the upper limit 34. If you leave it at 35, there's every chance that 35 will be the number returned and adding would make the number 36. That's bad.

Isn't this math stuff fun?

The Math Object

The Math object is amazing. Table 6.1 shows all the methods that can be attached. When using the Math object, think of it in the same way as you would the Date.get*Something*() method. It functions in a similar fashion and returns numbers the same way.

Where you see *argument* in the table, I mean a mathematical equation.

For example, the first Math.method(), Math.abs() could be written this way:

```
Math.abs((22*3) / 4)
```

Table 6.1 Math Object Methods

Method	Return Value
Math.abs(*argument*)	The absolute value of an argument
Math.acos(*argument*)	The arc cosine of the argument
Math.asin(*argument*)	The arc sine of the argument
Math.atan(*argument*)	The arc tangent of the argument
Math.atan2(*argument1*, *argument2*)	The angle of polar coordinates x and y
Math.ceil(*argument*)	The number one larger than or equal to the argument
Math.cos(*argument*)	The cosine of the argument
Math.exp(*argument*)	A natural logarithm
Math.floor(*argument*)	The number 1 less than or equal to the argument
Math.E	Base of natural logarithms
Math.LN2	Logarithm of 2 (appx: 0.6932)
Math.LN10	Logarithm of 10 (appx: 2.3026)
Math.log	Logarithm of positive numbers greater than 0
Math.LOG10E	Base-10 logarithm of E
Math.LOG2E	Base-2 logarithm of E
Math.max(*arg1*,*arg2*)	The greater of the two arguments
Math.min(*arg1*,*arg2*)	The lesser of the two arguments
Math.PI	The value of pi
Math.pow(*arg1*, *arg2*)	*arg1* raised to the *arg2* power
Math.random	A random number between 0 and 1
Math.round(*value*)	Rounds to the nearest number
Math.sin(*argument*)	The sine of the argument
Math.sqrt(*argument*)	The square root of the argument

continues

Table 6.1 continued

Method	Return Value
Math.SQRT1_2	The square root of 1/2
Math.SQRT2	The square root of 2
Math.tan(*argument*)	The tangent of the argument

Your Assignment

Set up the preceding script so that a prompt appears and asks the user for the upper limit number. The document should then read Here is your random number between 1 and *usersnumber*.

 You can see a possible answer to this assignment on your own computer by clicking on Lesson 33 Assignment in your download packet or see it online at http://www.htmlgoodies.com/ JSBook/assignment33.html.

Lesson 34: Producing Random Statements and Images

As referenced in Lessons 32 and 33, producing random numbers is good, but by itself, the technique doesn't do much besides post a number. Here we start to take that concept of randomness and apply it to other items. In this case, one of three statements will pop up on the screen. Which statement depends on which random number the computer comes up with.

In Lesson 21, you learned the concept of if and else. Here we pick that concept up once again to get the desired effect:

```
<SCRIPT LANGUAGE="JavaScript">
var0="An Apple A Day"
var1="A Stitch in Time"
var2="Bird in the Hand"
now=new Date()
num=(now.getSeconds() )%2
document.write("Random Number: "       + num + "<br>")
if (num == 0)
{cliche=var0}
if (num == 1)
{cliche=var1}
if (num == 2)
{cliche=var2}
document.write(cliche)
</SCRIPT>
<p>....as I always say.
```

You can see the script's effect in Figure 6.5.

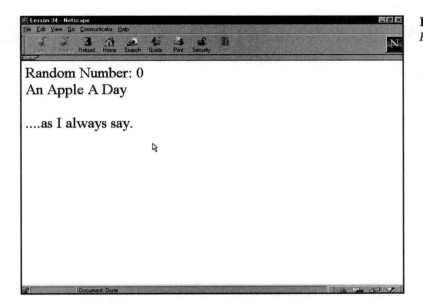

Figure 6.5
Random statement.

 To see the effect on your own computer, click on Lesson 34 Script's Effect in your download packet or see it online at http://www.htmlgoodies.com/JSBook/lesson34example.html.

Deconstructing the Script

This one reads very nicely from the top down. Here we start by giving three lines of text three variable names var0 through var2:

```
var0="Apple a Day";
var1="A Stitch in Time";
var2="Bird in the Hand";
```

We could have started with 1, but that would have meant we would need to set the random number generator code to add 1. It's not worth the concern. We're just starting with 0. Moving along:

```
now=new Date()
num=(now.getSeconds() )%2
```

Next, the script uses the two-line date code to draw a random number between 0 and 1. Note the number 2 after the % sign. Remember that means the numbers 0, 1, and 2 could come up.

The code has assigned the variable name `now` to the new date object and the variable `num` the result of the random number code.

Finally, this line writes the random number to the page through a `document.write` statement:

```
document.write("Random Number: "+ num + "<br>")
```

Getting the Random Statement

Now let's look at the second section of the JavaScript:

```
if (num == 0)
        {cliche=var0}
if (num == 1)
        {cliche=var1}
if (num == 2)
        {cliche=var2}
document.write(cliche)
```

The code that assigned the variable and chose a random number is now going to be used to choose one of these three statements. Let's take a look at just the first two lines of code:

```
if (num == 0)
        {cliche=var0}
```

This is a statement using the `if` method. Remember from Lesson 21 that any statement that follows `if` must be sitting inside parentheses.

Those two lines mean "If the number, `num`, created by the random number code is zero, `cliche` is equal to variable `var0`."

Notice the `cliche=` statement is within braces {}. The reason is that it's actually a function of the `if` method.

But you remembered that from Lesson 21.

Double and Single Equal Signs

You might have caught this already, but it's very important, so we'll drive the point home. In JavaScript, a double equal sign actually means *is equal to*.

A single equal sign simply acts as the verb *is*. Remember you use a single equal sign in assigning variable names. Think of that as meaning *is*. But, if you want to make the statement that something *is equal to* in JavaScript, you use the double equal signs.

Yes, we know it sounds backward, but that's the way it is.

154

We keep it straight by thinking that a double (==) means *is equal to*, and a single (=) means *is*.

Back to the Deconstruction

The code then sets two more cliché numbers to var1 and var2, depending on whether 1 or 2 is chosen:

```
if (num == 1)
        {cliche=var1}
if (num == 2)
        {cliche=var2}
document.write(cliche)
```

Finally, a document.write statement is used to write the cliché to the page. Because there is no text surrounding cliche, you don't need any plus signs.

What's Happening?

The process is quite linear. First, three variable names are set, attaching three text strings to the variables var0 through var2.

Next, a random number is chosen and written to the page.

Then that number is looked at through a series of if statements. If the first statement isn't true, num does not equal zero, and the next if statement is looked at. If that statement isn't true, the script goes on to the next.

One of those statements will be true because we know that we'll only have 0, 1, or 2 returned from the random number code.

Why Don't You Use an **else** with Your **if**?

It isn't needed. We know one of those if statements will be true. You could have just as easily written this so that the last if statement was an else. It would have worked just the same way, but again, it's not needed. Three ifs will do just fine.

Your Assignment

 We have three pictures for you at

- http://www.htmlgoodies.com/JSBook/pic1.gif
- http://www.htmlgoodies.com/JSBook/pic2.gif
- http://www.htmlgoodies.com/JSBook/pic3.gif

Modify this JavaScript program to display a random picture rather than text. Make the text under the image read describes my mood today.

 You can see a possible answer to this assignment on your own computer by clicking on Lesson 34 Assignment in your download packet or see it online at http://www.htmlgoodies.com/ JSBook/assignment34.html.

Lesson 35: Introduction to for Loops

All programming languages have a branching method. The branching method in JavaScript is if, which we just looked at. It allows you to say, "If this is that, execute these statements."

In addition, all programming languages also have looping techniques. Looping is a fancy way of saying, "Run the script again and again, rather than just once."

JavaScript has two looping methods: for loops and while loops.

In general, you use for loops when you know how many times you want to perform a loop. Use while loops when you are not sure how many times you want to perform a loop.

That probably didn't make a whole lot of sense, so let's get right to an example. We'll start with a for loop because we know how many times we want this script to loop (the next lesson discusses while loops):

```
We'll now count from one to five:
<script language="JavaScript">
for (i=1; i<=5; i=i+1)
{
document.write(i + "<BR>");
}
</SCRIPT>
...and we're done
```

The script's effect appears in Figure 6.6.

 To see the effect on your own computer, click on Lesson 35 Script's Effect in your download packet or see it online at http://www.htmlgoodies.com/JSBook/lesson35example.html.

Deconstructing the Script

First off, look at how short this script is. It's a nice break, don't you think?

If you haven't noticed, the for statement is seen as a function. See the braces {}?

Let's look at the syntax of a for statement:

```
for(i=1; i<=5; i=i+1)
```

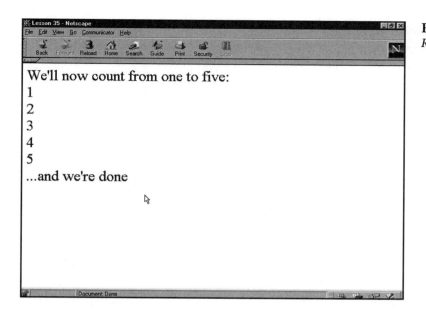

Figure 6.6
Results of a for *loop.*

There are three parts separated by semicolons. We'll take each part in order.

```
i=1
```

This sets the starting value of the variable used to control the loop. In this case it's set to 1, but it could be set to 10 or 100. Think of it simply as a starting point for the loop. That starting point has now been assigned the variable i.

```
i <= 5
```

This is the condition controlling the number of times the loop will be repeated. In this example, the loop will be repeated while i is less than or equal to 5.

From Joe Burns: You're probably familiar with that less than sign from middle-school math. I was always able to keep the greater than and less than signs apart by thinking of it as an alligator's mouth. The alligator always wants to bite the biggest number. It's a good tip, compliments of Miss Scovern, my sixth-grade math teacher. She was also the volleyball coach.

```
i=i+1
```

This defines the increment value. Every time the loop is run, the program will add 1 to i. The program can add any number you want. We just want it to add 1.

Finally, a document.write statement prints the number. Notice the <BR>. That makes each of the numbers break to the next line. You could just as easily have the numbers all in a row separated by commas, by just altering that section of text that appears after each number.

This JavaScript will be triggered, or looped, five times. Therefore, it will produce the numbers 1 through 5. We could have it count to 1,000,000 just as easily as 5, but that would take up too much Web page space.

Your Assignment

This is a great, and not so difficult, effect. You're going to use this for loop as a delay.

Write an HTML document that displays Counting Now with a white background. Then use JavaScript to count to 10,000. Yes, that is 10,000. Do not use commas in for statements or you'll get errors!

At the point the script is done counting, the background color should change to yellow and an alert box should pop up that reads done.

Do not have the numbers print to the page. You do not want them to be seen. They are only there to count.

Hint: You might want to try writing the script setting the number to 10 rather than 10,000 to start with. You don't want to get stuck in a 10,000-number loop.

 You can see a possible answer to this assignment on your own computer by clicking on Lesson 35 Assignment in your download packet or see it online at http://www.htmlgoodies.com/ JSBook/assignment35.html.

Lesson 36: Introduction to while Loops

This example looks at the while loop. Remember that usually you use for loops when you know how many times you want to perform a loop, and while loops when you are not sure how many times you want to perform a loop.

We're doing this to show you how to use variables to count iterations in a loop and to help you get ready for your assignment:

```
<SCRIPT LANGUAGE="JavaScript">
var usernum = prompt("How many time should I write Happy?","0")
loops=usernum
num=1
while (num <= loops)
{
document.write("Happy ")
num=num+1
}
```

```
document.write("Birthday")
</SCRIPT>
```

You can see the script's effect in Figures 6.7 and 6.8.

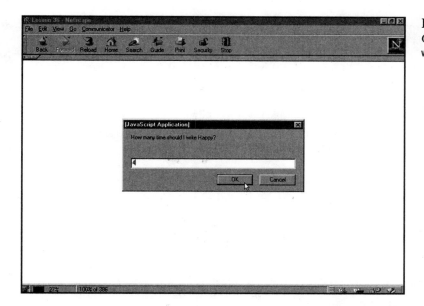

Figure 6.7
Getting information for the while *loop.*

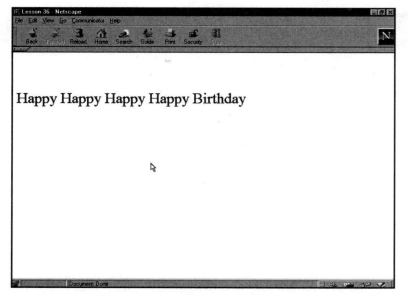

Figure 6.8
Results of a while *loop.*

To see the effect on your own computer, click on Lesson 36 Script's Effect in your download packet or see it online at http://www.htmlgoodies.com/JSBook/lesson36example.html.

The `while` Condition

The `while` loop is similar to the `for` statement in syntax. The difference is that in the `for` loop, we set the beginning index number and increment in the `for` statement.

The `while` statement just contains a condition and we wait for input from the user to get the loop underway.

The script in this example uses the statement `while(num <=loops)`.

The condition is actually just the <=. It stands for *less than or equal to*. Table 6.2 shows the other conditions that JavaScript recognizes.

Table 6.2   Conditions That JavaScript Recognizes

Condition	What It Means
==	Equal to
!=	Not equal to
<	Less than
>	Greater than
<=	Less than or equal to
>=	Greater than or equal to
?:	Conditional statement

The conditional statement is a pretty fancy item. It assigns a variable name depending on the outcome of one of the other conditions in the table. For example:

```
YearsWithCompany = (ywc >=45) ? "retire" : "notretire"
```

If the person has been with the company equal to or more years than 45, the value `retire` is attached to it. If the years value is less than 45, the `notretire` variable is attached.

Deconstructing the Script

Another short program. We'll whip right through it.

We start with a basic prompt asking the user for a number. Notice we have a 0 in the second set of quotes. That's done so that if the user simply hits OK without entering a number, the script will still run without errors.

That number is assigned the variable name usernum. The variable loops is set to represent the number the user put in.

The while(num<=loops) statement tells the program to do the loop over and over while the variable num is less than or equal to loops put in by the user. See the use of the <= condition?

It might seem that the variable num just came up and out of nowhere—basically, it did. We needed a number equal to 0. We could have set num to 0, but didn't need to. JavaScript counts everything and starts counting at 0. num is a new variable, so by default, it gets the value of 0. There's a new shortcut for you.

If the user enters the number 7, the loop will roll seven times.

Each time the program goes through the loop it writes Happy plus a space and adds 1 to num. The following code in the function does that:

```
document.write("Happy ")
num=num+1
```

Let's say the user put in the number 7. The loop would roll and 1 would be added to num. The script would roll again and check to see if the new number meets the criteria. This looping continues until the number 7, the number the user put in, is met. After that's done, the looping stops.

The finishing touch is added with the addition of Birthday at the end through a document.write statement.

So Happy, Happy, Happy, Happy, Happy, Happy, Happy Birthday to you.

Your Assignment

Here's another challenge. Set up this lesson's script so that the prompt asks how long a random number the user would like. Take the number that the user enters and create a random number that long.

Hint: You cannot create the number as a whole; you'll have to create it one number at a time.

 You can see a possible answer to this assignment on your own computer by clicking on Lesson 36 Assignment in your download packet or see it online at http://www.htmlgoodies.com/ JSBook/assignment36.html.

Lesson 37: End of Chapter Review—A Browser Detect Script

It's the end of a chapter, and that means review and do.

Look over the commands you have learned so far, shown in Table 6.3, and think about how you can use them to create useful and functional JavaScripts for your site. You've also been introduced to these JavaScript concepts:

- The `alert()`, `confirm()`, and `prompt()` methods
- The `If/Else` conditional statement
- These Event Handlers: `onBlur`, `onChange`, `onClick`, `onDblClick`, `onFocus`, `onKeyDown`, `onKeyPress`, `onKeyUp`, `onLoad`, `onMouseDown`, `onMouseMove`, `onMouseOut`, `onMouseOver`, `onMouseUp`, `onSubmit`
- Arithmetic operators: (+), (-), (*), (/), (%)
- Conditions: (==), (!=), (<), (>),(=<), (=>), (?:)
- The HTML 4.0 flag `<SPAN>`
- Creating variable names
- Creating a function
- `for` Loops
- HTML form items
- Form item attribute `NAME=`
- Form item properties: `length`, `value`, `selectedIndex`
- Form item methods: `toLowerCase`, `toUpperCase()`
- `while` loops

Table 6.3 Object-Related JavaScript Commands Demonstrated in Chapters 1 Through 6

Object	Methods	Properties
date	getDate() getDay() getHours() getMinutes() getMonth() getSeconds() getYear()	
document	write()	alinkColor, bgColor, fgColor, linkColor, lastModified, location, referrer, title, vlinkColor

Object	Methods	Properties
history	go()	length
location		host, hostname, href
Math	random(), round()	
navigator		appCodeName, appName, appVersion, userAgent
window	close()	defaultstatus, directories, location, menubar, resizable, self, scrollbars, status, toolbar

Event Handlers

Here's our example script:

```
<SCRIPT LANGUAGE="javascript">

if (navigator.appName == "Netscape")
{
location.href="nspage.html"
}
if (navigator.appName == "Microsoft Internet Explorer")
{
location.href="iepage.html"
}
if (navigator.appName != "Netscape")
{
location.href="textpage.html"
}
</SCRIPT>
```

The effect is difficult to show, so we'll describe it to you. The JavaScript is what is known as a browser detect script. The purpose of the script is to view the user's browser, and load a page made specifically for that browser. It's a script that is widely requested from the HTML Goodies site.

The script is set up to load nspage.html if the user's browser is Netscape Navigator, and iepage.html if the user's browser is Internet Explorer.

Finally, there's a statement to act as a catch-all for users who are not running either browser. Those users will be sent to textpage.html, a text-based version of the other two pages.

Deconstructing the Script

The script is made up of three `if` statements, but they only really check for two things.

The format of the script is set up to test for Netscape Navigator browsers first:

```
if (navigator.appName == "Netscape")
{
location.href="nspage.html"
}
```

The check is performed by asking whether the browser's `appName` is Netscape. If it is, end of script. The `nspage.html` is loaded and all's well.

If the user is not running Navigator, the second `if` statement comes into play, and it checks to see whether the browser's `appName` is Internet Explorer. If it is, end of script. The `iepage.html` loads:

```
if (navigator.appName == "Microsoft Internet Explorer")
{
location.href="iepage.html"
}
```

> **NOTE**
>
> By the way, we found the return from the `navigator.appName` to use in the script by simply writing a very small script that returned the value to the page. Then we ran the script in Netscape Navigator and Internet Explorer and wrote the values down.

If the browser is neither of those, the third `if` statement is checked:

```
if (navigator.appName != "Netscape")
{
location.href="textpage.html"
}
```

The third statement might seem a bit silly. We already know that the browser is not Netscape. If it were, the script would have sent us to the Netscape page.

But that's the beauty of it all. We know the browser is not Netscape because the script would have never gotten this far if the browser were one of the other two.

By writing the code to check whether it is not Netscape, we are guaranteeing that this `if` statement is true; therefore, the browser goes to the `textpage.html`.

Pretty clever, huh?

Placement of the Script

Where you place this script is quite important. It should be on a page all by itself. External text will not display anyway and will probably slow the page's completion.

The script will never be seen by the user. The reaction is usually so fast that all he sees is a fast blank page load, and then up comes the page for his browser.

So, make this a page unto itself and put the bells and whistles on the pages you write for the browsers.

Your Assignment

Your assignment, as it always is at the end of a chapter, is to create something you're proud to put on your Web pages. But we always make a suggestion.

Let's play the lottery. But not that silly three-number lottery, let's play the big six.

Set up a page with 12 small text boxes. Six of the boxes will be for the user to enter her six numbers between 1 and 47.

Then there should be a button that will randomly generate six numbers between 1 and 47.

Finally, a button should be created that will pop up an alert box to tell the user whether she wins.

Hint: The win button is a bit of a ploy.

 You can see a possible answer to this assignment on your own computer by clicking on Lesson 37 Assignment in your download packet or see it online at http://www.htmlgoodies.com/ JSBook/assignment37.html.

Chapter 7

Clocks, Counts, and Scrolling Text

This chapter contains the following lessons and scripts:

- Lesson 38: A Running Clock
- Lesson 39: A Fancy Digital Clock
- Lesson 40: Image Driven Clock
- Lesson 41: Countdown to Date
- Lesson 42: Scrolling Text
- Lesson 43: End of Chapter Review—Count to an Event

The purpose of this chapter is to take what you have learned so far and create real-time effects with it. It's nice to be able to post the time the user arrived, but that's a static number. Here, you'll learn to create a digital clock that runs right in the browser window.

You'll also learn to post text depending on what time of day it is. It's a nice way to wish someone a good morning at the right time.

You'll also learn to create counts and countdowns to dates and events.

Finally, you'll learn one of the most popular events available through JavaScript, scrolling text.

Lesson 38: A Running Clock

What we're going to do here is set up a script that will return the hour, minute, and second the user arrives at the page. It's a format you should be quite familiar with at this point.

This lesson takes one more step by setting the script so that it runs again and again, giving the appearance that the clock is advancing on its own.

The script is displayed in full HTML document format in order to show the placement of each of the parts of code:

```
<HTML>
<HEAD>
<SCRIPT LANGUAGE="javascript">

function RunningTime() {

var RightNow = new Date()
var hr = RightNow.getHours() + 1
var min = RightNow.getMinutes()
var sec = RightNow.getSeconds()

var printIt = "Time: " +hr+ ":" +min+ ":" +sec

document.clock.clockface.value = printIt

var KeepItGoing=setTimeout("RunningTime()","1000")

}
</SCRIPT>
</HEAD>
<body bgcolor="ffffff" onLoad="RunningTime()">

<FORM NAME="clock">
<INPUT TYPE="text" name="clockface">
</FORM>

</body>
</html>
```

You can see the script's effect in Figure 7.1.

 To see the effect on your own computer, click on Lesson 38 Script's Effect in your download packet or see it online at http://www.htmlgoodies.com/JSBook/lesson38example.html.

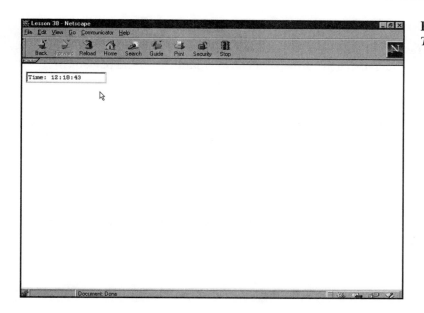

Figure 7.1
The digital clock.

Deconstructing the Script

We'll start from the bottom, and go over the JavaScript second:

```
<FORM NAME="clock">
<INPUT TYPE="text" name="clockface">
</FORM>
```

You've seen this before. It's a basic HTML form text box meant to receive and display what is returned from the JavaScript.

The form itself is named clock, and the text box is named clockface.

Next up from the bottom is the onLoad= trigger that starts the script rolling when the page loads into the browser window. You'll find that in the BODY flag.

It would be best to explain what happens before going into each smaller section of the script.

The script is set up to return a basic *hour:minute:second* time format. The returns from the getSomething() methods will display in a text box. You could probably figure that much out just by looking at the script.

The magic of this script is in the fact that it appears to be running, but it's not. Here's the deal: The script loads and posts the time to the text box. Then the script waits one second, and runs again. Then it waits one second, and runs again. Then it waits one second and...you know the rest. The effect of the script updating every second is that the seconds are counting up and the clock is running.

No Loop!

Let me point out that this is not done with a `for` or a `while` loop. If we were to achieve the effect through a loop—and you can get the same effect—we would tie up the page to the point where you couldn't even click on any links. You see, the method used in this lesson is controlled. It runs one time every second.

If this were done with a loop, the loop might run 500 times per second or more. It would be all the browser could do to keep updating the page. It wouldn't have time for you.

If you want a running clock, this is the way to go.

Getting the Time

Now we move on to the script's parts. We'll work from the middle out. This is the code that returns the *hour:minute:second* time format:

```
var RightNow = new Date()
var hr = RightNow.getHours() + 1
var min = RightNow.getMinutes()
var sec = RightNow.getSeconds()
```

The format is quite typical. The `Date` object is assigned the variable name `RightNow`. Then the hour, minute, and second are assigned the variable names `hr`, `min`, and `sec`, respectively. Notice that as the variable names are assigned, 1 is added the `RightNow.getHours()` format to compensate for JavaScript returning hours starting at 0.

The Function

The entire script to this point is set up as a function. The format looks like this:

```
function RunningTime()
{
Everything mentioned so far is in here

var KeepItGoing=setTimeout("RunningTime()","1000")
}
```

The function is titled `RunningTime()`. Each time `RunningTime()` is triggered, a new value from the `Date` object will be returned and posted to the text box.

So, as mentioned earlier, we need to find a method of getting the function to run, wait a second, and then run again. As you might have already guessed, this is what does the trick:

```
var KeepItGoing=setTimeout("RunningTime()","1000")
```

If you start to really get into writing JavaScript, this format will become very familiar. What we're doing is setting up a rest period. The `setTimeout()` method does just what its name implies. It sets a certain amount of time out. In this case, 1000/1000ths of a second, or one second.

The format to implement the `setTimeout()` method is the traditional format you would use to set up a variable.

The command `var` starts off the line of code. We then set up the variable name `KeepItGoing`. The equal sign denotes that what follows will be represented by that variable name.

The method `setTimeout()` is then given two parameters: the name of the function, `RunningTime()`, and the number of milliseconds that the timeout should be.

Remember, JavaScript counts everything, it starts counting at zero, and it counts time in milliseconds. Thus, `1000` is equal to one second. If you want the script to count up in 5-second intervals, set the number to `5000`.

The effect is that the script runs, waits a second, and then runs the function `RunningTime()`. Then it waits a second, and then runs the function `RunningTime()`, and then waits a second...you know the rest.

Just remember: The `setTimeout()` method command line is inside of the function. In fact, it is the last line of code before the second curly brace that finishes off the function.

Placement is important—get `setTimeout()` last.

But When Do We Call for **KeepItGoing**?

Strange, huh? You never do. The format for setting `setTimeout()` requires you to use the format for setting up a variable, but you never actually call for the variable. When the command is run as part of the variable line, the effect is generated. Very clever.

Your Assignment

For this assignment, see whether you can get the running clock to display in the status bar.

 You can see a possible answer to this assignment on your own computer by clicking on Lesson 38 Assignment in your download packet or see it online at `http://www.htmlgoodies.com/ JSBook/assignment38.html`.

Lesson 39: A Fancy Digital Clock

In Chapter 6, "Mathematics, Random Things, and Loops," we wrote about the `if` conditional statement a good bit. Here we're going to use those `if` conditions to redesign the clock in Lesson 38 so that it reads like a normal digital clock. It will read in normal time using only the hours 1 through 12 for the hour, rather than 1 through 24. In addition, we'll get the seconds to read 00 rather than 60 when the clock turns over to the new minute.

We'll even get an AM or PM to pop up at the end.

Here's the script:

```
<HTML>
<HEAD>
<SCRIPT LANGUAGE="javascript">

function RunningTime() {

var RightNow = new Date()

var ampm = RightNow.getHours()
if (ampm > 12)
 {nampm = "PM"}
else
 {nampm = "AM"}

var hr = RightNow.getHours()
if(hr >= 12)
 {nhr = hr -12}
else
 {nhr = hr}

if (hr == 0)
{nhr = "12"}
else
{nhr = nhr}
var min = RightNow.getMinutes()
if (min < 10)
 {nmin = "0" +min}
else
 {nmin = min}

var sec = RightNow.getSeconds()
if (sec < 10)
 {nsec = "0" +sec}
else
 {nsec = sec}

if (nsec >= 60)
 {nnsec = "00"}
```

```
else
  {nnsec = nsec}

var printIt = "Time: " +nhr+ ":" +nmin+ ":" +nnsec+ ":" +nampm

document.clock.clockface.value = printIt

var KeepItGoing=setTimeout("RunningTime()","1000")

}
</SCRIPT>

</HEAD>

<BODY BGCOLOR="ffffff" onLoad="RunningTime()">

<FORM NAME="clock">
<INPUT TYPE="text" name="clockface">
</FORM>

</BODY>
</HTML>
```

The script's effect appears in Figure 7.2.

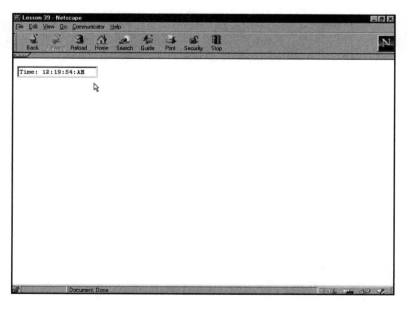

Figure 7.2
The fancy digital clock.

To see the effect on your own computer, click on Lesson 39 Script's Effect in your download packet or see it online at `http://www.htmlgoodies.com/JSBook/lesson39example.html`.

Deconstructing the Script

By now, we're going to assume you understand the concept of returning the *hour:minute:second* time format by assigning the Date object a variable name, and then assigning variables to the getHours(), getMinutes(), and getSeconds() methods to get the correct time.

In this script, that same format is followed, only after each of the get*Something*() methods, a series of if statements is set up to alter the number that is returned.

In addition, a series of if conditional statements is set up to assign text a variable name, depending on what number is being returned.

If this is all getting a little confusing, read on. We're going to take each new section in order.

The Hours

This is the code that returns the hour number and the if statements that alter it:

```
var ampm = RightNow.getHours()
if (ampm >= 12)
 {nampm = "PM"}
else
 {nampm = "AM"}

var hr = RightNow.getHours()
if(hr > 12)
 {nhr = hr -12}
else
 {nhr = hr}

if (hr == 0)
{nhr = "12"}
else
{nhr = nhr}
```

You might notice that the hour is called for twice. It is. But also take note that the variable name in each call for the hour number is different. The reason is because the first small block of code is using the hour to assign a variable name to the text *AM* and *PM*. The second block of code makes sure that the hour number returned is in the traditional 12-number format, rather than the 24-hour military time.

174

We'll look at the first small block of code first:

```
var ampm = RightNow.getHours()
if (ampm >= 12)
 {nampm = "PM"}
else
 {nampm = "AM"}
```

The number returned from the `RightNow.getHours()` `object.method` is assigned the variable `ampm`.

A basic `if` / `else` statement is set up that means, "If `ampm` is greater than 12, assign the variable `nampm` the text value of *PM*. If not, assign `nampm` the text value of *AM*." We chose the variable `nampm` to represent the new `ampm`. Get it?

Do you see what happened? The concept is that if the hour returned is after noon, the variable `nampm` is assigned `"PM"`, otherwise it will get `"AM"`.

Now we have this variable in our hip pocket. Later, in a `document.write` statement, we can call for this text value and it will show up on the page. Got it? Good. You have to love this math stuff. Now the second small block of code:

```
var hr = RightNow.getHours()
if(hr > 12)
 {nhr = hr -12}
else
 {nhr = hr}
```

This works like the first block, except it actually alters the number that is returned from the `RightNow.getHours()` method.

The `if` / `else` reads, "If the variable `hr` is greater than 12, `nhr` (new hr, just like above) is `hr` minus 12. If not, `nhr` equals `hr`."

The reason for subtracting 12 in the first instance is to lose the 24-hour format. If the script runs at 10 o'clock at night, the number returned is 22. By subtracting 12, we get the more familiar 10.

But what if it's 0 o'clock? That can happen. If you remember, the `getHours()` method returns the numbers 0 (midnight) through 23 (11:00 PM). Usually you can fix this situation by adding one to the return. That's how we got the correct number returned in the last lesson. But here we're not adding one to the mix.

Thus, we run the risk of 0 being returned from midnight through 1:00 AM. That's not good. So let's set up yet another `if` / `else` statement that looks like this:

```
if (hr == 0)
{nhr = "12"}
else
{nhr = nhr}
```

The block of code tests the hour return. If the return is 0, then the variable nhr is changed to 12 in order to represent the time between midnight and 1:00 AM. Otherwise, we let nhr's value display as returned.

Yes, we could have created a new variable, but why bother? It's only going to come into play one twenty-fourth of the time anyway. We just kept the variable name the same. Besides, we liked nhr.

Now remember, this is set up so that nhr is the correct number, the number we want to post to the page. That's the variable you need to call for in the document.write statements, not hr. That hr variable was just used as a means to an end.

The Minutes

This code should be pretty easy for you to figure out after rolling through the hours code. Here it is

```
var min = RightNow.getMinutes()
if (min < 10)
 {nmin = "0" +min}
else
 {nmin = min}
```

The minute is assigned the variable name min and is called for in the normal fashion and one is added. At this point, the number is correct. There's no need to manipulate it more, right? Well, sharp-eyed readers have probably noticed that when the minute is less than 10, the return is just the single number. The display would look better if we could get a zero in front when there is just that single digit. So that's what we're going to do.

The if / else statement reads, "If the variable min is less than 10, nmin (new min, remember?) will read zero followed by the number. If not, make nmin equal to min."

Now we have that variable nmin in the correct form to be used in the clock.

The Seconds

Here's the code that creates the correct second return:

```
var sec = RightNow.getSeconds()
if (sec < 10)
 {nsec = "0" +sec}
else
```

```
{nsec = sec}

if (nsec >= 60)
 {nnsec = "00"}
else
  {nnsec = nsec}
```

The first block of code is identical to what we just did with the minutes. If the second returned is less than 10, make the display two digits by writing a zero in front of the single digit. If not, let nsec be equal to sec.

The second block of code will only come into play once a minute, but it's a great look. You know by adding 1 to the end of the RightNow.getSeconds() that the numbers 1 through 60 will be returned. But 60 is not a normal number to see on a digital clock. Usually when the number gets to 59, the next number in line is double zero. That's what the second block of code is doing. It reads, "If the number returned by nsec is greater than or equal to 60, make nnsec (new, new sec) equal to 00. If not, let nnsec equal nsec."

See how one variable is built off the value assigned to another? That's one of the cornerstones of JavaScript programming. You get a value returned and then manipulate it before displaying it for the viewer.

The Rest of the Script

The rest of the script is identical to the script in Lesson 38. The script gives the impression it is running through the use of the setTimeout() command:

```
var KeepItGoing=setTimeout("RunningTime()","1000")
```

Finally, the output of the script is sent to an HTML form text box for display. It looks like this:

```
<FORM NAME="clock">
<INPUT TYPE="text" name="clockface">
</FORM>
```

It seems like a lot is going on again, and again, and again, and it is. But your computer's pretty smart. It can handle it.

Your Assignment

Rewrite a section of the script so that not only will the output of the script read AM and PM, but also read Good Morning between midnight and noon, Good Afternoon between noon and 6PM, and Good Evening after 6PM.

Hint: Set up the if statements with Good Evening as the result if the first if statement is true.

 You can see a possible answer to this assignment on your own computer by clicking on Lesson 39 Assignment in your download packet or see it online at http://www.htmlgoodies.com/ JSBook/assignment39.html.

Lesson 40: Image Driven Clock

This is a very popular effect. We'll use the template digital clock from Lesson 38 and set up a series of if statements so that the returns are images rather than text:

```
<SCRIPT LANGUAGE="javascript">

var RightNow = new Date()

var hr = RightNow.getHours()

if (hr == 0)
  {hrn = "<IMG SRC=1.gif><IMG SRC=2.gif>"}
if (hr == 01)
  {hrn = "<IMG SRC=0.gif><IMG SRC=1.gif>"}
if (hr == 02)
  {hrn = "<IMG SRC=0.gif><IMG SRC=2.gif>"}
if (hr == 03)
  {hrn = "<IMG SRC=0.gif><IMG SRC=3.gif>"}
if (hr == 04)
  {hrn = "<IMG SRC=0.gif><IMG SRC=4.gif>"}
if (hr == 05)
  {hrn = "<IMG SRC=0.gif><IMG SRC=5.gif>"}
if (hr == 06)
  {hrn = "<IMG SRC=0.gif><IMG SRC=6.gif>"}
if (hr == 07)
  {hrn = "<IMG SRC=0.gif><IMG SRC=7.gif>"}
if (hr == 08)
  {hrn = "<IMG SRC=0.gif><IMG SRC=8.gif>"}
if (hr == 09)
  {hrn = "<IMG SRC=0.gif><IMG SRC=9.gif>"}
if (hr == 10)
  {hrn = "<IMG SRC=1.gif><IMG SRC=0.gif>"}
if (hr == 11)
  {hrn = "<IMG SRC=1.gif><IMG SRC=1.gif>"}
if (hr == 12)
  {hrn = "<IMG SRC=1.gif><IMG SRC=2.gif>"}
if (hr == 13)
  {hrn = "<IMG SRC=0.gif><IMG SRC=1.gif>"}
```

```
if (hr == 14)
 {hrn = "<IMG SRC=0.gif><IMG SRC=2.gif>"}
if (hr == 15)
 {hrn = "<IMG SRC=0.gif><IMG SRC=3.gif>"}
if (hr == 16)
 {hrn = "<IMG SRC=0.gif><IMG SRC=4.gif>"}
if (hr == 17)
 {hrn = "<IMG SRC=0.gif><IMG SRC=5.gif>"}
if (hr == 18)
 {hrn = "<IMG SRC=0.gif><IMG SRC=6.gif>"}
if (hr == 19)
 {hrn = "<IMG SRC=0.gif><IMG SRC=7.gif>"}
if (hr == 20)
 {hrn = "<IMG SRC=0.gif><IMG SRC=8.gif>"}
if (hr == 21)
 {hrn = "<IMG SRC=0.gif><IMG SRC=9.gif>"}
if (hr == 22)
 {hrn = "<IMG SRC=1.gif><IMG SRC=0.gif>"}
if (hr == 23)
 {hrn = "<IMG SRC=1.gif><IMG SRC=1.gif>"}


var min = RightNow.getMinutes() + 1

if (min == 01)
 {nmin = "<IMG SRC=0.gif><IMG SRC=1.gif>"}
if (min == 02)
 {nmin = "<IMG SRC=0.gif><IMG SRC=2.gif>"}
if (min == 03)
 {nmin = "<IMG SRC=0.gif><IMG SRC=3.gif>"}
if (min == 04)
 {nmin = "<IMG SRC=0.gif><IMG SRC=4.gif>"}
if (min == 05)
 {nmin = "<IMG SRC=0.gif><IMG SRC=5.gif>"}
if (min == 06)
 {nmin = "<IMG SRC=0.gif><IMG SRC=6.gif>"}
if (min == 07)
 {nmin = "<IMG SRC=0.gif><IMG SRC=7.gif>"}
if (min == 08)
 {nmin = "<IMG SRC=0.gif><IMG SRC=8.gif>"}
if (min == 09)
 {nmin = "<IMG SRC=0.gif><IMG SRC=9.gif>"}
if (min == 10)
 {nmin = "<IMG SRC=1.gif><IMG SRC=0.gif>"}
```

```
if (min == 11)
 {nmin = "<IMG SRC=1.gif><IMG SRC=1.gif>"}
if (min == 12)
 {nmin = "<IMG SRC=1.gif><IMG SRC=2.gif>"}
if (min == 13)
 {nmin = "<IMG SRC=1.gif><IMG SRC=3.gif>"}
if (min == 14)
 {nmin = "<IMG SRC=1.gif><IMG SRC=4.gif>"}
if (min == 15)
 {nmin = "<IMG SRC=1.gif><IMG SRC=5.gif>"}
if (min == 16)
 {nmin = "<IMG SRC=1.gif><IMG SRC=6.gif>"}
if (min == 17)
 {nmin = "<IMG SRC=1.gif><IMG SRC=7.gif>"}
if (min == 18)
 {nmin = "<IMG SRC=1.gif><IMG SRC=8.gif>"}
if (min == 19)
 {nmin = "<IMG SRC=1.gif><IMG SRC=9.gif>"}
if (min == 20)
 {nmin = "<IMG SRC=2.gif><IMG SRC=0.gif>"}

if (min == 21)
 {nmin = "<IMG SRC=2.gif><IMG SRC=1.gif>"}
if (min == 22)
 {nmin = "<IMG SRC=2.gif><IMG SRC=2.gif>"}
if (min == 23)
 {nmin = "<IMG SRC=2.gif><IMG SRC=3.gif>"}
if (min == 24)
 {nmin = "<IMG SRC=2.gif><IMG SRC=4.gif>"}
if (min == 25)
 {nmin = "<IMG SRC=2.gif><IMG SRC=5.gif>"}
if (min == 26)
 {nmin = "<IMG SRC=2.gif><IMG SRC=6.gif>"}
if (min == 27)
 {nmin = "<IMG SRC=2.gif><IMG SRC=7.gif>"}
if (min == 28)
 {nmin = "<IMG SRC=2.gif><IMG SRC=8.gif>"}
if (min == 29)
 {nmin = "<IMG SRC=2.gif><IMG SRC=9.gif>"}
if (min == 30)
 {nmin = "<IMG SRC=3.gif><IMG SRC=0.gif>"}

if (min == 31)
 {nmin = "<IMG SRC=3.gif><IMG SRC=1.gif>"}
```

```
if (min == 32)
 {nmin = "<IMG SRC=3.gif><IMG SRC=2.gif>"}
if (min == 33)
 {nmin = "<IMG SRC=3.gif><IMG SRC=3.gif>"}
if (min == 34)
 {nmin = "<IMG SRC=3.gif><IMG SRC=4.gif>"}
if (min == 35)
 {nmin = "<IMG SRC=3.gif><IMG SRC=5.gif>"}
if (min == 36)
 {nmin = "<IMG SRC=3.gif><IMG SRC=6.gif>"}
if (min == 37)
 {nmin = "<IMG SRC=3.gif><IMG SRC=7.gif>"}
if (min == 38)
 {nmin = "<IMG SRC=3.gif><IMG SRC=8.gif>"}
if (min == 39)
 {nmin = "<IMG SRC=3.gif><IMG SRC=9.gif>"}
if (min == 40)
 {nmin = "<IMG SRC=4.gif><IMG SRC=0.gif>"}

if (min == 41)
 {nmin = "<IMG SRC=4.gif><IMG SRC=1.gif>"}
if (min == 42)
 {nmin = "<IMG SRC=4.gif><IMG SRC=2.gif>"}
if (min == 43)
 {nmin = "<IMG SRC=4.gif><IMG SRC=3.gif>"}
if (min == 44)
 {nmin = "<IMG SRC=4.gif><IMG SRC=4.gif>"}
if (min == 45)
 {nmin = "<IMG SRC=4.gif><IMG SRC=5.gif>"}
if (min == 46)
 {nmin = "<IMG SRC=4.gif><IMG SRC=6.gif>"}
if (min == 47)
 {nmin = "<IMG SRC=4.gif><IMG SRC=7.gif>"}
if (min == 48)
 {nmin = "<IMG SRC=4.gif><IMG SRC=8.gif>"}
if (min == 49)
 {nmin = "<IMG SRC=4.gif><IMG SRC=9.gif>"}
if (min == 50)
 {nmin = "<IMG SRC=5.gif><IMG SRC=0.gif>"}

if (min == 51)
 {nmin = "<IMG SRC=5.gif><IMG SRC=1.gif>"}
if (min == 52)
 {nmin = "<IMG SRC=5.gif><IMG SRC=2.gif>"}
```

```
if (min == 53)
 {nmin = "<IMG SRC=5.gif><IMG SRC=3.gif>"}
if (min == 54)
 {nmin = "<IMG SRC=5.gif><IMG SRC=4.gif>"}
if (min == 55)
 {nmin = "<IMG SRC=5.gif><IMG SRC=5.gif>"}
if (min == 56)
 {nmin = "<IMG SRC=5.gif><IMG SRC=6.gif>"}
if (min == 57)
 {nmin = "<IMG SRC=5.gif><IMG SRC=7.gif>"}
if (min == 58)
 {nmin = "<IMG SRC=5.gif><IMG SRC=8.gif>"}
if (min == 59)
 {nmin = "<IMG SRC=5.gif><IMG SRC=9.gif>"}
if (min == 60)
 {nmin = "<IMG SRC=0.gif><IMG SRC=0.gif>"}

document.write(hrn+ "<IMG SRC=sc.gif>" +nmin)
</SCRIPT>
```

You can see the script's effect in Figure 7.3.

Figure 7.3
Clock displaying images.

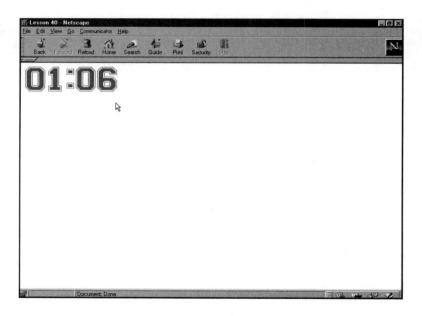

Click Here *To see the effect on your own computer, click on Lesson 40 Script's Effect in your download packet or see it online at* http://www.htmlgoodies.com/JSBook/lesson40example.html.

Deconstructing the Script

To start with, we create 11 images. They are the numbers 0 through 9 and a colon. The 11 images are shown in Figure 7.4.

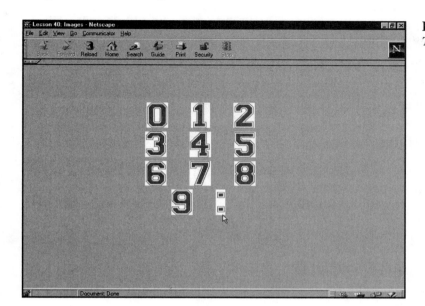

Figure 7.4
The clock images.

If you have grabbed the download packet from the HTML Goodies Web site, you already have the images on your computer. They are named 0.gif through 9.gif and sc.gif for the colon.

If you need to get them online, point your browser to http://www.htmlgoodies.com/JSBook/ 0.gif through http://www.htmlgoodies.com/JSBook/9.gif, as well as to http:// www.htmlgoodies.com/JSBook/sc.gif for the colon.

The script is very long compared to the size of the scripts we've been working with up to this point. But if you take another look, you'll notice that the script is little more than the same *hour:minute:second* return format that we used in the previous two lessons with a whole lot of `if` statements underneath.

The Hour

The hour is returned using the basic `RightNow.getHours()` *object.method* statement and is assigned the variable name `hr`. We are dealing with the military time format here, 0 through 23 will be returned, so there's no need to add one to the `getHours` return. We'll just allow an `if` statement for a return of zero.

Then the if statements start to roll. Here's the first one:

```
if (hr == 0)
  {hrn = "<IMG SRC=1.gif><IMG SRC=2.gif>"}
```

The first if statement deals with a getHours return of 0. That would be midnight. It reads, "If the hr variable, the number returned, is equal to 0, hrn (hour new is what we meant) is equal to these two images: <IMG SRC=1.gif><IMG SRC=2.gif>." That represents midnight.

Now we have the variable hrn set to return the 1 image and the 2 image.

Here's the second if statement that will be enacted if the getHours return is equal to 01:

```
if (hr == 01)
  {hrn = "<IMG SRC=0.gif><IMG SRC=1.gif>"}
```

In this if statement we're dealing with 1:00 AM. The return will be 01, so we set the two numbers to display as zero and one.

We didn't have to use 0 and 1; we could have just returned the 1 image. It would have worked just as well, but we think it looks better to have all numbers in the time set to display double images. It's just personal preference.

The if statements roll on until all numbers, 0 through 23, are represented. Notice we have the 0 and the 1 image set to return for the number 13 so that the clock will display the traditional 1 through 12 hours.

There is no need for an else statement at the end because we know that the number returned has to be 0 through 23. One of those if statements will come true every time.

The Minutes

Now this was a lot of coding. The concept is exactly the same as the earlier example, except we set 60 different if statements, one each for the numbers 1 through 60.

The code is the same except for one small difference. For the number 60, we set the images 0 and 0 to be returned. Clock readouts usually don't display 60, but rather 00, so we wanted to equal that.

The Display

This might be the shortest display since Lesson 1. The hour variable hrn is returned, the colon is placed, and then the minute variable nmin is returned. It looks like this:

```
document.write(hrn+ "<IMG SRC=sc.gif>" +nmin)
```

Because the variables are returning text representing four images, two for each, what you get is a series of five images across.

For example, if the time is 5:24, the `document.write` line will read:

```
<IMG SRC=0.gif><IMG SRC=5.gif><IMG SRC=sc.gif>
➥<IMG SRC=2.gif><IMG SRC=4.gif>
```

Get it?

Where's the `setTimeout()`?

This script is not actually set to rest, but you can do it simply by adding a function name and the `setTimeout()` format at the end of the function. By not setting this script to run, we got to stop and talk about using images in these running clocks.

The images we are using here are about 3KB each. That's a lot to ask of a browser to load every second, even if you do pre-load each image. Of course, this script only displays images for the hours and minutes, so you could set the `onTimeout()` to `60000` so the script would only update every minute.

If you do want to use this format to create a running clock, make a point of using very, very low byte images. If you don't, the script will show nothing. It won't be able to display the images fast enough.

So go way low on the bytes that make up your images, and do your darnedest to pre-load. If you use seconds, you might also want to set up the script to count every two seconds, or every five seconds. It will still be a good look.

Your Assignment

Add some code to the end of this script so that it also displays the seconds.

 You can see a possible answer to this assignment on your own computer by clicking on Lesson 40 Assignment in your download packet or see it online at `http://www.htmlgoodies.com/ JSBook/assignment40.html`.

Lesson 41: Countdown to Date

How many days is it to your birthday, Christmas, the new year? You can figure it out automatically as long as you know how to set a date in the future. After you have that future point, you can perform mathematics to find out the number of days until the date you set.

Of course, you can also get the minutes and seconds too, but first things first:

```
<SCRIPT LANGUAGE="javascript">

RightNow = new Date()
```

```
mil = new Date("January 1, 2001")
mil.setYear = RightNow.getYear;
day = (1000*60*60*24)
computeDay = (mil.getTime() - RightNow.getTime()) / day;
DayResult = Math.round(computeDay);

document.write("<center> "+DayResult+" days until the new Millennium,
➥ January 1<sup>st</sup>, 2001</center>");

</SCRIPT>
```

The script's effect appears in Figure 7.5.

Figure 7.5
Display of days until the millennium.

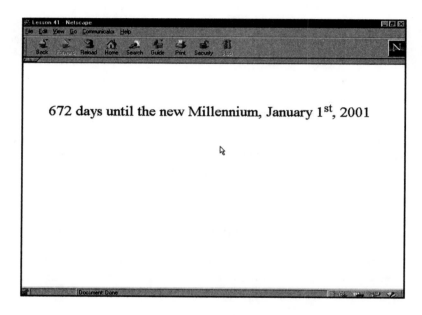

672 days until the new Millennium, January 1st, 2001

 To see the effect on your own computer, click on Lesson 41 Script's Effect in your download packet or see it online at http://www.htmlgoodies.com/JSBook/lesson41example.html.

Deconstructing the Script

The concept of the script is pretty simple. We first set a date off in the distance. That's our ending point. We then grab the current date. Now that we have these two points, it's possible, through mathematics, to figure out the number of days, minutes, or seconds from this point to the one we set way off in the future.

Here's script from the top down:

```
RightNow = new Date()

mil = new Date("January 1, 2001")
mil.setYear = RightNow.getYear;
```

The first three lines of the script set up the Date object and assign it the variable name RightNow.

Next, we assign a new date to the variable mil because this is a script to figure out the days to the millennium. But take a second look. See how the instances now have a date in the middle, "January 1, 2001"? That's where we set a date off in the distance. Now we have our future point.

Set It!

Next, we set the current year into stone. mil.setYear is a method used to set a year point and not allow it to move.

You see, when you use getSomething() the number that is returned is ever-changing, especially the second. By changing the text get to set, we carve the date in stone. That will work for hours, minutes, seconds, days, months, and as shown here, years.

JavaScript Counts by the Thousand

As if you didn't have enough to remember about how JavaScript counts, here's one more fact. 1000 is equal to one second. JavaScript counts time in 1/1000ths of a second (milliseconds).

Remember the Math.random() statement we used earlier to return a random number between 000 and 999? Well, it could be done because of JavaScript counting in milliseconds.

So we move along.

What's a Day?

This is a day:

```
day = (1000*60*60*24)
```

Because we have set our point in the future, now we need to create some mathematical statements so we can start figuring the days.

1000 equals a second, multiplied by 60 is a minute, multiplied by 60 equals an hour, multiplied by 24 equals a day. See how that works? Now we have a variable, day, that represents one 24-hour period.

Figure the Days

Now let's do the math. We'll set a variable name, computeDay, to figure the days between the point we set in the future and right now. It looks like this:

```
computeDay = (mil.getTime() - RightNow.getTime()) / day;
DayResult = Math.round(computeDay);
```

The variable mil.getTime() is new to this book. The method getTime() works under the object Date, just like any of the other get*Something*() or set*Something*() methods do.

Where getTime() differs is that it represents right now. When this method is run, it grabs all the dates and times at once. This will represent our second point in time, right now.

The math is performed by subtracting right now from our date in the future and dividing it by a day.

The number returned will most likely not be a round number, so we need to round it off using the Math.round() object.method statement.

The result is assigned the variable name DayResult.

Putting It on the Page

The result is put to the page through a basic document.write statement and some fancy HTML coding to create the superscript *st*:

```
document.write("<center> "+DayResult+" days until the new Millennium,
➡ January 1<sup>st</sup>, 2001</center>");
```

The script looks complicated at first, but after you break it down to its smallest parts, you can see it's a simple math problem where you display the results.

Your Assignment

Add some code to our script so it will also display the number of minutes until the new millennium.

Hint: It's not as simple as multiplying the number of days by 60.

 You can see a possible answer to this assignment on your own computer by clicking on Lesson 41 Assignment in your download packet or see it online at http://www.htmlgoodies.com/ JSBook/assignment41.html.

Lesson 42: Scrolling Text

Scrolling, scrolling, scrolling. Keep those letters scrolling.

Setting up scrolling text is a little tricky. It's done by setting a line of text, and then moving it a little to the left after a certain amount of time, again and again.

But after you get the scroll to roll, you can get it to scroll in the status bar, in an HTML division, an HTML layer, or in a text box like we did here:

```
<HTML>
<HEAD>
<SCRIPT LANGUAGE="JavaScript">

var space = "                                                    "
var scr = space + "This text is scrolling along..."

function ScrollAlong()
{

   temp = scr.substring(0,1);
   scr += temp
   scr = scr.substring(1,scr.length);
   document.Scroll.ScrollBox.value = scr.substring(0,55);
   var counts = setTimeout("ScrollAlong()",50);
 }
</SCRIPT>

</HEAD>

<BODY BGCOLOR="#FFFFFF" onLoad="ScrollAlong()">

<FORM NAME="Scroll">
<INPUT TYPE="text" size="50" name="ScrollBox" value="">
</FORM>

</BODY>
</HTML>
```

You can see the script's effect in Figure 7.6.

Figure 7.6
Scroll in text box.

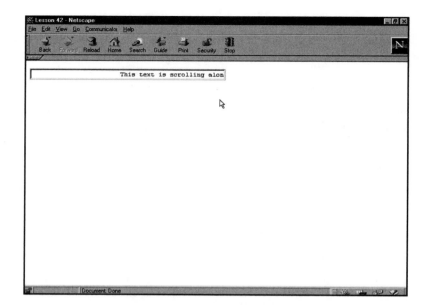

 To see the effect on your own computer, click on Lesson 42 Script's Effect in your download packet or see it online at http://www.htmlgoodies.com/JSBook/lesson42example.html.

Deconstructing the Script

The JavaScript that produces the scroll actually sits in between the HTML <HEAD> flags. The script that creates the scroll is contained in a function named ScrollAlong() that is triggered by an onLoad= event handler in the <BODY> flag.

The output of the script is displayed in a text box that looks like this:

```
<FORM NAME="Scroll">
<INPUT TYPE="text" size="50" name="ScrollBox" value="">
</FORM>
```

The name of the entire form is Scroll, and the name of the text box that will receive the scrolling text is ScrollBox.

Now that we understand the set up and the names of all the external parts, let's concentrate on the script.

190

The Text That Scrolls

The first two lines of the script, before the function, set the text that will scroll:

```
var space = "                                                   "
var scr = space + "This text is scrolling along..."
```

If the first line looks a little strange, there's a good reason. It's meant to produce space before the scroll. The variable name space is assigned to around 50 spaces. Then, the variable name scr is assigned to space and the text "This text is scrolling along...".

Now we have a long set of spaces and then text. The reason is aesthetic. If you didn't put a bunch of space before, or after the scrolling text, one scroll would just bump right into another.

Yes, we could have put all this on one line, but showing it this way was better because it gave us a chance to write this little section telling you to add a bunch of spaces before and after your scrolling text.

The Scrolling Script

This script, surrounded by the function ScrollingAlong(), actually creates the scroll. In reality, nothing is actually scrolling. The script is just taking all those spaces and text moving them to the left a nudge, again and again. The effect is the appearance that the text is scrolling.

Let's break it down. First, the variable temp is assigned to scr.substring(0,1). scr, you'll remember, represents the text that will scroll along:

```
temp = scr.substring(0,1);
```

The substring(0,1) command is new. It returns a portion, or sub, of a text string depending on an index. The index is contained within the instance, zero and one. Basically, this command will return part of the text to the scroll when called upon. At this point, it is set to return only one character. This is what actually creates the scroll.

Next, scr is given a new value. Here's the code:

```
scr += temp
```

The operator in the middle is what does the trick. That += operator means to add what is before the operator to what is beyond the operator. So, scr += temp could actually have been written as scr = scr + temp. The += is just a little shorthand we thought you'd like to know.

So what has happened? The substring scr is now the entire text string plus the entire text string one character in. If that happens again and again, the text will build adding one more character from the string each time to the next letter or space in the string to create the next display. That will give the effect that the start point keeps moving one space to the left, eating away at the substring text. The text will keep displaying one letter to the right and give the effect that it's actually scrolling out from the right-hand side of the text box.

The script continues to build up again using scr as the variable of choice.

```
scr = scr.substring(1,scr.length);
```

Now, scr is assigned a value that's a substring of itself, working with the two indexes 1 and the text string's length. This might seem a little confusing at this point, but what you are asking for here is a subset of the text string. If you put in a number, only that many letters would be returned. By setting the argument of the subset to the length of the substring, you can be assured the entire string will be returned, rather than just the string each time missing one letter.

At this point, the code that came before is making the return keep moving one to the left. And then this line, posting the text in full, is starting at that one space to the left again and again. That'll look like a scroll, right?

```
document.Scroll.ScrollBox.value = scr.substring(0,55);
```

The output of scr.substring is now being sent to the text box through the hierarchy statement document.Scroll.ScrollBox.value. The two numbers in the instance are, again, two arguments. Yet this time, we're not dealing with text, but rather that return space within the text box. This line is set up to provide 55 spaces of visible text in which the text will scroll.

You can prove that to yourself by setting the 55 to 25 and rerunning the script. The space in which the text scrolls will be cut almost in half.

Now we need to make the script keep repeating itself, because if it doesn't, this would be a one-character space scroll. That would be too quick and pretty boring. Here's what does it:

```
var counts = setTimeout("ScrollAlong()",50);
```

Here's that setTimeout() statement you've come to know and love. This time around, the variable name is counts and it will run the next substring every 50/1000ths of a second.

Set the number higher to go slower and set it lower to go faster. Just remember you're not setting a speed here. You're setting the 1/1000ths of a second before the script runs again. The result is that the scroll appears faster or slower.

Scrolls are rough, but after you have the very basics of them, you should be able to scroll with the best of them.

Your Assignment

Alter the code in this lesson so that the text that scrolls is different, the scroll occurs in the status bar, and finally, it scrolls much faster than it is set to scroll now.

 You can see a possible answer to this assignment on your own computer by clicking on Lesson 42 Assignment in your download packet or see it online at http://www.htmlgoodies.com/ JSBook/assignment42.html.

Lesson 43: End of Chapter Review—Count to an Event

Up until now, we have had events that run consistently or figured out set times. Now let's get a countdown to roll in much the same fashion as we got the scroll to roll.

The script in this lesson is set up to count five seconds and then perform an event.

Table 7.1 shows the object-related JavaScript commands you've been given up to now. You've also been introduced to these JavaScript concepts:

- String and the substring() method
- The alert(), confirm(), and prompt() methods
- The If/Else conditional statement
- These Event Handlers: onBlur, onChange, onClick, onDblClick, onFocus, onKeyDown, onKeyPress, onKeyUp, onLoad, onMouseDown, onMouseMove, onMouseOut, onMouseOver, onMouseUp, onSubmit
- Arithmetic Operators: (+), (-), (*), (/), (%)
- Conditions: (==), (!=), (<), (>), (=<), (=>), (?:), (+=)
- The HTML 4.0 flag <SPAN>
- Creating variable names
- Creating a function
- for Loops
- HTML form items
- Form item attribute NAME=
- Form item properties: length, value, selectedIndex
- Form item methods: toLowerCase, toUpperCase()
- while loops

Table 7.1   Object-Related JavaScript Commands Demonstrated in Chapters 1 Through 7

Object	Methods	Properties
date	getDate() getDay() getHours() getMinutes() getMonth() getSeconds() getTime() setYear() setDate() setDay() setHours() setMinutes() setMonth() setSeconds() setYear()	
document	write()	alinkColor, bgColor, fgColor, linkColor, lastModified, location, referrer, title, vlinkColor
history	go()	length
location		host, hostname, href
Math	random(), round()	
navigator		appCodeName, appName, appVersion, userAgent
window	close() setTimeout()	defaultstatus, directories, location, menubar, resizable, self, scrollbars, status, toolbar

Here's a script that puts some of these concepts to work:

```
<HTML>
<HEAD>
<TITLE>Lesson 43</TITLE>

<SCRIPT LANGUAGE="JavaScript">

RightNow = new Date();
StartPoint = RightNow.getTime();

function StartTheCount()
{
```

```
    var RightNow2 = new Date();
        var CurrentTime = RightNow2.getTime();
        var timeDifference = CurrentTime - StartPoint;
        this.DifferenceInSeconds = timeDifference/1000;
        return(this.DifferenceInSeconds);
}

function TheSeconds()
{
        var SecCounts = StartTheCount();
        var SecCounts1 = " "+SecCounts;
SecCounts1= SecCounts1.substring(0,SecCounts1.indexOf(".")) +
➥ " seconds";

if (DifferenceInSeconds >= 6)
 {alert("done")}
else
{
        document.FormCount.CountBox.value = SecCounts1
       window.setTimeout('TheSeconds()',1000);}
}
</SCRIPT>

</HEAD>

<BODY BGCOLOR="FFFFFF" onLoad="window.setTimeout('TheSeconds()',1)">

<FORM NAME="FormCount">
<INPUT TYPE="text" size=9 NAME="CountBox">
</FORM>

</HTML>
```

The script's effect appears in Figure 7.7.

 To see the effect on your own computer click on Lesson 43 Script's Effect in your download packet or see it online at http://www.htmlgoodies.com/JSBook/lesson43example.html.

Figure 7.7
Alert box after countdown.

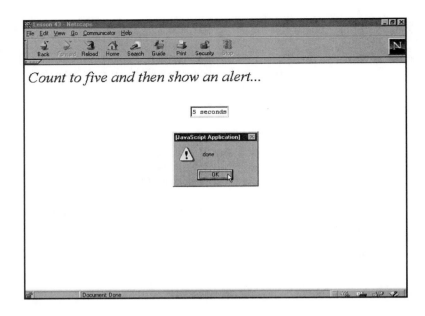

Deconstructing the Script

For this chapter wrap up, we're going to go with a rather large effect. The script is made up of objects you already know, but there are a lot of them. Also, there are two functions. So we better get started.

We'll start again from the bottom:

```
<FORM NAME="FormCount">
<INPUT TYPE="text" size=9 NAME="CountBox">
</FORM>
```

The preceding code creates an HTML form text box that will receive the output of the script. The form itself is named FormCount and the box that will receive the value is named CountBox. Now we know the names and can start tearing down the script.

The Script

The script begins in a familiar fashion, by assigning the value RightNow to the Date object:

```
RightNow = new Date();
StartPoint = RightNow.getTime();
```

Because we will be figuring out seconds until an event, we'll need to set a point in time, so we assigned the variable StartPoint to the second in time the script runs, RightNow.getTime().

The First Function

The first function is named `StartTheCount()`, appropriately enough. The code is similar to the code from Lesson 41 that figured the number days until a set point:

```
function StartTheCount()
{

var RightNow2 = new Date();
        var CurrentTime = RightNow2.getTime();
        var timeDifference = CurrentTime - StartPoint;
        this.DifferenceInSeconds = timeDifference/1000;
        return(this.DifferenceInSeconds);
}
```

The variable `RightNow2` is assigned to a brand-new `Date` object. Then the variable `CurrentTime` is assigned to the exact point in time at which the script runs, as returned by `RightNow2.getTime()`.

The time difference in seconds between the `CurrentTime` and `StartPoint` is figured by subtracting one from the other. The answer is then divided by 1000, JavaScript's representation of a second. The result is assigned the variable name `DifferenceInSeconds`.

Now, we take our answer and run the second function.

The Second Function

The second function, named `TheSeconds()`, is actually a couple of events put together. The first event creates the count; the second event watches the numbers roll by and enacts an alert box when the count reaches 6.

The first event looks like this:

```
var SecCounts = StartTheCount()
var SecCounts1 = " "+SecCounts;

SecCounts1= SecCounts1.substring(0,SecCounts1.indexOf(".")) +
➥ " seconds";
```

The variable name `SetCount` is assigned to the output of the first function `DifferenceInSeconds`. Obviously, we didn't have to do this. It just seemed good to assign a new name because we were in a whole new function.

The variable `SecCounts1` is assigned to a space plus the results of the first function. This is much like the scrolling script was put together, adding space to a value.

SecCounts1 is then given a value, the substring of itself. Remember that a substring returns the greater of the two indexes in its instance. In the preceding code, the two indexes are 0 and the indexOf() SecCounts1.

Yes, that indexOf() is new. That command returns a count of what you point it toward. In this case, we have pointed it toward the results of the first script. That means the indexOf() starts to count from the point returned by the mathematics in the first function, probably 1 or less than 1.

Only now the substring will not return a letter as in the scroll script, but rather will return the number, and the indexOf() will begin the count.

But how does it count up? Look at the last line of the second function:

```
window.setTimeout('TheSeconds()',1000);}
```

It's a basic setTimeout() method that reruns the function TheSeconds() every second. That's why the script counts. It is run again and again and again until…

Stopping the Count

One of the selling points of this script is that it will count up to a certain point, and then throw up an alert box, or whatever you set it to do.

The count is watched, and then the alert box is enacted by the following code:

```
if (DifferenceInSeconds >= 6)
 {alert("done")}
else
{
document.FormCount.CountBox.value = SecCounts1
window.setTimeout('TheSeconds()',1000);}
}
```

It is a simple if / else statement that says if the output of the first script, DifferenceInSeconds, is greater than or equal to 6, post an alert. If not, continue to post the output of SecCounts1 to the text box CountBox in the form named FormCount.

Why Count from the First Function?

Ah, you noticed that. We're not relying on the count from the second function to set off the alert. You see, the second function is just a display. The first function is the one that is really keeping count. That's why we're using the result, DifferenceInSeconds, to count for the if / else statement.

It's a true count using that number. The count that displays is for show only.

Your Assignment

Set up a greeting for your users. This is a great effect. Get the text Good Morning, Afternoon, or Evening, to scroll in the status bar. The text should then be followed by the text Welcome to my page.

 You can see a possible answer to this assignment on your own computer by clicking on Lesson 43 Assignment in your download packet or see it online at http://www.htmlgoodies.com/ JSBook/assignment43.html.

Chapter 8

Arrays

This chapter contains the following lessons and scripts:

- Lesson 44: Two Different Array Formats
- Lesson 45: Combining User Input with Arrays
- Lesson 46: Random Quotes
- Lesson 47: A Guessing Game Using Arrays
- Lesson 48: A Password Script
- Lesson 49: End of Chapter Review—A Quiz

One of the staples of any programming language is the ability to create an indexed, ordered list of items for the program to use, manipulate, or display. That indexed list is called an *array*.

JavaScript offers two basic formats for presenting an array. Each works equally well, although after we get into the scripts in this chapter, you'll see how using one format or the other in particular cases is best, simply to keep it all straight your own mind.

Setting up an array is a little tricky at first. You have to be concerned with the order of the items, whether the items are data or literal strings, and how the data will be used. Plus there's the concern that JavaScript counts everything, and it starts counting at 0.

But after you grasp the concept of setting up arrays, the possibilities of what you can do with them are endless.

Lesson 44: Two Different Array Formats

Sharp-minded readers might remember that way back in Lesson 15, we put together an array. The array was set up to present the day of the week. Here, we set up the exact same array and result—only this time we'll follow a different method of presenting an array.

Both formats are included for explanation purposes. We'll start with the format you haven't seen yet:

```
<SCRIPT LANGUAGE="JavaScript">

var dayName=new Array(7)
dayName[0]="Sunday"
dayName[1]="Monday"
dayName[2]="Tuesday"
dayName[3]="Wednesday"
dayName[4]="Thursday"
dayName[5]="Friday"
dayName[6]="Saturday"

var y=new Date();
var Today = y.getDay()

document.write("Today is "+dayName[Today] + ".");

</SCRIPT>
```

The script's effect appears in Figure 8.1.

 To see the effect on your own computer, click on Lesson 44 Script's Effect in your download packet or see it online at http://www.htmlgoodies.com/JSBook/lesson44example.html.

Deconstructing the Script

Immediately following the <SCRIPT LANGUAGE=javascript> flag is the array that presents the days of the week. It looks like this:

```
var dayName=new Array(7)
dayName[0]="Sunday"
dayName[1]="Monday"
dayName[2]="Tuesday"
dayName[3]="Wednesday"
dayName[4]="Thursday"
dayName[5]="Friday"
dayName[6]="Saturday"
```

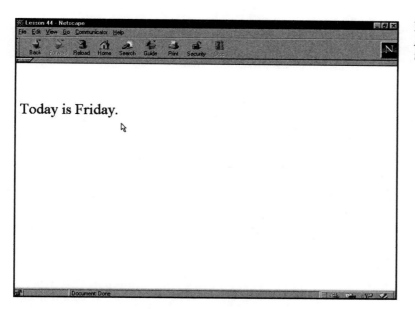

Figure 8.1
*Day of the week posted
through an array.*

Notice the order. Remember that JavaScript counts everything and starts counting at 0. The order of the days above starts with 0 for Sunday. We chose to put Sunday first because when you call for the dates of the week using the getDays() method, Sunday will return the number 0, Monday will return 1, and so on. So the order is not up for discussion.

The Format of a New Array

Look at the format of the array. The array itself is seen by the browser as a variable name. That's extremely handy because after the variable name is assigned, we can call on the array, and an index number, and just that piece of data or literal string is returned.

The array is assigned the variable name dayName. Notice the format you use to set a new array. It is quite similar to the format used when setting a new Date object. You assign the variable name, specify that the assigned item is new, and then declare it as an array: new Array(7).

The number that appears in the array's instance (the parentheses) is the number of items in the array. Remember, even though the array starts numbering items at 0, you still need to count the first item as a member of the array. It has happened too many times that because the first element in the array was listed as 0, it was not counted by the author. JavaScript counts it, so you must count it, too.

Listing the Array Items

This format of listing array items is good in that the number assigned to the array item is right there for all the world to see. The first items looks like this:

```
dayName[0]="Sunday"
```

dayName is the variable name assigned to the entire array. To set apart an item as an element in the dayName array, you use the variable name and then the number that will be assigned by JavaScript, starting at 0 and simply counting up by 1. The number assigned to the indexed items in the array is referred to as the *index number.*

Notice the number is within square brackets. We always keep that usage straight because square brackets are all that's left. We can't use parentheses because they are used for instances, and we can't use braces because they are used for enclosing functions. Okay, it's not a good method of remembering, but it sure works for us.

Next is the single equal sign used to assign a value to the *variable*[#]. In this case, the value is a literal string, Sunday. It is text, nothing more. We do not want to manipulate this data or do anything with it other than display it if needed. Because it is only text, double quotation marks surround it.

Later in this chapter, we make arrays that consist of numbers and answers to a quiz. That numeric data is not to be returned. We want to manipulate it and return something else depending on the outcome. That numeric data does not appear within quotation marks. Here, though, we're using literal strings. They sit within the double quotation marks. Have we driven that point home?

To complete the array, you work down the line, assigning the same variable name and adding 1 to the number until you reach the end of your list. When all items have been listed, you've finished your array.

More Than One in a JavaScript

It is more common to have multiple arrays in a JavaScript than it is to have only one. Your assignment today requires you to put more than one array in the script.

The format for each new script is the same as we've already described. However, each new array must be assigned a new variable name. Then when you list the items in the array, you need to assign them numbers using that new variable name.

However, every new array starts counting at 0.

Here's an example of three small arrays that could all go on the same page:

```
var tree=new Array(3)
tree[0]="Elm"
```

```
tree[1]="Pine"
tree[2]="Maple"

var NumberData=new Array(3)
NumberData[0]=15
NumberData[1]=30
NumberData[2]=45

var Cats=new Array(3)
Cats[0]="Fido"
Cats[1]="Chloe"
Cats[2]="Stimpy"
```

All three arrays have different variable names, and each list starts counting at 0. You can include 1,000 arrays on a page as long as you come up 1,000 different variable names and number them all starting with 0.

Returning from the Array

Now that we have gone over the concept of setting up the array, we need to discuss how to get one of the items returned. And not just any item, let's get the one we want. Here's the code that calls for the day of the week:

```
var y=new Date();
var Today = y.getDay()

document.write("Today is "+dayName[Today] + ".");
```

The first two lines should look familiar. The new Date object is assigned the variable name y. Then the *object.method* statement y.getDay() is assigned the variable name Today. When all is said and done, Today will return the number representing the day of the week.

The document.write statement is where the magic happens. It starts off posting the text Today is , leaving the space for appearance. Then a return is called for. Notice the plus signs. The return is the variable name we assigned to the array. We know that the string to be returned will come from that array. But which one?

Notice that within the square brackets is the output of y.getDay(), Today. That value is a number. If the number returned is 0, today must be Sunday. If the number returned is 4, today must be Thursday.

Whatever the number, the value is placed within the square brackets. That value is then used to go to the array and return the string that is attached to that number.

And the day of the week appears on the page.

But what about adding 1 to the `y.getDate()` statement to get the number up to snuff? It's not needed. You added 1 when you were returning just a number. Because of the 0 being in the mix, you needed to add 1 because everything starts counting at 0. If you didn't, the month, the year, the hour, and so on, would all be off by 1.

Here, there's no need to add 1. In fact, you'll mess things up by doing it. The array allows for 0 to be a correct answer. If you add 1, 0 will never be returned, and it will never get to be Sunday. And we can't have that.

A Different Type of Array

Now, let's look at the script we wrote in Lesson 15. It does the same thing as the script we've just discussed in this lesson, but the arrays are set up differently:

```
<SCRIPT LANGUAGE="JavaScript">
var dayName=new Array("Sunday","Monday","Tuesday",
➡"Wednesday","Thursday","Friday","Saturday")
var y=new Date();
var Today = y.getDay()
document.write("Today is "+dayName[Today] + ".");
</SCRIPT>
```

This is the line that creates the array:

```
var dayName=new Array("Sunday","Monday","Tuesday",
➡"Wednesday","Thursday","Friday","Saturday")
```

The same rules described earlier still apply. The array is assigned a variable name and the array is noted as being new, just like setting up a `Date` object.

The difference between the two arrays is that in this format, you're allowing the JavaScript to assign the values for the array items, rather than doing it yourself. Sunday is 0, Monday gets a 1, Tuesday gets 2, and so on.

The results will be the same, and both scripts will run just fine.

The main difference is that in this format, you cannot tell at a glance what number is assigned to each element. I found myself counting more times than I wanted to.

When Do I Use One or the Other?

After writing the scripts in the chapter, we found that the format you use is as much as personal preference as anything else. However, the straight-line format worked best when we were comparing two lines of arrays. That way the arrays were listed on two lines and we could quickly see which data went with which in the arrays.

When simply returning data based upon the user's input, the vertical list was best.

But the choice is yours. Either one will work, and both are useful. Just remember that strings are surrounded by double quotation marks, and when you use the all-in-a-row format like the script from Lesson 15, the items are separated by a comma and no spaces.

Your Assignment

Add a second array to the script, following the same pattern, to complete the phrase It is day in the month of month.

 You can see a possible answer to this assignment on your own computer by clicking on Lesson 44 Assignment in your download packet or see it online at http://www.htmlgoodies.com/ JSBook/assignment44.html.

Lesson 45: Combining User Input with Arrays

Joe is a huge fan of the *Rocky* movies. He wrote this script. The concept is pretty basic. There are five *Rocky* movies. The user is asked to enter a number, 1 through 5, into a text box and then click a button.

When the button is clicked, the title of the movie and a very brief plot summary appears in two other text boxes.

There are two arrays in the script. Depending on what number the user puts in, that number in both arrays is returned. So here again, both arrays are locked into an order. One number, two arrays, two returns.

While you read through the list, keep in mind that there was no *Rocky 0*. So you have to make allowances for those users who try to be funny and enter a goose egg.

Here's the script:

```
<SCRIPT LANGUAGE="javascript">

function Balboa()
{
var num = document.RockyForm.RockyUser.value

var Movie = new Array(6)
Movie[0]="There was no Rocky 0"
Movie[1]="Rocky"
Movie[2]="Rocky II"
Movie[3]="Rocky III"
Movie[4]="Rocky IV"
Movie[5]="Rocky V"
```

```
var Outcome = new Array(6)
Outcome[0]="No Outcome"
Outcome[1]="Rocky Loses"
Outcome[2]="Rocky Wins"
Outcome[3]="Rocky Loses, then Wins"
Outcome[4]="Apollo Dies, Rocky Wins"
Outcome[5]="Rocky Wins Street Brawl"

document.RockyForm.RockyTitle.value=Movie[num]

document.RockyForm.RockyOutcome.value=Outcome[num]

}

</SCRIPT>

<FORM NAME="RockyForm">Enter a Rocky Movie Number (1-5):
<INPUT NAME="RockyUser" TYPE="text" SIZE="2">

<INPUT TYPE="button" Value="Tell Me What Happens"
➥onClick="Balboa()"><P>

You chose: <INPUT NAME="RockyTitle" TYPE="text" SIZE="26"><BR>
The outcome was: <INPUT NAME="RockyOutcome" TYPE="text" SIZE="26">
</FORM>
```

You can see the script's effect in Figure 8.2.

 To see the effect on your own computer, click on Lesson 45 Script's Effect in your download packet or see it online at http://www.htmlgoodies.com/JSBook/lesson45example.html.

Deconstructing the Script

As is often the case when the script includes a form element, we will start from the bottom:

```
<FORM NAME="RockyForm">Enter a Rocky Movie Number (1-5):
<INPUT NAME="RockyUser" TYPE="text" SIZE="2">

<INPUT TYPE="button" Value="Tell Me What Happens"
➥onClick="Balboa()"><P>

You chose: <INPUT NAME="RockyTitle" TYPE="text" SIZE="26"><BR>
The outcome was: <INPUT NAME="RockyOutcome" TYPE="text" SIZE="26">
</FORM>
```

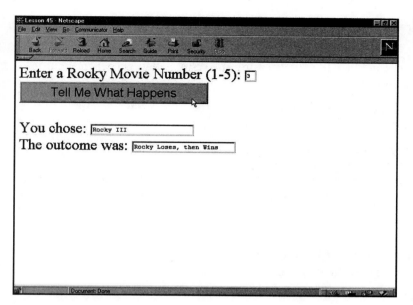

Figure 8.2
Output from user input.

This HTML form code is constructed to provide a box to accept data, a button to start the process, and then two text boxes to receive the output of the script. Let's take them in order.

The name of the entire form is `RockyForm`.

The box that will receive the user's number is named `RockyUser`. Now we know enough to start creating hierarchy statements to represent this box. This particular text box will be referred to as `document.RockyForm.RockyUser.value`.

Next, there's a form button that will read Tell Me What Happened. When clicked, the button will trigger a function named `Balboa()`.

The final two boxes will receive the output of the script. The first will get the title of the movie. Its name is `RockyTitle`. The second box will receive the brief plot line. Its title is `RockyOutcome`.

Okay, now we know the players on the field, let's move on to the function.

The Function

The first three lines of the script play a very important role:

```
function Balboa()
{
var num = document.RockyForm.RockyUser.value
```

The first line sets the entire script into a function called Balboa(). Remember that from the button?

The second line has the opening brace to start encasing the script. Then we get to the line that takes the information from the user.

In the preceding code, while identifying the text boxes, we stopped and wrote out the hierarchy of the box that will receive the user's number. The line

```
var num = document.RockyForm.RockyUser.value
```

now assigns the variable num to whatever the user puts in. That's important because later we will use that num value to call on a specific array object from both arrays.

The Arrays

Both arrays contain six elements. The titles of the films are assigned the variable name Movie and the brief plot lines are assigned the variable name Outcome:

```
var Movie = new Array(6)
Movie[0]="There was no Rocky 0"
Movie[1]="Rocky"
Movie[2]="Rocky II"
Movie[3]="Rocky III"
Movie[4]="Rocky IV"
Movie[5]="Rocky V"

var Outcome = new Array(6)
Outcome[0]="No Outcome"
Outcome[1]="Rocky Loses"
Outcome[2]="Rocky Wins"
Outcome[3]="Rocky Loses, then Wins"
Outcome[4]="Apollo Dies, Rocky Wins"
Outcome[5]="Rocky Wins Street Brawl"
```

Notice right off that the two arrays are set in the same order. If you look at array item number three in each, the title and the outcome line up. We are going to use one number, represented by num, to pull from both arrays. If you don't have the two arrays in the same order, either the title or the outcome will be wrong.

There are only five *Rocky* movies, yet there are six items in the array. The reason is that you simply cannot ignore that 0 exists. JavaScript loves it. It has to have it. So you make a point of offering it an array value. In this case, we simply specified that there was no *Rocky 0*, and there was no outcome.

Pulling from the Arrays

The following code enters information into the two text boxes when the button is clicked:

```
document.RockyForm.RockyTitle.value=Movie[num]
```

```
document.RockyForm.RockyOutcome.value=Outcome[num]
```

The first line returns the array item represented by the number the user entered from the `Movie` array.

The second line returns the array item represented by the number the user entered from the `Outcome` array.

Because both arrays are set up in the same order, the same number will return the same array item number, and the two results will jibe with each other. That means you won't get the title of *Rocky II* and the outcome of *Rocky IV*.

This type of script can be used to create numerous returns as long as the items being returned are in a set order. This technique could be used to create a listing of presidents, Super Bowl winners, World Series winners, or any other numeric rundown of items. It could be set up as a great teaching tool.

Your Assignment

Add code to the sample script so that a third text box receives a rating. When the user clicks on the button, he should see three things: the new rating, the name of the movie, and what happens.

 You can see a possible answer to this assignment on your own computer by clicking on Lesson 45 Assignment in your download packet or see it online at http://www.htmlgoodies.com/ JSBook/assignment45.html.

Lesson 46: Random Quotes

One of the biggest selling points of JavaScript is how easy it is to set up a random event. Arrays lend themselves to randomization very well.

In this lesson, we'll set up a script that returns one of ten quotes chosen at random.

Remember that even though we're using quotes, anything that you list in the array can be returned in a random fashion: links, images, or a greeting are some of the more popular items.

So read through this lesson, think about how you could apply this concept of grabbing a random array item, and apply it to your own pages.

Here's the script:

```
<SCRIPT LANGUAGE="JavaScript">

var quote = new Array(10);
quote[0] = " Education is going to college to learn
➥to express your ignorance in scientific terms ";
quote[1] = "Chance favors the prepared mind";
quote[2] = "A stitch in time, saves nine.";
quote[3] = "The only difference between bravery
➥and stupidity is the outcome";
quote[4] = "One should never let a formal education
➥get in the way of learning";
quote[5] = "Happiness is two kinds of ice cream.";
quote[6] = "If you choose not to make a choice,
➥you still have made a decision.";
quote[7] = "Do, or do not. There is no try";
quote[8] = "Reality is merely an illusion,
➥albeit a very persistent one.";
quote[9] = "No one ever said life would be easy.";

var now=new Date()
var num=(now.getSeconds())%9

document.write(quote[num])

</SCRIPT>
```

The script's effect appears in Figure 8.3. Note that we've added the text A Random Quote to the figure. The script does not post that text.

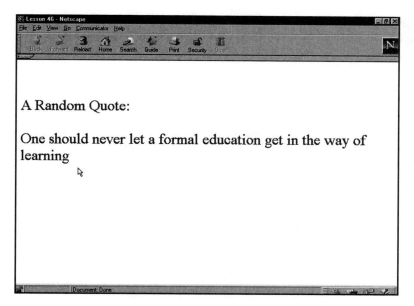

Figure 8.3
Random quote.

 To see the effect on your own computer, click on Lesson 46 Script's Effect in your download packet or see it online at `http://www.htmlgoodies.com/JSBook/lesson46example.html.`

Deconstructing the Script

Do you like the quotes? If not, change them, or add more. Either way, let's get started tearing this script apart. Here's the array:

```
var quote = new Array(10);
quote[0] = " Education is going to college to learn to
➥express your ignorance in scientific terms ";
quote[1] = "Chance favors the prepared mind";
quote[2] = "A stitch in time, saves nine.";
quote[3] = "The only difference between bravery
➥and stupidity is the outcome";
quote[4] = "One should never let a formal education
➥get in the way of learning";
quote[5] = "Happiness is two kinds of ice cream.";
quote[6] = "If you choose not to make a choice,
➥you still have made a decision.";
quote[7] = "Do, or do not. There is no try";
quote[8] = "Reality is merely an illusion,
➥albeit a very persistent one.";
quote[9] = "No one ever said life would be easy.";
```

The format is the same as seen in the last lesson. But just to drive a point home, we could have used the array format where all ten quotes were listed in a row, in quotation marks, and separated by commas, and no spaces. It would have worked just fine, but think of what it would have looked like. The line of code that contained the array items would have been a mile long and couldn't have been easily understood at a glance. Using the preceding format, you can quickly see each of the array items and its number.

Let's get back to the array. The array has been assigned the variable name quote. There are 10 items in the array. Notice though that the array only goes up to 9. Again, that is because there is a 0 in the count. We know we keep pointing it out, but it can be very confusing and very easy to overlook.

From Joe Burns: I have seen JavaScripts that use random arrays set up so that 0 never comes into play. The random number is set to return 1 as its lowest number. Still, the author had to make a point of putting a 0 array item in the run. It didn't have a useful value because it was never going to come up, but there had to be some value or the JavaScript would throw an error. Then, even though the author was only working with 10 items, he had to make a point of the array being listed as 11 items because even though the zero item would never come into play, it still had to be counted. Ugh! What a pain. Follow the format above and just remember that there has to be a 0 line. Your life and your math will be a whole lot easier.

The Random Number Code

We're using the same random number code found throughout the book. The Date object is assigned the variable name now:

```
var now=new Date()
var num=(now.getSeconds())%9
```

The variable num will represent the random number produced by dividing the returned second by 9 and using the remainder. Did you remember that the % sign actually returns the remainder of the division? If not, now you will.

This code will return a number between 0 and 9. Of course, you know those are the same numbers we have set up in our array. See how all the pieces are coming together?

Putting It on the Page

Because we're only dealing with a returned value and no other text surrounding it, there is no need for plus signs or quotation marks. What we want returned is one of the quote array items. Which item is settled by entering the result of the random number code into the square brackets:

```
document.write(quote[num])
```

Depending on the number, that quote will be returned to the page.

Random Anything

As long as the array is set up correctly and you set up the `document.write` statement in the correct fashion, just about anything can be returned randomly to the page. The HTML Goodies email box receives a great deal of mail asking how to create random images, links, banners, and the like. This is how it's done. You'll have to play with the code a little to make it all display correctly, but we've shown you the base methodology and format.

So be random.

Your Assignment

Add five more quotes to the scripts. That might seem easy, but look closely. You have to do more than just add the text.

 You can see a possible answer to this assignment on your own computer by clicking on Lesson 46 Assignment in your download packet or see it online at `http://www.htmlgoodies.com/JSBook/assignment46.html`*.*

Lesson 47: A Guessing Game Using Arrays

Let's play a game. In this example, the user is asked to guess the JavaScript's favorite state from a list of states. The prompt statement is repeated until the user guesses the state correctly. But it's not as easy as it seems. The user cannot just keep guessing down the line until she gets it right by process of elimination. Each time the button is pressed, a new random state is selected.

This script will use the randomization you just read about and take you in a new direction, testing user input against what is returned from the array:

```
<SCRIPT LANGUAGE="JavaScript">
var states=new Array()
states[0]="CT"
states[1]="PA"
states[2]="NJ"
states[3]="NY"
states[4]="RI"

function pickstate()
{
var now=new Date()
var num=(now.getSeconds())%4
```

```
var guess=prompt("What's my favorite state: CT, PA, NJ, NY, or RI?")
if (states[num] == guess.toUpperCase())
{alert("That's my favorite state!")}
else
{alert("No, Try again")}
}

</SCRIPT>

<FORM>
<INPUT TYPE="button" VALUE="Guess My Favorite State"
➥onClick="pickstate()">
</FORM>
```

You can see the script's effect in Figure 8.4.

Figure 8.4
Random array game.

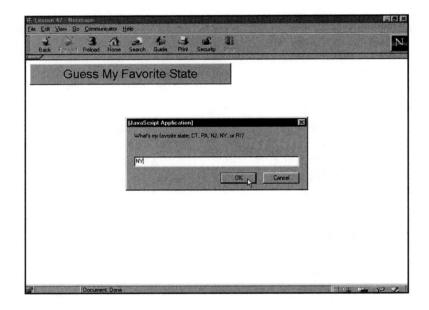

 To see the effect on your own computer, click on Lesson 47 Script's Effect in your download
packet or see it online at http://www.htmlgoodies.com/JSBook/lesson47example.html.

Deconstructing the Script

It might be more tradition at this point, but there are form elements in this script, so we will
start from the bottom:

```
<FORM>
<INPUT TYPE="button" VALUE="Guess My Favorite State"
➥onClick="pickstate()">
</FORM>
```

The form element is simply a button to get the entire process under way. When the button is clicked, a function named pickstate() will be triggered and run.

The Array

```
var states=new Array()
states[0]="CT"
states[1]="PA"
states[2]="NJ"
states[3]="NY"
states[4]="RI"
```

The array is the vertical format listing five possible favorite states. The state names are in double quotation marks, so they are simple literal strings that will be returned later through a piece of random code.

The Game Function pickstate()

Now let's look at the pickstate() function:

```
function pickstate()
{
var now=new Date()
var num=(now.getSeconds())%4


var guess=prompt("What's my favorite state: CT, PA, NJ, NY, or RI?")
if (states[num] == guess.toUpperCase())
{alert("That's my favorite state!")}
else
{alert("No, Try again")}
}

</SCRIPT>
```

The random number is returned as it was in the last lesson. The Date object is assigned the variable now. Then the variable num is assigned the returned number created by dividing the current second by 4 and using the remainder of the equation.

That means there is a possibility of five numbers being returned, 0 though 4. Those are the same five numbers represented in our array.

The game is played by first asking the user to name a favorite state:

```
var guess=prompt("What's my favorite state: CT, PA, NJ, NY, or RI?")
```

Notice that the prompt offers the choices the user can make. One of the five must be the choice. If the user does not enter one of those choices, the answer and the return from the array will simply match. The variable name guess is assigned to the user's entry.

Then an if statement asks whether the array item returned by the random number generator is equal to the guess the user made:

```
if (states[num] == guess.toUpperCase())
```

We've tried to compensate for the fact that JavaScript sees lowercase and uppercase letters differently by adding the method toUppercase() to the end of the guess variable. (You might remember the toUpperCase() method from Chapter 5, "Forms: A Great Way to Interact with Your Users." It sets a literal string to all capital letters.) By using toUpperCase(), we ensure that the guess will always be uppercase and a user will not lose the game simply because he or she entered lowercase letters rather than the required uppercase letters.

Next, the if statement posts an alert box that reads That's my favorite state! if the user's state and the state returned from the random code are the same. If the two are not the same, an alert box pops up to say No, Try again:

```
{alert("That's my favorite state!")}
else
{alert("No, Try again")}
```

The game might seem simple at first, a basic one-in-five chance. Not so. At the start of every game, a new state is generated. Therefore, from game to game, the chance of choosing the winner stays the same. That means you just can't keep choosing the same state and winning by simple state elimination. That would be cheating.

Your Assignment

This one can be done a few different ways. Alter the script so that it produces a form button. When the user clicks the button, he will be sent to one of three randomly chosen links.

 You can see a possible answer to this assignment on your own computer by clicking on Lesson 47 Assignment in your download packet or see it online at http://www.htmlgoodies.com/ JSBook/assignment47.html.

Lesson 48: A Password Script

Password protection is very popular on the Web. Whether what is being protected really requires protection is a matter of personal opinion. The thinking might be that if you need a password to see what is behind the curtain, it must be more important than what is just sitting out for all the world to see.

An array offers a fantastic method for setting up a password-protected page or directory.

The password script in this lesson offers an array of seemingly random letters. The user is asked to enter three numbers. Those numbers are checked against the array and a page URL is created. The many different number combinations make it quite difficult to guess at the name of the page that is being protected.

But because you, the JavaScript author, know the page name, you can set up the script to return the correct three letters to form the protected page's address.

As you look down the script, I'll tell you that the page name that is being protected is joe.html and the password is 1, 4, 5:

```
<SCRIPT LANGUAGE="javascript">

function GoIn()
{
var Password = new Array("p","j","l","t","o","e","o","b","x","z")

function getNumbers()
{
return document.userInput.u1.value
return document.userInput.u2.value
return document.userInput.u3.value
}

var input1 = document.userInput.u1.value
var input2 = document.userInput.u2.value
var input3 = document.userInput.u3.value

var pw1 = Password[input1]
var pw2 = Password[input2]
var pw3 = Password[input3]

var pw = pw1 + pw2 + pw3
if (pw == pw1+pw2+pw3)
{location.href = pw+ ".html"}
}
</SCRIPT>
```

```
Put in Your Three-Number Password to Enter:
<FORM NAME="userInput">
<INPUT TYPE="text" Name ="u1" SIZE="2">
<INPUT TYPE="text" Name ="u2" SIZE="2">
<INPUT TYPE="text" Name ="u3" SIZE="2">
<INPUT TYPE="button" VALUE="Enter" onClick="GoIn()">
</FORM>
```

The script's effect appears in Figure 8.5.

Figure 8.5
Accepting the password.

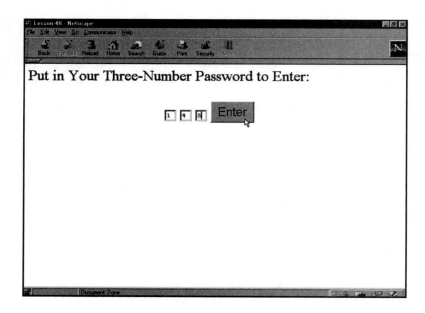

 To see the effect on your own computer, click on *Lesson 48 Script's Effect in your download packet or see it online at* http://www.htmlgoodies.com/JSBook/lesson48example.html.

Deconstructing the Script

What's that? You say you didn't see the password in the script? Of course not. What good would a password script be if all you had to do was look at the script and pull out the password? That's like writing the combination to a lock on the back of the lock. This script is a little hard to crack just by looking at the source code.

The Form Elements

This script contains form elements, so we will start from the bottom and meet the players:

```
Put in Your Three-Number Password to Enter:
<FORM NAME="userInput">
<INPUT TYPE="text" Name ="u1" SIZE="2">
<INPUT TYPE="text" Name ="u2" SIZE="2">
<INPUT TYPE="text" Name ="u3" SIZE="2">
<INPUT TYPE="button" VALUE="Enter" onClick="GoIn()">
</FORM>
```

The form itself is named userInput. That makes sense.

The first text box is named u1, the second is named u2, and the third is named u3.

Finally, there's a form button that, when clicked, starts a function called GoIn().

Now you know the names, and will understand the hierarchy statements, so we go back to the top.

The Script

Here's the function GoIn() being created. The brace always comes right after the function name:

```
function GoIn()
{
var Password = new Array("p","j","l","t","o","e","o","b","x","z")
```

Next is the array. To the viewer, it looks like a run of random letters. Good. That's what we want. It should look like there is no rhyme or reason to why the letters are set in the order they are. In reality, there is an order—at least an order we know—so that as the script progresses, we can call for array letter number 1, number 4, and number 5, put them all together and create joe.html.

Now, do you see a little pattern emerging? The other letters will never enter into it. We are only interested in the second letter in the list. That letter is represented by the number 1, and the letter is j.

The second number in the password script is 4. The letter represented by the number four is o. Remember, count up from 0!

The third number in the password is 5. The letter represented by the number five is e.

By putting those three array items together and adding .html, we get the URL joe.html.

We made the order of the letters of joe correct. You can further attempt to confuse the reader by putting the letters out of order. Just make sure the numbers you call for are the numbers that coincide with the page name you are attempting to create.

Get the Results into the Function

This is new. The purpose of this function is to make sure that the data the user entered into the three text boxes are in the function so we can work with them. It basically pulls the values into the script.

```
function getNumbers()
{
return document.userInput.u1.value
return document.userInput.u2.value
return document.userInput.u3.value
}
```

There was no need to do this in the game script in the last lesson because we were only dealing with one piece of data. Now we have three. So by setting up a function and calling for the return of the values found in the text boxes, we now have those three numbers in the function.

It is a good idea to do this any time you have multiple input values from a user.

The following lines aren't needed, but it is a good idea to assign a much simpler variable name to the data the user has entered into the text boxes. That way we do not have to write out those long hierarchy statements again and again:

```
var input1 = document.userInput.u1.value
var input2 = document.userInput.u2.value
var input3 = document.userInput.u3.value
```

Now we start to build the page's URL from the data the user has given. The three variable names pw1 through pw3 are assigned to the letters returned by taking the three numbers entered by the user and grabbing that letter in the array:

```
var pw1 = Password[input1]
var pw2 = Password[input2]
var pw3 = Password[input3]
```

For example, if the user entered the number 3 in the first box, pw1 would be equal to t. That happens two more times using the data in the second and third text boxes.

The variable name pw is created using the values pw1, pw2, and pw3:

```
var pw = pw1 + pw2 + pw3
```

Finally, an `if` statement asks whether pw is equal to pw1+pw2+pw3. Of course it is. The variable pw was created by using those three pw# variables:

```
if (pw == pw1+pw2+pw3)
{location.href = pw+ ".html"}
}
```

Because pw will always equal pw1+pw2+pw3, the script attempts to find a page with the URL made up of the three letters returned.

Unless the three letters are correct, the browser won't find the page. An error message will pop up saying the page made up of the three letters the user posted cannot be found. Because the user is given no indication whether his or her answer is even close, every try is a random shot.

There are ten letters and three of them must be correct. That means a one-in-ten shot times three. Do the math. That's a pretty hard shot at just guessing the correct three numbers.

Now, those odds of guessing the password ring true only if you make your array out of purely random letters or groupings of letters. A smart person might be able to go into the code above after seeing what it is looking for and pick out joe through a little brain power. But if I made the name of the protected page bjz, the fight to figure it out would much harder because that's just a run of letters that means nothing.

Toughen It Up

Try setting up the text array with multiple letters in each position.

Try setting up the script so that you require four numbers.

Try setting up the script so that each of the text boxes pulls from a different array. Make each array a different grouping of ASCII text characters.

You could make this JavaScript even more challenging by rewriting it so the script contains two arrays. The first is a series of random numbers. Those numbers coincide with letters in a second array. Use the number from the first array to pull a letter from the second.

For example, suppose the user enters the number 0. In the first array, the number in the 0 position is 4. Now use that 4 to pull out the letter at the number 4 index position in the second array. I can't even begin to think of the odds of guessing that one correctly.

Your Assignment

This time around, you won't need to do much, but you will need to pay close attention to what you are changing. Take the script from this lesson and alter it so that the new password is 3, 6, 4.

You can see a possible answer to this assignment on your own computer by clicking on Lesson 48 Assignment in your download packet or see it online at `http://www.htmlgoodies.com/JSBook/assignment48.html`.

Lesson 49: End of Chapter Review—A Quiz

The purpose of this end-of-chapter review is the same as all the other ones. You are to take everything you have learned up to this point and create a new and useful script to place on your own pages.

Of course, we'll offer one ourselves and then make a suggestion or two.

Table 8.1 shows the object-related JavaScript commands you've been given up to now. You've also been introduced to these JavaScript concepts:

- String and the `substring()` method
- Arrays
- The `alert()`, `confirm()`, and `prompt()` methods
- The `If/Else` conditional statement
- These Event Handlers: onBlur, onChange, onClick, onDblClick, onFocus, onKeyDown, onKeyPress, onKeyUp, onLoad, onMouseDown, onMouseMove, onMouseOut, onMouseOver, onMouseUp, onSubmit
- Arithmetic operators: (+), (-), (*), (/), (%)
- Conditions: (==), (!=), (<), (>), (=<), (=>), (?:), (+=)
- The HTML 4.0 flag <SPAN>
- Creating variable names
- Creating a function
- `for` loops
- HTML form items
- Form item attribute `NAME=`
- Form item properties: `length`, `value`, `selectedIndex`
- Form item methods: `toLowerCase`, `toUpperCase()`
- `return`
- `while` loops

Table 8.1   Object-Related JavaScript Commands Demonstrated in Chapters 1 Through 8

Object	Methods	Properties
date	getDate() getDay() getHours() getMinutes() getMonth() getSeconds() getTime() setYear() setDate() setDay() setHours() setMinutes() setMonth() setSeconds() setYear()	
document	write()	alinkColor, bgColor, fgColor, linkColor, lastModified, location, referrer, title, vlinkColor
history	go()	length
location		host, hostname, href
Math	random(), round()	
navigator		appCodeName, appName, appVersion, userAgent
window	close() setTimeout()	defaultstatus, directories, location, menubar, resizable, self, scrollbars, status, toolbar

This lesson's script is a quiz. There are five form element drop-down boxes with three answers each. The user will choose the answers she feels are correct and click the button to see her score:

```
<SCRIPT LANGUAGE="javascript">

function Gradeit()
{

function getselectedIndex(){
return document.quiz.q1.selectedIndex
return document.quiz.q2.selectedIndex
return document.quiz.q3.selectedIndex
return document.quiz.q4.selectedIndex
return document.quiz.q5.selectedIndex
}
```

```
var Answers=new Array(1,2,2,3,1)
var UserAnswers = new Array(document.quiz.q1.selectedIndex,
➥document.quiz.q2.selectedIndex,document.quiz.q3.selectedIndex,
➥document.quiz.q4.selectedIndex,document.quiz.q5.selectedIndex)
var count0 = 0

if (Answers[0] == UserAnswers[0])
{count0 = count0 + 1}
else
{count0 = count0}

if (Answers[1] == UserAnswers[1])
{count1 = count0 + 1}
else
{count1 = count0}

if (Answers[2] == UserAnswers[2])
{count2 = count1 + 1}
else
{count2 = count1}

if (Answers[3] == UserAnswers[3])
{count3 = count2 + 1}
else
{count3 = count2}

if (Answers[4] == UserAnswers[4])
{count4 = count3 + 1}
else
{count4 = count3}

alert("You got " + count4 + "/5 right.")

}
</SCRIPT>

<FORM NAME="quiz">

<b>#1: What is 2 + 2?</b>
<SELECT NAME="q1">
<OPTION SELECTED>Choose One
<OPTION>4
<OPTION>2
<OPTION>22
```

```
</SELECT>
<P>

<b>#2: Trees have: </b>
<SELECT NAME="q2">
<OPTION SELECTED>Choose One
<OPTION>engines
<OPTION>leaves
<OPTION>dogs
</SELECT>
<P>

<b>#3: This book is about:</b>
<SELECT NAME="q3">
<OPTION SELECTED>Choose One
<OPTION>Nothing
<OPTION>JavaScript
<OPTION>Love and Romance
</SELECT>
<P>

<b>#4: Who sang "Yesterday"?</b>
<SELECT NAME="q4">
<OPTION SELECTED>Choose One
<OPTION>Van Halen
<OPTION>Metallica
<OPTION>The Beatles
</SELECT>
<P>

<b>#5 What color is blue?</b>
<SELECT NAME="q5">
<OPTION SELECTED>Choose One
<OPTION>blue
<OPTION>green
<OPTION>off-blue
</SELECT>
<P>

<INPUT TYPE="button" VALUE="Grade Me" onClick="Gradeit()">

</FORM>
```

The beauty of this script is that it uses two arrays to get the final score. The first array consists of the correct answers. The second array consists of the answers given by the user.

One by one, the answers are checked against each other. If the answer is correct, 1 is added to the score. If not, the score remains the same.

The results of the script are then displayed in an alert box.

You can see the script's effect in Figure 8.6.

Figure 8.6
The results of the quiz.

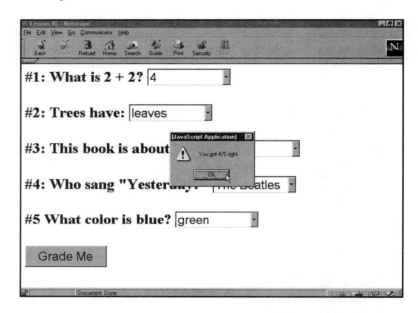

 To see the effect on your own computer, click on Lesson 49 Script's Effect in your download packet or see it online at `http://www.htmlgoodies.com/JSBook/lesson49example.html`.

Deconstructing the Script

Okay, this is a long script and it looks scary, but don't be put off. It's a lot of the same elements again, and again, and again.

There are form elements in this script, so we will start at the bottom.

The Form Elements

Rather than display all five drop-down boxes, let's only look at the first one. The other four work exactly the same way. Hopefully, you can get the answer to this one:

```
<FORM NAME="quiz">

<b>#1: What is 2 + 2?</b>
<SELECT NAME="q1">
```

```
<OPTION SELECTED>Choose One
<OPTION>4
<OPTION>2
<OPTION>22
</SELECT>
<P>
```

The name of the entire form is `quiz`. Remember that the entire form will contain all five drop-down menu boxes. You are only seeing the first one here. Look back at the full script if you need to.

The name of the first drop-down menu box is q1. We decided on that because it represented question one. That makes sense.

The next four drop-down menu boxes all are set up the same, except they are named q2 through q5, respectively.

Remember: JavaScript counts everything and it starts counting at 0. In each of these drop-down menu boxes, each selection is assigned a number by the JavaScript. The first is 0, and it counts up from there.

Notice that the first select choice, the one that will receive the number 0, is not a viable answer. It simply displays Choose One so the user knows to click to choose an answer.

Finally, there is a form button after the five drop-down menu boxes:

```
<INPUT TYPE="button" VALUE="Grade Me" onClick="Gradeit()">
```

That button will trigger a function named Gradeit().

Still with us? Good.

The Script

The script is a little long, but there's nothing new in it and its inner workings are pretty straightforward.

The script begins by being surrounded by the function Gradeit(). This is the function that the HTML form button will trigger when the user clicks:

```
function Gradeit()
{
```

You probably remember the next part from the last lesson. This function is making a point of bringing up the answers the user chose so that the data can be manipulated in this script. Notice the q1 through q5 names in the hierarchy statements:

```
function getselectedIndex(){
return document.quiz.q1.selectedIndex
```

```
return document.quiz.q2.selectedIndex
return document.quiz.q3.selectedIndex
return document.quiz.q4.selectedIndex
return document.quiz.q5.selectedIndex
}
```

Notice how I am not asking for the value the user entered because the input device is not a text box. It's a drop-down menu box, and the command you use to return that value is selectedIndex. Remember that from Chapter 5?

Next come the answers. The array was created as a key:

```
var Answers=new Array(1,2,2,3,1)
```

The answers that are taken from the drop-down menu boxes will be tested against these numbers. If the numbers returned from the menu boxes are the same, the user gets 5 out of 5. If not, the user gets a lower score.

Here are the results of the quiz as given by the user:

```
var UserAnswers = new
 Array(document.quiz.q1.selectedIndex,
➥document.quiz.q2.selectedIndex,document.quiz.q3.selectedIndex,
➥document.quiz.q4.selectedIndex,document.quiz.q5.selectedIndex)
```

Yes, the format is a little long setting it up in the single-line array format, but the answers are in the single-line format, so we felt this should be, too.

We could have made this line shorter by assigning variable names to the long hierarchy statements. However, we're only writing the statement once, so assigning variable names would be a step that just isn't required.

Grade the Test

Grading is achieved by comparing the Answers array and the UserAnswers array, one array item at a time. The 0 items in both arrays will be compared. If they match, add 1. If not, do nothing and go on to the next one.

Each time you grade another answer, you have to change the variable name. It gets a little confusing, but follow it along.

First, a variable, count0, is created and assigned a 0 value:

```
var count0 = 0
```

You have to do this in case the user doesn't get any of the answers right. Without setting the count to 0 to start with, the JavaScript would throw an error if the result was 0 out of 5.

Now we move to the grading itself. Let's look at only the first two questions being graded:

```
if (Answers[0] == UserAnswers[0])
{count0 = count0 + 1}
else
{count0 = count0}

if (Answers[1] == UserAnswers[1])
{count1 = count0 + 1}
else
{count1 = count0}
```

The first `if` statement compares the two numbers in the 0 position in the `Answers` and `UserAnswers` arrays.

If they are the same, `count0` gets 1 added. If not, `count0` remains keeps the same value, 0.

The next two numbers in both arrays—the numbers in the 1 position—are now compared. If they are the same, `count1`, a new variable, equals `count0` plus 1.

If not, `count1` equals `count0`, or still 0.

The process continues this way, creating a new variable name to coincide with each new question's grading. It looks like this. Follow the new variable names along:

```
if (Answers[2] == UserAnswers[2])
{count2 = count1 + 1}
else
{count2 = count1}

if (Answers[3] == UserAnswers[3])
{count3 = count2 + 1}
else
{count3 = count2}

if (Answers[4] == UserAnswers[4])
{count4 = count3 + 1}
else
{count4 = count3}
```

When all is said and done, `count4` will have the final score out of five. An alert box is set to pop up with `count4`'s value displayed as a grade. It looks like this:

```
alert("You got " + count4 + "/5 right.")
```

Altering the Display

Okay, we agree that displaying the score on an alert box is a little cheesy. The point of showing you this script was to provide an example of getting a JavaScript to grade a quiz.

The display is up to you. You easily have enough knowledge at this point to take the count4 variable and post it all over the place.

In fact, look back through the script. You can pretty easily display the user's choices right along with his score. You can even make all that information pop up in a new browser window.

All we provided here was a way to get the math done. Now it's up to you to make it pretty. Think about it for a moment. There must be 50 ways to get this script to display the results.

Your Assignment

For this assignment, put together an entirely new script. The script should post a random image. Furthermore, the random image should have a URL attached to it. The URL should not be random. It should always be attached to that image when it displays.

 You can see a possible answer to this assignment on your own computer by clicking on Lesson 49 Assignment in your download packet or see it online at http://www.htmlgoodies.com/JSBook/assignment49.html.

Chapter 9

Putting It All Together

This chapter contains the following lessons and scripts:

- Lesson 50: JavaScript Animation
- Lesson 51: Background Color-Changing Script
- Lesson 52: A Floating, Moving, New Browser Window
- Lesson 53: Form Validation
- Lesson 54: Self-Typing Typewriter
- Lesson 55: Scrolling Credits

This chapter is a series of six rather difficult scripts. The effects are quite different than any of the other scripts in the book. Here we'll deal with animation, wildly changing background colors, a browser window that flies around the screen, HTML form validation, a typewriter that types by itself, and finally, scrolling credits, just like in the movies.

The scripts are difficult on purpose. We wanted the last chapter to be a showcase for some of the higher-end effects you can get through JavaScript. But don't worry: Each script is explained in detail, and you'll understand them well enough to make changes and place them on your page.

Lesson 50: JavaScript Animation

You already know about image flips that occur when the mouse passes over an image. Here you'll go one step farther. This script takes a series of 10 images and plays them one after another, like a movie.

We simply count our images from zero to nine, but if you use images in the correct order, this script will play them at whatever speed you want to create a basic animation:

```
<SCRIPT LANGUAGE="JavaScript">
var num=1
  img1 = new Image (55,45)
  img1.src = "0.gif"

  img2 = new Image (55,45)
  img2.src = "1.gif"

  img3 = new Image (55,45)
  img3.src = "2.gif"

  img4 = new Image (55,45)
  img4.src = "3.gif"

  img5 = new Image (55,45)
  img5.src = "4.gif"

  img6 = new Image (55,45)
  img6.src = "5.gif"

  img7 = new Image (55,45)
  img7.src = "6.gif"

  img8 = new Image (55,45)
  img8.src = "7.gif"

  img9 = new Image (55,45)
  img9.src = "8.gif"

  img10 = new Image (55,45)
  img10.src = "9.gif"


  function startshow()
```

```
      {
  for (i=1; i<50; i=i+1)
   {document.mypic.src=eval("img"+num+".src")
      for(x=1; x<1000; x=x+1)
    {}
      num=num+1
      if(num==10)
      {num=1}
      }
      document.mypic.src=img1.src
      }
  </SCRIPT>

  <IMG SRC="0.gif" NAME="mypic" BORDER=0>
  <p>

  <A HREF="JavaScript:startshow()">Display animation</a>
```

You can see the script's effect in Figure 9.1.

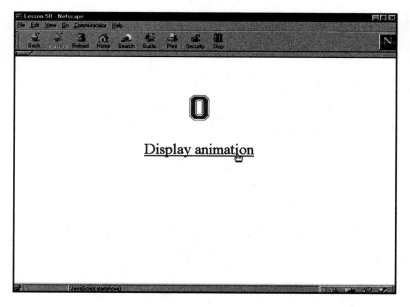

Figure 9.1
The first cell of the animation count to 10.

To see the effect on your own computer, click on Lesson 50 Script's Effect in your download packet, or see it online at http://www.htmlgoodies.com/JSBook/lesson50example.html.

Deconstructing the Script

Let's begin by talking about the 10 small blocks of code that start the script:

```
img1 = new Image (55,45)
  img1.src = "0.gif"


  img2 = new Image (55,45)
  img2.src = "1.gif"
```

We're only showing the first two blocks of code here because the same format is followed again and again. Notice each of the small blocks of code calls for a new image, `0.gif` through `9.gif`.

The code is pre-loading the images. Remember what we're trying to do here. The latter portions of the script, which we'll get to in a moment, will create an animation by showing 10 images right in a row.

Well, if you have to wait for the server to be contacted every time a new image is called for, it wouldn't be much of an animation. You want all 10 images in the cache and ready to go when the user clicks to start the animation show. That's why you need to pre-load all the images.

The format is pretty basic. It reads as if you were setting a new `Date` object. A variable name is assigned to a new `Image` object. The numbers in the parentheses are the height and width, in that order, of the image.

In the next line, the image source is offered in an `object.property` format: `img1.src = "0.gif"` Note the double quotes. If you don't surround the name of the image in quotes, the script will think that dot separates an object from a property or a method and throw an error. But by inserting double quotes, you set `"0.gif"` apart as a string.

And so it goes 10 times. Each time, a new object is set with a new variable name, and then a source is offered.

The result is a download of the image. Now, when the animation is called for, all the images are already in the browser cache and the viewer gets a good show.

The Animation

Okay, now that we have all 10 images loaded and ready to go, let's get to the meat of the script.

The script is surrounded by the function `startshow()`. That way, we have the ability to use an Event Handler later on to start the animation when a user clicks.

The actual animation is created through a couple of `for` loops. Here's the first:

```
for (i=1; i<50; i=i+1)
{document.mypic.src=eval("img"+num+".src")
```

Remember that we've created the variable `num` and assigned it a value of one. Did you catch that? It's way at the very tip top of the script, even before the pre-loading code. That's important. If we didn't assign a value of one, the script would start with zero as the starting point. It's also important for that variable setting to be outside of the function. We'll explain why in a moment.

The first `for` loop states that the loop will go 50 times. The number 50 is quite arbitrary. We simply chose a high number because we wanted the animation to run a lot of times.

The loop states that the `document.mypic.src` hierarchy statement is equal to `img`, the returned value of `num` and then `.src`. It's building a source for the next image.

Remember that `num` is equal to one. We set that up as a variable earlier, remember? So without doing a thing, we have two images. The first is `0.gif`, which is on the page to start with. You'll see the code in a moment. We also have `1.gif`, the first image source built from the `for` loop.

Don't worry about the number building up past `9.gif`, the last image in the sequence. We'll fix that concern a little later.

Now we hit the second `for` loop:

```
for(x=1; x<1000; x=x+1)
    {}
```

Think of this loop as timing. Notice there are no commands in the curly brackets; thus nothing happens while the loop counts to 1000. And as we know, 1000 equals a second. So when this loop is run, all it does is count, stalling the animation.

If you want the animation to go faster, make the number this loop is counting smaller. If you want it to go slower, make the number larger.

Okay, so we have the animation. Now we need to make a point of telling the JavaScript to add one each time it rolls around. This code does that for us:

```
num=num+1
```

That seems simple enough. But what happens when the number reaches 9 and `9.gif` is the last image in the animation? This happens:

```
if(num==10)
{num=1}
```

An `if` statement says that if the variable `num` reaches `10`, set it back to `1`.

Why 10 rather than 9? Remember that we want `num` to reach nine, and before this statement we add one. When `num` gets to nine, one will be added before the `if` statement is reached. Thus, when `num` gets to 10, we become concerned.

We created `num` at the very top of the script and gave it the value of `one` to get it out of the function. If `one` was in the function, we couldn't reset it as we're doing because it would have to retain that number while in the function. By putting it outside of the function, we make it a piece of data and it can be manipulated and changed.

Finally, we're back to one. The statement

```
document.mypic.src=img1.src
```

is added to set the source to `0.gif`, calling again on the original image so that the animation starts again at the beginning, `0.gif`, rather than at `1.gif`.

Calling for the Animation

Here's the code that posts the first image to the page and starts the animation:

```
<IMG SRC="0.gif" NAME="mypic" BORDER=0>
<p>
<A HREF="JavaScript:startshow()">Display animation</a>
```

The first line is a basic HTML image flag with a NAME= attribute included so that this image space is attached to the preceding script. Any image changes will take place within this space. That's why it's a good idea to make all the images the same size, just like when you created an image flip.

Now, here's something new. Look at the format of the hypertext link that starts the animation. It is pointing at `JavaScript:startshow()` rather than a hypertext link.

That's a quick way to put active text on a page to trigger a function. By putting `JavaScript:` into the hypertext formula, the browser knows that a script, contained within the document, will be enacted. The function name that follows will tell the browser which script to trigger. It's very clever.

The effect is an animation in which each new image is loaded into the image space every time the second `for` loop counts to 1000 (that is, every second).

This animation will run five times. Remember that the first `for` loop is set to 50. There are ten images in this animation. Ten divided into 50 goes 5 times.

Your Assignment

This one will take a bit of thought. Change the script so that the animation is no longer in it. Then make it so that when you click, you get the next image in line, again and again, until you have rolled through the entire set of 10 images.

 You can see a possible answer to this assignment on your own computer by clicking on Lesson 50 Assignment in your download packet or viewing it online at http://www.htmlgoodies.com/JSBook/assignment50.html.

Lesson 51: Background Color-Changing Script

This script is another animation of sorts. The script runs in a loop and changes the background color slightly every time it loops around. And because we're setting not one, but two colors, the background loops around for all the blues, then the greens, then the yellows, and so on.

It's annoying and great all at the same time. Here's the script:

```
<SCRIPT LANGUAGE="JavaScript">

b = 10;
f = 99;
a = true;

function BGChange() {
if(a == true) {
b++;
f--;
}

if(b==10) {
b++;
f--;
a = true;
}

document.bgColor=b+"00"+f;

setTimeout ("BGChange()",10);
}

BGChange();

</SCRIPT>
```

You can see the script's effect in Figure 9.2.

Figure 9.2
Color-changing background script.

To see the effect on your own computer click on Lesson 51 Script's Effect in your download packet or see it online at http://www.htmlgoodies.com/JSBook/lesson51example.html.

What's Happening?

It will be helpful if you know what happens in this script first before I explain what the script does.

The entire purpose of the script is to create different hexadecimal (hex) codes that will then be used to create background colors.

A hex code is made up of three sets of two numbers representing saturation of red, green, and blue. For example, the code FF FF FF indicates red, green, and blue all turned up to their highest color saturation. That combination of all colors at their highest level produces white. 00 00 00 is just the opposite. There's no red, green, or blue. It's black.

This JavaScript will create a new background hex code by changing the first and last sets of two numbers. One set of two numbers will increase while the other decreases. The green setting, represented by the two middle numbers in the hex code, will remain the same.

Because the script runs again and again so fast, the change in color looks quite fluid.

That's the concept; now let's tear it apart.

Deconstructing the Script

This JavaScript carries with it a lot of the same thinking as the script in Lesson 50. A few variables are created outside of a function and then manipulated within the function. Those manipulations are then used to create a new element and the browser displays that element. In this case, the elements are new background colors rather than the images from last lesson.

We'll start from the top and work our way down.

First we set up three variables and assign values to them:

```
b = 10;
f = 99;
a = true;
```

The first two variables, b and f, will be used make up the new hex codes. The third variable, a, is set to true so we can set up a condition later that if a equals true, something should be done. Of course, by setting a up as being true, we know that a will be true and thus the condition will run.

That's a good trick to keep in your hip pocket. Set a variable to true so that later you can set up a condition to run off of it.

Now we get into the function and the first condition. It's an if statement:

```
function BGChange() {
if(a == true) {
b++;
f--;
}
```

The function is given the name BGChange(). That seems logical.

Here we use the condition that if a is true, do something. Of course we know a is true, so we know the condition will run. There's no need for an else statement. You only need an else statement if you want something to happen if the condition isn't true. We know the condition will always be true, so there's no need for the else statement.

Now, here's something new. Notice that b is followed by a double plus sign (++) and f is followed by a double negative (--). Those are operators that set up increments, a count.

We know that b is equal to 10 and f is equal to 99. We just set that up in the preceding variables. So by setting b aside with double plus signs, we know it will count up from 10. And f will count down from 99. One goes one way, and one goes the other. That's what gives that nice fading color to the script.

But what happens when b can longer count down? We reset the numbers just like we did in the last script. Here's the code:

```
if(b==10) {
b++;
f- -;
a = true;
}
```

If b equals 10, count one more time and set a to true. This will make sense when we cycle back to the top of the script again.

Now the code that makes the background magic:

```
document.bgColor=b+"00"+f;
```

You've seen this before. This code alters the background of the document object. But notice now that the first two numbers of the hex code are represented by b and the last two are represented by f. One is counting down and the other is counting up.

Each time the script cycles through, a new color is created and sent to the background. And because the color change is very slight each time, you get a very pretty flow.

The set line of code should look familiar:

```
setTimeout ("BGChange()",10);
}
```

It is a setTimeOut() command that will run the BGChange() function after waiting 10/1000 of a second. Set the number higher to make the change in color go slower.

Finally, the script ends with a clever trick. This is the last line of code:

```
BGChange();
```

You probably recognize it as the name of the function. But why is it last? To start the cycle. Sure, we could have used an onLoad= Event Handler to trigger the function, but why not try something new?

By placing the name of the function right after the function itself, the name triggers the function to run.

Now, that's clever.

This JavaScript is very clever and very annoying at the same time. Try changing around the b and the f to get different color combinations.

Also, try using two copies of this script (remember to change the function name in one), so you get two running at the same time. It's a very strange effect.

Your Assignment

We want you to play around with the script so that you get a whole new range of colors. Change the hex code that is produced for the background and change out the levels of colors.

Hint: There's no new code required. Just change what you see in the script.

 You can see a possible answer to this assignment on your own computer by clicking on Lesson 51 Assignment in your download packet or see it online at `http://www.htmlgoodies.com/ JSBook/assignment51.html`.

Lesson 52: A Floating, Moving, New Browser Window

If nothing else, this effect will certainly grab someone's attention: The page loads and then a smaller browser window pops up and flies around the screen.

We have it set so the browser flies in a circle, but you can change coordinates so that it will fly around in just about any pattern, and you can set how many times it flies around. We have set ours set to only fly around once and then stop.

You have to see this one to believe it. Here's the code:

```
<SCRIPT LANGUAGE="javascript">

a=275;
b=275;
r=50;
x=1;

function rotateObjects(r)
{
var newWin = window.open ('movingAround.html', 'newwindow',
➥ config='height=150,width=350,toolbar=no,menubar=yes,
➥scrollbars=yes,resizable=no,location=no,directories=no,
➥status=no');

for (var i = 0; i <360; i++) {
x = (r * Math.cos((i * Math.PI)/180)) + a;
y = (r * Math.sin((i * Math.PI)/180)) + b;
newWin.moveTo(x,y);
}


}
```

```
while (r<=100)

{  for (r=60;r<=100;r+=1)

{
rotateTimer = setTimeout("rotateObjects(r)", 1000);

r+= 45;
 }

}
</SCRIPT>
```

The script's effect appears in Figure 9.3.

Figure 9.3
Moving browser window.

 To see the effect on your own computer, click on Lesson 52 Script's Effect in your download packet or see it online at http://www.htmlgoodies.com/JSBook/lesson52example.html.

Deconstructing the Script

This is a difficult script, but it reads rather easily, top to bottom. The concept is pretty straightforward. You open a window and then move it around the browser screen. We'll start at the top.

Once again we are setting a few variables before we get to the function of the script:

```
a=275;
b=275;
r=50;
x=1;
```

The function is named `rotateObjects(r)`:

```
function rotateObjects(r)
{
var newWin = window.open ('movingAround.html', 'newwindow',
➥ config='height=150,width=350,toolbar=no,menubar=yes,
➥scrollbars=yes,resizable=no,location=no,directories=no,
➥status=no');
```

Note that r in the parentheses of the function. Remember it is now set to represent 50.

The first order of business is to open a new window. It will be 150 pixels tall by 300 pixels wide and will not have any of the configurations except a scrollbar if need be. The name of the page that will be displayed in the new window is `MovingAround.html`.

Now that we've got the new browser window open, we'd better get it moving or this won't be much of a script.

A `for` loop does the dirty work:

```
for (var i = 0; i <360; i++) {
x = (r * Math.cos((i * Math.PI)/180)) + a;
y = (r * Math.sin((i * Math.PI)/180)) + b;
newWin.moveTo(x,y);
```

The variable i is set to 0. The next condition of the `for` loop is that i must be less than 360. Finally, the loop wants i to increase in increments. Note the double plus sign.

Think of the 360 in the `for` statement not as a count to be reached, but rather the degrees of a circle. The next two mathematical equations are set up to create points upon that 360 circle.

The variable x is created by taking r, which is set to 50, and multiplying it by the cosine (`Math.cos`) of i times PI (`Math.PI`) divided by 180 plus a, which is set to 275.

The variable y is created using the same math equation, except at the end, b is added. b is also set to 275.

Each time the loop runs, the variable i is raised by one so the output of the x and y variables gradually increase. And because we are figuring the results of x and y using PI and a cosine, the results of running the equations again and again will be an arc.

If you run the entire equation 360 times, that will create a full circle. Still with me?

The last line above tells the browser to move the window that was just opened to the new x and y points. When the new window is moved again and again quickly, the impression is that it is smoothly rolling in a circle.

But the loop doesn't run forever. Something must be set up to tell the browser window to stop. It's a while loop:

```
while (r<=100)

{   for (r=60;r<=100;r+=1)

{
    rotateTimer = setTimeout("rotateObjects(r)", 1000);

r+= 45;
  }

}
```

The preceding code states that while r is equal to or less than 100, the script should keep running the for loop within the while loop's curly brackets.

Inside the while loop's brackets is yet another for loop. It uses the variable r to count with as well. It sets r to 60 and will run until r equals 100, adding one each time the loop runs.

The for loop contains a setTimeout() that will wait a second to start the function rotateObjects(r) again.

Finally, r is set to itself plus 45. Notice the += operator.

The script rolls through its series of loops until one of the loops meets its quota.

If you set the r=+ 45 to a lower number, the window loops more because it takes longer to complete the loop. Setting 360 to a lower number shortens the arc the window takes.

This is a great script to alter. Because there are three loops to contend with, one will affect the others each time you change out a loop's condition.

But when all is said and done, this is a fantastic, attention-grabbing JavaScript.

Your Assignment

This shouldn't be so tough. Alter the code so that the window only rolls one half a circle, and move the new window more to the left.

You can see a possible answer to this assignment on your own computer by clicking on Lesson 52 Assignment in your download packet, or see it online at http://www.htmlgoodies.com/ JSBook/assignment52.html.

Lesson 53: Form Validation

The HTML Goodies email box is always receiving letters asking how to set up a form that requires users to fill in all the blanks. And furthermore, how can the form be set up to ensure that the information the user enters is valid?

The short answer is that you'll never be able to force someone to fill in your forms, or to fill them in correctly. But you can certainly take a shot at suggesting they do.

This script will check for both empty fields and, to a point, check to see if the field is filled out correctly:

```
<SCRIPT LANGUAGE="JavaScript">

function TheFormCheck() {
if (document.TheForm.email.value=="" && document.TheForm.phone.value=="")
{
alert("It would be helpful to include both your name and email");
document.TheForm.email.focus();return false
}

if (document.TheForm.email.value!="")
{if (document.TheForm.email.value.indexOf("@")==-1 ||
➥ document.TheForm.email.value.indexOf(".")==-1 ||
➥ document.TheForm.email.value.indexOf(" ")!=-1 ||
➥ document.TheForm.email.value.length<6)
{alert("Sorry, your email address is not valid.");
document.TheForm.email.focus();return false}
}


if (document.TheForm.TextBox.value.indexOf("://")!=-1)
{
alert("The string :// is not allowed in the TextBox field.");
document.TheForm.TextBox.focus();return false
}
}
</SCRIPT>

<FORM NAME="TheForm" METHOD=POST ACTION=""
➥onSubmit="return TheFormCheck()">
```

```
<b>Name: </b><INPUT NAME="name" SIZE=30 MAXLENGTH=34><BR>
<b>Email: </b><INPUT NAME="email" SIZE=30 MAXLENGTH=34><BR>
<b>Phone: </b><INPUT NAME="phone" SIZE=30 MAXLENGTH=34><BR>

<TEXTAREA NAME="TextBox" WRAP=VIRTUAL ROWS=8 COLS=48></TEXTAREA><BR>
<INPUT TYPE=SUBMIT VALUE="Submit"><INPUT TYPE=RESET>
</FORM>
```

You can see the script's effect in Figure 9.4.

Figure 9.4
Testing the form.

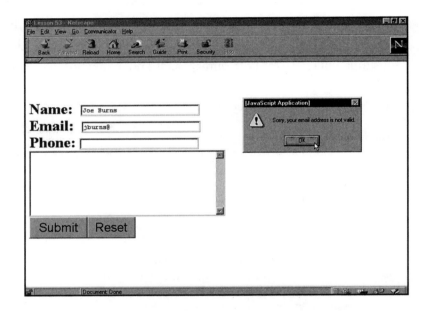

To see the effect on your own computer, click on Lesson 53 Script's Effect in your download packet, or see it online at http://www.htmlgoodies.com/JSBook/lesson53example.html.

Deconstructing the Script

As we have done before, we'll begin deconstructing this script by starting at the bottom with the HTML form elements:

```
<FORM NAME="TheForm" METHOD=POST ACTION=""
➥onSubmit="return TheFormCheck()">
<b>Name: </b><INPUT NAME="name" SIZE=30 MAXLENGTH=34><BR>
<b>Email: </b><INPUT NAME="email" SIZE=30 MAXLENGTH=34><BR>
<b>Phone: </b><INPUT NAME="phone" SIZE=30 MAXLENGTH=34><BR>
```

```
<TEXTAREA NAME="TextBox" WRAP=VIRTUAL ROWS=8 COLS=48></TEXTAREA><BR>
<INPUT TYPE=SUBMIT VALUE="Submit"><INPUT TYPE=RESET>
</FORM>
```

The entire form is named TheForm. It's not a very clever name, but it'll do. Because this form is set up to mail the contents of the text boxes like a simple guestbook, we have also set the METHOD to POST and offered a spot for the action. That is where one would write in mailto:your@email.address.com.

Notice the onSubmit= Event Handler too. When this form is submitted, the contents of the entire form are to be returned to a JavaScript function named TheFormCheck().

Then there are three text boxes for the user to enter his or her name, email, and phone. So we also made those three terms the names of the three boxes.

Next is a TEXTAREA box named TextBox, and finally a Submit button to send the output of the form items.

Okay, now we're up to speed on the HTML. Let's go back up to the top and look at the JavaScript.

The Script

The JavaScript is set up to take the information returned from the form and check it. The checking is done through a series of if statements.

While we're moving through the JavaScript, be aware that the code that checks each form element is in the same order as the form elements themselves. The email box is checked before the TEXTAREA box, and so on. That's important because we want any errors in filling out the form to appear in the same order as the boxes themselves. By checking the boxes in order, we will get that effect.

But what should be checked? Should all text boxes be verified? That's up to you. Here you'll learn the basic process of how to set up a verification. It's up to you to then choose what topics the verification will look for. Sometime you really need to be clever about what you're looking for. Following you'll see some rather interesting methods of checking whether an email address is valid or not.

Verifying the Email and Phone Text Boxes

This first block of JavaScript will check the text boxes that receive the user's email address and phone number:

```
function TheFormCheck() {
if (document.TheForm.email.value=="" && document.TheForm.phone.value=="")
{
```

```
    alert("It would be helpful to include both your name and email");
    document.TheForm.email.focus();return false
    }
```

The code `document.TheForm.email.value==""` is checking if the value of that specific form element is empty.

The double ampersands (&&) means and.

The same format is followed again to check if the text box for the phone number is empty.

There is an alert box that will pop up if the condition is correct. Next comes the line `document.TheForm.email.focus();return false`. That line of code is triggered when the alert button is enacted. It basically states that focus should be put back on the email form element. This step disallows the sending of the form.

Put it all together and the `if` statement states that if the email and the phone text box are empty, an alert box should be posted telling the user to enter some information. The form should not be sent until the user complies. It's very efficient code.

Verifying the Email Text Box Alone

The purpose of the following block of script is to verify if what is written in the text box is a valid email address:

```
    if (document.TheForm.email.value!="")
    {if (document.TheForm.email.value.indexOf("@")==-1 ||
    ➥ document.TheForm.email.value.indexOf(".")==-1 ||
    ➥ document.TheForm.email.value.indexOf(" ")!=-1 ||
    ➥ document.TheForm.email.value.length<6)
    {alert("Sorry, your email address is not valid.");
    document.TheForm.email.focus();return false}
    }
```

The format is a familiar `if` statement, but look at the condition. There are four checks made of the data put into the check box. In the check of the email and phone text boxes earlier, there were only two conditions, so a double ampersand (&&) was sufficient. Here there are four conditions, so you need to denote them differently.

The method is to place a double vertical line (¦¦)between each condition. That sets each condition apart in the browser's mind as a separate check, but also tells the browser to perform each one. So each time the script is run, each of the four checks will be performed on the text returned from the email text box.

The code checks the input four different ways:

- `document.TheForm.email.value.indexOf("@")==-1`. This code checks if the text includes the @ sign, as all email addresses do. The check is performed by checking if the number of @ signs in the text is equal to negative one. Negative one is used to represent no @ signs because what we're asking for here is an index of the number of @ in the text. Remember that JavaScript counts everything and it starts counting at zero. So asking if there is a zero index is the same as asking if there is a @. So we use -1 to represent zero occurrences of @. It's a little confusing, but that's the method.

- `document.TheForm.email.value.indexOf(".")==-1`. This code checks to see if there are any dots (.) in the text as there will always be in an email address. Again, the negative one means zero occurrences.

- `document.TheForm.email.value.indexOf(" ")!=-1`. This code makes sure that there are *no* empty spaces. Notice the != meaning "not equal to". Email addresses will not have any spaces in them.

- `document.TheForm.email.value.length<6`. Finally, this code checks if the length of the email address is fewer that six characters. Six is checked because technically the smallest email address would be *x@xx.xx*. For example, an email address from Canada could be `j@xx.ca`.

If all the conditions are met, the script moves along to the next set of code. If the conditions are not met, an alert box pops up stating that the email address is not valid and focus is put on the email box. That, once again, stops the form from being sent.

The TEXTAREA *Box*

This code checks the TEXTBOX for any instances of the string `://`:

```
if (document.TheForm.TextBox.value.indexOf("://")!=-1)
{
alert("The string :// is not allowed in the TextBox field.");
document.TheForm.TextBox.focus();return false
}
```

That would suggest someone is putting in a Web page address. This is sometimes used to create spam email using the server of the person receiving the email. This check will stop that practice. Of course, it also stops people from sending you full Web addresses. It's up to you whether to use it or not.

If the condition is met, then an alert box pops up, focus is put upon the TEXTAREA box, and the form does not send.

If all the conditions are met, the `if` statements are all bypassed and the form does its job, sending the information off to the person who posted the form.

The script can be altered and added to almost endlessly. You simply need to find clever methods of checking if the information entered is valid.

Your Assignment

The Phone text box right now is only checked to see if anything is filled in. Write some extra code so the validation script checks to see if the data the user entered is a valid phone number.

 You can see a possible answer to this assignment on your own computer by clicking on Lesson 53 Assignment in your download packet, or see it online at `http://www.htmlgoodies.com/ JSBook/assignment53.html`.

Lesson 54: Self-Typing Typewriter

This is a fantastic effect. A text box appears and the computer appears to be typing into it. Its uses can range from a simple greeting, to page instructions, to simply keeping a viewer's attention.

Here's the script:

```
<SCRIPT LANGUAGE="javascript">
var i = 0
var typeString= "All work and no play makes Jack a dull boy."
+" All work and no play makes Jack a dull boy.
➡All work and no play makes Jack a dull boy. "
+" All work and no play makes Jack a dull boy.
➡All work and no play makes Jack a dull boy. "
+" All work and no play makes Jack a dull boy.
➡All work and no play makes Jack a dull boy. "

function type()
{
var typeLength= typeString.length
document.typewriterScreen.typepage.value=
➡document.typewriterScreen.typepage.value + typeString.charAt(i)
i++
var timeID= setTimeout("type()",70)
}
</SCRIPT>
```

```
<BODY onLoad= "type()">
<FORM NAME="typewriterScreen">
<TEXTAREA ROWS=6 COLS=45 WRAP="virtual" NAME="typepage"></TEXTAREA>
</FORM>
```

The script's effect appears in Figure 9.5.

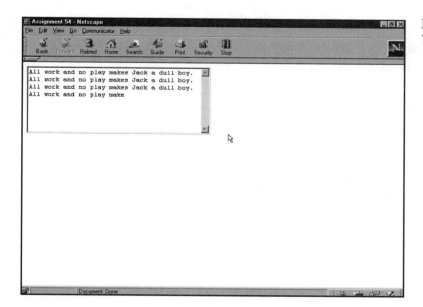

Figure 9.5
Typewriter typing.

 To see the effect on your own computer, click on *Lesson 54 Script's Effect* in your download packet, or see it online at http://www.htmlgoodies.com/JSBook/lesson54example.html.

What's Happening?

Here's the scoop on how the typing effect is created.

Each time the JavaScript is run, the script posts the value of the TEXTBOX with the next letter in the string, chosen by i. It works a lot like a scroll, working one letter into the string each time it runs.

The first time the JavaScript runs, the return is a blank TEXTBOX and the letter *A* from the string. That return is posted.

The next time it runs, the return from the TEXTBOX is *A* and the next letter in the string, *l* is added. That return is also posted.

The next time the script runs, the return from the TEXTBOX is *Al* and the next letter in the string, *l* is added. That is posted.

253

If this happens again and again, the effect is the letters typing themselves to the screen. Now, let's dig into the script.

Deconstructing the Script

Usually we would start by naming the HTML form elements, but not this time. The form elements actually play a role in the effect, so we will discuss them last after you understand the typing effect.

This script begins by setting up a variable i and setting it to one. Then a very long literal string is given the variable name typeString. It looks like this:

```
var i = 0
var typeString= "All work and no play makes Jack a dull boy."
+" All work and no play makes Jack a dull boy.
All work and no play makes Jack a dull boy. "
+" All work and no play makes Jack a dull boy.
All work and no play makes Jack a dull boy. "
+" All work and no play makes Jack a dull boy.
All work and no play makes Jack a dull boy. "
```

Notice that each statement in quotes is connected by a plus sign so that one will just follow the other in one long line of text.

The Typing Function

The function is named type():

```
function type()
{
var typeLength= typeString.length
document.typewriterScreen.typepage.value=
document.typewriterScreen.typepage.value + typeString.charAt(i)
i++
var timeID= setTimeout("type()",70)
}
```

It will be triggered to run through an onLoad= Event Handler in the BODY flag.

First the variable typeLength is created and given the value of the number of letters in the literal string, typeString.length.

Next, the TEXTBOX of the following HTML form is set up to receive the output of the script. Even though we haven't talked about the HTML form elements, you can probably guess just from this line of code that the form itself is named typewriterScreen and the TEXTBOX is named typepage. They are.

The typing effect is created by taking the value of the TEXTBOX and adding the first character of typeString. That's done with the following code:

```
= document.typewriterScreen.typepage.value + typeString.charAt(i)
```

Remember that i is equal to one.

After that occurs, i starts to move incrementally up. Notice the double plus signs.

Finally the code var timeID= setTimeout(type(),70) sets a timeout for the script of 70/1000 of a second before it runs through the function again.

The HTML Form Elements

As we said earlier, the name of the form is typewriterScreen and the name of the TEXTAREA box is typepage. You can see that in the following code:

```
<FORM NAME="typewriterScreen">
<TEXTAREA ROWS=6 COLS=45 WRAP="virtual" NAME="typepage"></TEXTAREA>
</FORM>
```

This form element differs from the others we've used because this one plays a part in the effect. Notice the attribute WRAP="virtual". That forces the text to wrap at the edge of the TEXTBOX rather than continue going off to the right.

But it's the size that gets the look. The COLS attribute is set two letters longer than the text *All work and no play makes Jack a dull boy*. By doing that, we were able to create what appear to be carriage returns right where we wanted them. Without each new line of text appearing on a new line, a great deal of the effect would have been lost.

Your Assignment

Add some code to the preceding script so that after the entire string of text has posted, an alert box pops up.

Hint: It should happen when the count is equal to the number of characters in the string.

 You can see a possible answer to this assignment on your own computer by clicking on Lesson 54 Assignment in your download packet, or see it online at http://www.htmlgoodies.com/ JSBook/assignment54.html.

Lesson 55: Scrolling Credits

When you go to the movies, do you stick around and watch the credits? Wouldn't it be great to get that kind of scroll on a Web page credit list?

That's what this script does. It scrolls the page rather than the text. It's a great effect, and a fitting end to the book's last lesson:

```
<SCRIPT LANGUAGE="javascript">

var I = 0;
function scrollit() {
if (I == 1000) {stop = true}
else {
self.scroll(1,I);
I = eval(I + 1);
setTimeout("scrollit()", 20);
}
}

</SCRIPT>

<BODY OnLoad="scrollit()">

<CENTER>

<BR><BR><BR><BR><BR><BR><BR><BR><BR><BR><BR>
<BR><BR><BR><BR><BR><BR><BR><BR><BR><BR><BR>

<font size="+5" color="008000" FACE="arial">
➥<b>JavaScript Goodies</b></font>
<P>

<font size="+2" color="FFFFFF">by</font><P>

<font size="+3" color="ff00ff">Joe Burns, Ph.D.</font> <BR>

<font size="+2" color="ffffff">&</font><BR>

<font size="+3" color="ff00ff">Andree Growney</font> <BR><BR><BR>

</CENTER>
```

The script's effect appears in Figure 9.6.

 To see the effect on your own computer, click on Lesson 55 Script's Effect in your download packet, or see it online at http://www.htmlgoodies.com/JSBook/lesson55example.html.

Figure 9.6
Credits scrolling.

Deconstructing the Script

Okay, first off, let me explain what this is all about:

```
<BR><BR><BR><BR><BR><BR><BR><BR><BR><BR><BR>
<BR><BR><BR><BR><BR><BR><BR><BR><BR><BR><BR>
```

Do you see that code, right below the BODY flag and right above the HTML that will appear in the document window? It's there to add space before the text. If there is no space above the text, the page can't scroll.

Now remember, when you use this script, either make the page that will scroll longer than the browser's viewing area, or add a bunch of breaks above the text so that the page is long enough to scroll.

Plus, if you create enough space so that the text is pushed down out of the browser screen, you get the effect of the text scrolling up and out of the bottom, like during a movie's credits.

The script starts again by setting the variable I to 0 outside of a function.

The function is then set and named scrollit():

```
var I = 0;
function scrollit() {
```

The function starts by setting up an `if` condition that states when I equals 1000, the scroll is to stop:

```
if (I == 1000) {stop = true}
```

Because that won't be true for 1000 cycles of the script, something else has to happen.

The following code sets the scroll of the page, denoted by `self.scroll`, to scroll up one line:

```
else {
self.scroll(1,I);
```

Then one is added to I:

```
I = eval(I + 1);
```

Notice the `eval()` method. You should remember that it is used to set the results of the items within the parentheses to a numeric value.

Finally, the script is given a rest for 20/1000 of a second and the function is run again:

```
setTimeout("scrollit()", 20);
```

The process occurs again and again until I reaches 1000, or until you reach the end of the page and it can't scroll anymore.

The rest of the code is basic HTML to make the page long enough to actually have something to scroll.

Here's a hint about using this script. It looks best if the script starts the scroll on a blank page. That way, the text pops up from the bottom of the browser screen like normal movie credits.

In order to get that effect, you need to add enough blank lines of code above the first line of text to literally push the text off of the screen. Then when the scroll begins, the text comes up from the bottom. That's the way we have the coding set in the example.

Now take this code and make some credits. Make sure to remember Andree and me. Heck, we showed you how to do all this stuff. The least you could do is give us a credit.

Your Assignment

The assignment is to create your site's own scrolling credits, plus one more thing…create good and useful scripts.

 You can see a possible answer to this assignment on your own computer by clicking on Lesson 55 Assignment in your download packet, or see it online at `http://www.htmlgoodies.com/ JSBook/assignment55.html`*.*

JavaScript Basic Concepts

Literals

A *literal* is a name assigned to a variable. It is an unchanging title that remains throughout the script. For example:

```
var browser = navigator.Appname
```

This has created a variable called browser that is now equal to the browser name.

A *literal string* is any set of characters with quotation marks around it. This set of characters doesn't change. For example:

```
document.write("Hello there")
```

"Hello there" is a literal string.

Boolean Literals

Boolean literals are literals that only have two values, 1 and 0. The Boolean literal is often used to represent true (1) and false (0). It helps to think of the true and false as yes and no. For example:

```
window.open("" NAME="newwindow" HEIGHT=300,WIDTH=300,TOOLBAR=1;)
```

The toolbar=1 is a Boolean literal that means yes, you want a toolbar.

Comments

Comments are lines of text that are written to the page but do not affect the script's workings. The most common use is to add lines into a script along the way as a description of what is happening:

```
<SCRIPT>
//This prompt requests user name and assigns it the variable 'username'
var username = prompt("What is Your Name?")
</SCRIPT>
```

Above is the double-slash comment command. The double slash (//) will comment out everything that follows it as long as it stays on the same line. If you allow the text to go to another line without another set of double slashes, the script will think the comment is part of the code and will most probably throw an error.

Multiple-line comments can be created using this format:

```
/*In between the slash and star, you can have
   multiple lines of text.  As long as the code is surrounded
   it will all comment out.*/
```

Rule of thumb: Keep the star next to the text.

Document Object Model

The concept of hierarchy is of the utmost importance to JavaScript. An example is writing a line to denote a specific text box HTML form element. Let's say the form itself was named FormA and the text box was named Tbox.

The HTML code would look like this:

```
<FORM NAME="FormA">
<INPUT TYPE="text" NAME=Tbox">
</FORM>
```

If you were to write a line of JavaScript representing the text that a user might write into that text box, the code would look like this:

```
window.document.FormA.Tbox.value
```

That statement shows the hierarchy of the page. The browser window is the largest overriding element in the statement. All events will happen within the browser window. The document is the next largest, and then the form itself, the text box, and finally value representing what the user has written into the text box.

The concept of hierarchy is consistent throughout JavaScript and is known as the Document Object Model (DOM).

The name DOM, however, is not very descriptive. So, throughout this book, the term *hierarchy statement* is used to represent the DOM in any JavaScript.

Event Handlers

An Event Handler is a JavaScript command that sits inside an HTML flag, and does not require the beginning <SCRIPT> flag to work. An example is using an onClick Event Handler inside the HTML code for a button. When the mouse clicks on the button, the Event Handler performs the event it's set up to do. Here's an example:

```
<FORM>
<INPUT TYPE="button" VALUE="Click For An Alert"
onClick="alert("Thanks for clicking!")">
</FORM>
```

When the button is clicked, the alert button will pop up. Table A.1 shows some of the more popular Event Handlers. You can get a more complete example in Appendix B, "JavaScript Command Reference."

Table A.1 Popular Event Handlers

Event Handler	The Event Is Enacted When:
onBlur	Focus is off the item
onClick	The mouse button is clicked on the item
onFocus	Focus is brought to the item
onKeyDown	A keyboard key is pressed down
onKeyPress	A keyboard key is pressed
onKeyUp	A keyboard key is let up after being pressed down
onLoad	The page is loaded
onMouseOut	The mouse is moved off the item
onMouseOver	The mouse is passed over the item
onMouseMove	The mouse is moved
onMouseDown	The mouse is clicked down
onMouseUp	The mouse is released after clicking down
onUnload	The user leaves the page

Literal Integers

A *literal integer* is any whole number. For instance, 9 is a literal integer, whereas 9.23 is not. Literal integers can also be hexadecimal notation employing the numbers 1 through 9 and the letters *a* through *f*. This hex color code for purple is an example of a literal integer: 800080.

Methods

A *method* is any function that acts upon an object. The command `window.open()` is used to open a new browser window. In this case, `window` is the object and `open()` is the method acting upon the object.

Methods can be easily recognized by the two parentheses immediately following them. Sometimes those parentheses, called the *instance*, are given certain parameters by putting those parameters between the parentheses. When the parentheses are empty, the method acts fully upon the object it follows.

Objects

Objects are items that already exist to JavaScript or are created through JavaScript code. Objects are items that can be acted upon, or that have certain properties or characteristics attached to them. An HTML document is an object, as are the status bar and the `Date`.

Operators

Think of an operator as something that connects or works between two literals. The binary operators shown in Table A.2 are the most common.

Table A.2   Binary Operators

Operator	Meaning
+	Add
-	Subtract
*	Multiply
/	Divide
%	Divide and return remainder

The operators in Table A.3 show the relationships between literals.

Table A.3 Operators Showing Relationships Between Literals

Operator	Meaning
<	Less Than
>	Greater Than
<=	Less Than or Equal To
>=	Greater Than or Equal To
=	Assignment
==	Equal To
!=	Not Equal To
¦¦	Or||||
&	And (adding JavaScript commands together)
&&	And (literal)
?:	Conditional

The operators in Table A.4 are used to separate and end JavaScript commands and lines.

Table A.4 Operators That Separate and End JavaScript Commands

Operator	Meaning
,	Separates commands
;	Ends a line of JavaScript

Properties

A *property* is a characteristic or portion of a larger object. An example of a property is the status bar of the browser window written this way: `window.status` (*object.property*).

String

A *string* is any number of characters inside of double or single quotation marks. For example:

```
document.write("This is a string")
```

This example would simply write that string to the HTML document.

Variable

The ability to assign variable names to lines of code is paramount in JavaScript. Except for JavaScript commands themselves and an additional short list of unacceptable variable names in Appendix C, "JavaScript Reserved Variable Words," a variable can be any series of letters, numbers or a combination of both.

JavaScript allows for two levels of variables, local and global.

Local variables are variables that are only viable within a function. JavaScript understands that whenever a variable is encased within a function, that variable name is only viable inside that function. That way, if you copy and paste a script onto a page that already has a script on it, any variables that are equally named will not clash as long as that variable name is found within a function.

Global variables are variables that are not found within functions, and therefore *can* clash with the variables on the same page.

Here's an example:

```
<SCRIPT LANGUAGE="javascript">
var joe = 12
function writeit()
{
var joe = "Joe Burns"
document.write(joe)
}
</SCRIPT>
```

The variable joe is used twice, but because one occurrence is found outside the function—the global variable—and one is found inside of the function—the local variable—the two will not clash.

Now, with all that said, it is not a good idea to follow this format and use like variable names within your scripts. The purpose of the local variables being hidden is far more for protection against clashes with other scripts on the same page than with variable names within the same script.

JavaScript Command Reference

The following appendix is arranged in alphabetical order. It covers the commands found in this book, plus commands that can be substituted in some of the scripts in this book.

Please note that JavaScript is case sensitive. The capitalization pattern used below is how the commands must appear in your scripts, or they will not work.

action Property

An action works with the return of an HTML form. It works the same as the value you assign to the ACTION attribute when you define a form, and it's primarily used to call server-side CGI scripts. It's used to actually do something with the form information. Let's say you have a form you have named forma. It looks like this:

```
<FORM NAME="forma">
<INPUT TYPE="text" NAME="Tbox">
</FORM>
```

You could send the output of that form to an email address by using the following command:

```
<FORM NAME="forma">
<INPUT TYPE="button"
➥onClick="forma.action='mailto:jburns@htmlgoodies.com'">
</FORM>
```

alert Method

The alert method displays a JavaScript modal dialog box containing the text noted in the command. The alert box will only offer an OK button, unlike the confirm box that will offer both an OK and a Cancel button. Follow this format to have an alert box open upon the loading of the page:

```
<BODY onLoad="alert("This is an Alert Box!")">
```

The alert box is shown in Figure B.1.

Figure B.1
An alert box.

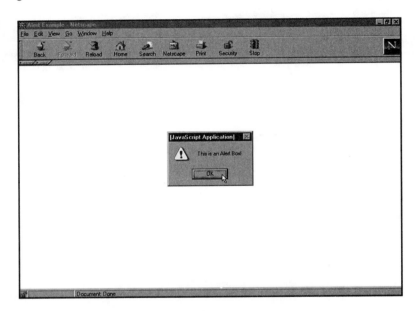

You can find alert used as part of a JavaScript example in Chapter 2, Lesson 6.

See also: confirm and prompt.

alinkColor Property

You use alinkColor to return the active link color using a document.write statement:

```
<SCRIPT LANGUAGE="javascript">
document.write("The active link color " +document.alinkColor+ ".")
</SCRIPT>
```

You can find alinkColor used as part of a JavaScript example in Chapter 1, Lesson 3.

See also: bgColor, fgColor, linkColor, and vlinkColor.

appCodeName Property

The appCodeName command will return the codename string of the browser. The command uses this format:

```
<SCRIPT LANGUAGE="javascript">
document.write("You are using " +navigator.appCodeName+ ".")
</SCRIPT>
```

You can find appCodeName used as part of a JavaScript example in Chapter 1, Lesson 3.

See also: appName, appVersion, navigator, and userAgent.

appName Property

This will return the official name of the browser string:

```
<SCRIPT LANGUAGE="javascript">
document.write("You are using " +navigator.appName+ ".")
</SCRIPT>
```

You can find appName used as part of a JavaScript example in Chapter 1, Lesson 3.

See also: appCodeName, appVersion, navigator, and userAgent.

appVersion Property

This command will return the browser version number string:

```
<SCRIPT LANGUAGE="javascript">
document.write("You are using " +navigator.appVersion+ ".")
</SCRIPT>
```

You can find appVersion used as part of a JavaScript example in Chapter 1, Lesson 3.

See also: appCodeName, appName, navigator, and userAgent.

array Method

Arrays are variables. For the most part, variables have only one value. However, an array is a variable with multiple values. An array can be an ordered collection of many numbers, letters, words, objects, or a combination of those four.

When you create an array, the items are assigned a number, starting at 0 and counting up:

```
var NewArray=("item0", "item1", "item2", "item3")
```

You can also set up arrays of literals by numbering them in this fashion:

```
var dayName=new Array(7)
dayName[0]="Sunday"
dayName[1]="Monday"
dayName[2]="Tuesday"
dayName[3]="Wednesday"
dayName[4]="Thursday"
dayName[5]="Friday"
dayName[6]="Saturday"
```

After creating an array, you can call for only one item of the array by calling for the item by number. Using the array of the days of the week above, this code would return Friday:

```
<SCRIPT LANGUAGE="javascript"
document.write(dayName[5])
</SCRIPT>
```

You can find array first used as part of a JavaScript example in Chapter 3, Lesson 15. Chapter 8 is devoted to arrays.

back Method

The back method is used in conjunction with the history object to move throughout the browser's history list:

```
<SCRIPT LANGUAGE="javascript">history.back()  //one page back in history
history.back(-3)  //moves three pages back in history
</SCRIPT>
```

You can set the number so the back command moves as many pages as you would like. Be careful that the user actually has as many pages in his history as you call for.

Please note that if back is used within a frameset, the entire frameset will not reload. Each frame that was changed will load the page that came before it.

You can find back used as part of a JavaScript example in Chapter 2, Lesson 9.

See also: forward, go, and history.

bgColor Property

This sets or returns the document background color. Here, bgColor is used inside an HTML radio button and the onClick Event Handler to set the background color:

```
<FORM>
<INPUT TYPE="radio" onClick="document.bgColor = green">
</FORM>
```

You can find bgColor used as part of a JavaScript example in Chapter 1, Lesson 3.

See also: alinkColor, fgColor, linkColor, and vlinkColor.

big Method

The big method is used to alter a text string. It sets the string to print to the document one font size bigger than default:

```
<SCRIPT LANGUAGE="javascript">
var textString = "Hello there!"
document.write(textString.big())
</SCRIPT>
```

See also: blink, bold, fixed, fontcolor, fontsize, italics, small, and strike.

blink Method

The blink method sets a text string to blink on and off in the browser window:

```
<SCRIPT LANGUAGE="javascript">
var textString = "Hello there!"
document.write(textString.blink())
</SCRIPT>
```

This is a Netscape Navigator–only command. Internet Explorer will not recognize it. Besides, this is an unwelcome command. For the most part, people do not like blinking text. Use it sparingly if at all.

See also: big, bold, fixed, fontcolor, fontsize, italics, small, and strike.

bold Method

The bold method sets a text string to appear in bold text font:

```
<SCRIPT LANGUAGE="javascript">
var textString = "Hello there!"
document.write(textString.bold())
</SCRIPT>
```

See also: big, blink, fixed, fontcolor, fontsize, italics, small, and strike.

close Method

The `close` method acts upon its object, the `window` or `self`, to close the window. The following code shows how a button can close the main window using an `onClick` Event Handler:

```
<FORM>
<INPUT TYPE="button" VALUE="Close the Window" onClick="self.close()">
</FORM>
```

See also: `clear`, `open`, `window`, `write`, and `writeln`.

confirm Method

The `confirm` method displays a dialog box that offers both an OK and a Cancel button. Refer to "The `alert` Method" earlier in this appendix for a different type of box. This script uses a function to offer a confirm box as a test when entering a page:

```
<SCRIPT LANGUAGE="javascript">
function confirmit()
{if (!confirm ("Are you sure you want to enter?"))
history.go(-1);return " "}
</SCRIPT>
```

The confirm box is shown in Figure B.2.

Figure B.2
The confirm box.

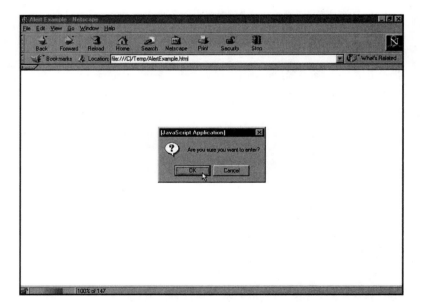

You can find `confirm` used as part of a JavaScript example in Chapter 4, Lesson 21.

See also: `alert` and `prompt`.

Date Object

`Date` is an overriding object that contains all date and time information, allowing for the return of both specific date and time strings. This is the simplest use of the object to return a full date and time string:

```
<SCRIPT LANGUAGE="javascript">
var  dayandtime = new Date()
document.write("It is " +dayandtime+ ".")
</SCRIPT>
```

You can find `Date` used as part of a JavaScript example in Chapter 3, Lesson 12.

See also: `getDate`, `getDay`, `getFullYear`, `getHours`, `getMinutes`, `getMonth`, `getSeconds`, `getTimezoneOffset`, and `getYear`.

defaultStatus Property of window

The `defaultStatus` property of the `window` object is used to display a string message in the browser's status bar:

```
<SCRIPT LANGUAGE="javascript">
defaultStatus = "This page's title is " +document.title+ "."
</SCRIPT>
```

You can find `defaultStatus` used as part of a JavaScript example in Chapter 3, Lesson 14.

See also: `status` and `window`.

document Object

The `document` object represents the current HTML document loaded into the browser. Here, `document` is acted upon by a `write` method to post text to the page:

```
<SCRIPT LANGUAGE="javascript">
document.write("Hello there!")
</SCRIPT>
```

You can find `document` used as part of a JavaScript example in Chapter 1, Lesson 1.

See also: `write` and `writeln`.

`document` Property

`document` is both an object and a property. The `document` property is part of the `window` object. You don't see `window` a great deal because the `window` object is often implied, as it is in this example:

```
document.bgColor = red
```

The technically correct method of writing the line above is

```
window.document.bgcolor = red
```

However, because `window` is the overriding, highest-level object in JavaScript, `window` is not required at the beginning of hierarchy statements. It is simply implied.

See also: `alinkColor`, `anchor`, `bgColor`, `cookie`, `fgColor`, `lastModified`, `linkColor`, `location`, `referrer`, `title`, and `vlinkColor`.

`eval` Method

`eval` is a method that that forces a string value to evaluate to a string expression. For example:

```
<SCRIPT LANGUAGE="javascript">
eval(Math.round(Math.PI/180))
</SCRIPT>
```

You can find `eval` used as part of a JavaScript example in Chapter 6, Lesson 36.

`fgColor` Property

The `fgColor` property represents the foreground color (actually the text color) of the current HTML document. You could return the `fgColor` color (text color) using a `document.write` statement:

```
<SCRIPT LANGUAGE="javascript">
document.write("The text color " +document.fgColor+ ".")
</SCRIPT>
```

You can find `fgColor` used as part of a JavaScript example in Chapter 1, Lesson 3.

See also: `alinkColor`, `bgColor`, `linkColor`, and `vlinkColor`.

fixed Method

The fixed method sets a string to a font much like the typewriter text <TT> font in HTML:

```
<SCRIPT LANGUAGE="javascript">
var textString = "Hello there!"
document.write(textString.fixed())
</SCRIPT>
```

See also: big, bold, fontcolor, fontsize, italics, small, and strike.

fontcolor Method

fontcolor works much like the <FONT COLOR> flag in HTML. It sets a string to a specific color:

```
<SCRIPT LANGUAGE="javascript">
var textString = "this will be red text"
document.write(textString.fontcolor("red"))
</SCRIPT>
```

See also: big, bold, fixed, fontsize, italics, small, and strike.

fontsize Method

fontsize sets a text string to a relative sized font much like the <FONT SIZE> HTML flag:

```
<SCRIPT LANGUAGE="javascript">
var textString = "this will be red text"
document.write(textString.fontsize("4"))
</SCRIPT>
```

See also: big, bold, fixed, fontcolor, italics, small, and strike.

for Loop

The for loop is used to run a group of code statements repeatedly, by setting a series of parameters that have to be true for the looping to stop. Traditionally, for loops are used when you know how many times you want a loop to run. This is the format for a for loop:

```
<SCRIPT LANGUAGE="javascript">
for (i=1; i<=5; i=i+1)
{
JavaScript event
}
</SCRIPT>
```

The event will loop as long as i is less than or equal to 5. Notice that each time the loop runs, i has one added to it; therefore, this script will loop 5 times.

You can find the for loop used as part of a JavaScript example in Chapter 6, Lesson 35.

See also: while.

forward Method

forward is used with the history object to move through the browser's history list:

```
<SCRIPT LANGUAGE="javascript">
history.forward()      //moves one page forward in the history
history.back(-3)  //moves three forward back in the history
</SCRIPT>
```

You can set the number of pages higher or lower than 1, but remember that the user might not have visited enough pages for the button created by this code to work. It's best to stay with 1.

You can find forward used as part of a JavaScript example in Chapter 2, Lesson 9.

Also see: back, go, and history.

frames Property

The frame property is used to denote a specific frame window, usually in terms of a hypertext link. Remember that frames are given a numeric order, starting with 0, in the order they appear on the HTML document. This example will load page.html into the second frame in the list of frame commands:

```
<FORM>
<INPUT TYPE="BUTTON" OnClick="parent.frames[1].location='page.html'">
</FORM>
```

frame can also be written as an object representing a portion of the browser window set aside through HTML FRAMESET flags. The frame itself is named in the HTML as shown in the following code:

```
<FRAMESET COLS="50%,50%">
<FRAME SRC="page1.html" NAME="frame1">
<FRAME SRC="page2.html" NAME="frame2">
</FRAMESET>
```

After it is named, each frame window is an object and can be targeted to receive a hypertext link output through JavaScript as shown in the following code:

```
parent.frame1=page3.html
```

function Object

The purpose of the function command is to both combine and name a group of JavaScript events specifically to create a single event. By assigning a function name to a set of JavaScript commands, the entire group of events can be called later in the script by using just the function name.

The format for creating a function is shown below. This function will be named bob:

```
<SCRIPT LANGUAGE="javascript">
function bob()
{
JavaScript commands and statements
}
</SCRIPT>
```

The function can be triggered to run in different ways. The format below calls the function when the HTML document loads into the browser window. Note the parentheses following the function name. It's the same format used with a method to act upon an object.

```
<BODY onLoad="bob()">
```

You can find function first used as part of a JavaScript example in Chapter 3, Lesson 14.

getDate Method

The getDate method will return the numeric integer of the day of the month (1 through 31, if the month has that many days).

```
<SCRIPT LANGUAGE="javascript">
RightNow = new Date();
document.write("Today's day is " + RightNow.getDate()+ ".")
</SCRIPT>
```

You can find getDate used as part of a JavaScript example in Chapter 3, Lesson 12.

See also: getDay, getFullYear, getHours, getMinutes, getMonth, getSeconds, getTimezoneOffset, and getYear.

getDay Method

The getDay method will return the numeric integer of the day of the week, where Sunday is 0 and Saturday is 6:

```
<SCRIPT LANGUAGE="javascript">
RightNow = new Date();
document.write("Today's day is " + RightNow.getDay()+ ".")
</SCRIPT>
```

This numeric representation is not very helpful. You'll need to write a script to change the number into a day text string using an array.

You can find getDay used as part of a JavaScript example in Chapter 3, Lesson 12.

See also: getDate, getFullYear, getHours, getMinutes, getMonth, getSeconds, getTimezoneOffset, and getYear.

getFullYear Method

The getFullYear method will return a four-digit integer (rather than two) representation of the current year:

```
<SCRIPT LANGUAGE="javascript">
RightNow = new Date();
document.write("The hours is " + RightNow.getFullYear()+ ".")
</SCRIPT>
```

This command was created as a repair to the Y2K bug.

You can find getFullYear used as part of a JavaScript example in Chapter 3, Lesson 12.

See also: getDate, getDay, getHours, getMinutes, getMonth, getSeconds, getTimezoneOffset, and getYear.

getHours Method

The getHours method will return the numeric integer of the current hour in military format, 0 through 23:

```
<SCRIPT LANGUAGE="javascript">
RightNow = new Date();
document.write("The hours is " + RightNow.getHours()+ ".")
</SCRIPT>
```

You can find getHours used as part of a JavaScript example in Chapter 3, Lesson 12.

See also: getDate, getDay, getFullYear, getMinutes, getMonth, getSeconds, getTimezoneOffset, and getYear.

getMinutes Method

The getMinutes method will return the numeric integer of the current minute, 0 through 59.

```
<SCRIPT LANGUAGE="javascript">
RightNow = new Date();
document.write("The minute is " + RightNow.getMinutes()+ ".")
</SCRIPT>
```

You can find getMinutes used as part of a JavaScript example in Chapter 3, Lesson 12.

See also: getDate, getDay, getFullYear, getHours, getMonth, getSeconds, getTimezoneOffset, and getYear.

getMonth Method

The getMonth method will return the numeric integer of the current month. In one of the more interesting JavaScript quirks, this method is actually always off by 1 because it sees January as 0. To fix that you should always add 1 to the output of the method. Here's the format:

```
<SCRIPT LANGUAGE="javascript">
RightNow = new Date();
NewMonth = [RightNow.getMonth+1]
document.write("The Month is " + NewMonth + ".")
</SCRIPT>
```

You can find getMonth used as part of a JavaScript example in Chapter 3, Lesson 12.

See also: getDate, getDay, getFullYear, getHours, getMinutes, getSeconds, getTimezoneOffset, and getYear.

getSeconds Method

The getSeconds method will return the numeric integer of the current second, 0 through 59:

```
<SCRIPT LANGUAGE="javascript">
RightNow = new Date();
document.write("The seconds are " + RightNow.getSeconds()+ ".")
</SCRIPT>
```

You can find getSeconds used as part of a JavaScript example in Chapter 3, Lesson 12.

See also: getDate, getDay, getFullYear, getHours, getMinutes, getMonth, getTimezoneOffset, and getYear.

getTimezoneOffset Method

The getTimezoneOffset method will return the number of minutes difference between your user's computer and Greenwich mean time (GMT):

```
<SCRIPT LANGUAGE="javascript">
RightNow = new Date();
document.write("The minutes offset is "
➥+ RightNow.getTimezoneOffset()+ ".")
</SCRIPT>
```

See also: getDate, getDay, getFullYear, getHours, getMinutes, getMonth, getSeconds, and getYear.

getYear Method

The getYear method will return a two-digit representation of the year, created by taking the current year and subtracting 1900:

```
<SCRIPT LANGUAGE="javascript">
RightNow = new Date();
document.write("The year is " + RightNow.getYear()+ ".")
</SCRIPT>
```

You can get the full four-digit year representation by using the getFullYear method or by re-adding the 1900.

For years past 1999, getYear returns a three-digit value, instead of a two-digit value.

You can find getYear used as part of a JavaScript example in Chapter 3, Lesson 12.

See also: getDate, getDay, getFullYear, getHours, getMinutes, getMonth, getSeconds, and getTimezoneOffset.

go Method

go works with the history object to load pages from the user's history file:

```
<SCRIPT LANGUAGE="javascript">
history.go(-2)  // Go back two pages in the history
</SCRIPT>
```

You can find go used as part of a JavaScript example in Chapter 2, Lesson 9.

See also: forward and history.

history Object

history is an object representing the browser's history file, which is the list of pages the viewer has visited during the current session. The following example will return the number of items listed in the history file. The command value is used to retrieve the number:

```
<SCRIPT LANGUAGE="javascript">
document.write("You've been to " + history.length + "pages.")
</SCRIPT>
```

You can find history used as part of a JavaScript example in Chapter 1, Lesson 3.

See also: back and forward.

host Property

The host property returns the name of the user's host and the port being used to connect to the Internet. If no port is specified, just the host name will be returned:

```
<SCRIPT LANGUAGE="javascript">
document.write("You're from " +location.host+ ".")
</SCRIPT>
```

The line might return www.joe.com:80.

You can find host used as part of a JavaScript example in Chapter 1, Lesson 3.

See also: hostname, href, location, and protocol.

hostname Property

The hostname property returns the user's host in the same manner as host, but without the port number attached:

```
<SCRIPT LANGUAGE="javascript">
document.write("You're from " +location.hostname+ ".")
</SCRIPT>
```

The line might return www.joe.com.

You can find hostname used as part of a JavaScript example in Chapter 1, Lesson 3.

See also: host, href, location, and protocol.

href Property of location

href is used to denote a string of the entire URL of a specified window object. Using this property, you can open a specified URL in a window:

```
<FORM>
<INPUT TYPE="button" onClick="location.href='page.html'">
</FORM>
```

You can find href used as part of a JavaScript example in Chapter 2, Lesson 6.

See also: host, hostname, location, and protocol.

if / else

The if / else structure is a conditional statement. The format states that if something is true, enact a specified JavaScript event. If not, enact a different JavaScript event.

The format follows this pattern:

```
<SCRIPT LANGUAGE="javascript">
if (condition to be met)
{JavaScript event}
else
{some other JavaScript event}
</SCRIPT>
```

If the condition following the `if` condition is met, the function in the first set of braces is enacted. If not, the function in the second set of braces runs.

It is also possible to set up a series of `if` conditions with no `else`. You would write one `if` statement after another, as shown in the following code:

```
<SCRIPT LANGUAGE="javascript">
if (condition to be met)
{JavaScript event}
if (condition to be met)
{some other JavaScript event}
if (condition to be met)
{some other JavaScript event}
if (condition to be met)
{some other JavaScript event}
</SCRIPT>
```

However, if you follow this format, you must make sure that one of the `if` statements will be true every time. If the script checks each of the `if` statements and finds an instance in which none of them is true, the script will simply not complete running.

You can find `if` / `else` first used as part of a JavaScript example in Chapter 4, Lesson 21.

`indexOf` Method

The method `indexOf` returns the numeric location of a specific string or character. Because JavaScript counts everything, and begins counting at 0, every string has an ordered set of letters. By using `indexOf`, you can return just a specific letter or portion of a text string.

In addition, `indexOf` can be used to check whether something does not appear in a string through the use of the –1 condition. For example

```
<SCRIPT LANGUAGE="javascript">
if (document.TheForm.email.value.indexOf("@")==-1)
{alert("there's no @, this is not a valid email address")}
else
{alert("Go on")}
</SCRIPT>
```

This code will check to see whether the text string entered in the text box email includes an @ or not. You use –1 because 0 is actually an index number in the mind of JavaScript. Therefore, you cannot ask whether there are 0 instances of @. If an @ appears in the text box, there is a 0 index number. The –1 format checks for no instances.

You can find `indexOf` used as part of a JavaScript example in Chapter 7, Lesson 43.

italics Method

The `italics` method is used to make a string print to a document in italics:

```
<SCRIPT LANGUAGE="javascript">
var textString = "Hello there!"
document.write(textString.italics())
</SCRIPT>
```

See also: `big`, `bold`, `fontcolor`, `fontsize`, `small`, and `strike`.

lastModified Property

When a document is altered and saved, or placed on a server, a date is recorded. The `lastModified` method will return that date to the current document:

```
<SCRIPT LANGUAGE="javascript">
document.write("I updated this page on " +document.lastModified+ ".")
</SCRIPT>
```

But remember that `lastModified` depends on the server's records. It's not always accurate, so use it as a guide, rather than as an end-all for the last updated date.

You can find `lastModified` used as part of a JavaScript example in Chapter 1, Lesson 3.

See also: `alinkColor`, `anchor`, `bgColor`, `cookie`, `fgColor`, `lastModified`, `linkColor`, `location`, `referrer`, `title`, and `vlinkColor`.

length Property

The `length` property returns a number representing the number of items that appear within the object it is attached to. The following example returns the number of pages the user has visited by returning the length of the `history` object:

```
<SCRIPT LANGUAGE="javascript">
document.write("You've been to " +history.length+ "pages")
</SCRIPT>
```

This property can also be used to return the number or characters in a string or HTML form text box.

You can find `length` used as part of a JavaScript example in Chapter 5, Lesson 24.

See also: `array` and `history`.

`linkColor` Property

The `linkColor` property denotes or returns the color of the links within the current document.

You could return the `linkColor`, in hexadecimal form, using a `document.write` statement:

```
<SCRIPT LANGUAGE="javascript">
document.write("The link color " +document.linkColor+ ".")
</SCRIPT>
```

You can find `linkColor` used as part of a JavaScript example in Chapter 1, Lesson 3.

See also: `alinkColor`, `fgColor`, and `vlinkColor`.

`location` Object

`location` represents Internet address information about the current HTML document. You can use the current location to jump to another location. The event will look like a simple hypertext link being clicked:

```
<FORM OnSubmit="location.href = 'page.html'">
<INPUT TYPE="text">
<INPUT TYPE="submit">
</FORM>
```

You can find `location` used as part of a JavaScript example in Chapter 2, Lesson 6.

See also: `host`, `hostname`, `href`, `location`, `pathname`, `port`, and `protocol`.

`location` Property

The `location` property represents the location of the current document. Use it to return the page's URL:

```
<SCRIPT LANGUAGE="javascript">
document.write("You're looking at " +document.location+ ".")
</SCRIPT>
```

You can find `location` used as part of a JavaScript example in Chapter 1, Lesson 3.

Math **Object**

Note the capitalization: The *M* is uppercase. Math is an object, but by itself means nothing other than it represents mathematics. But after you attach a method to Math, it can represent a number or a method of manipulating numbers. Table B.1 lists many of the Math object's methods. Again, notice the capitalization down the line.

Table B.1   Math Object Methods

Method	Return Value
Math.abs(*argument*)	The absolute value of an argument
Math.acos(*argument*)	The arc cosine of the argument
Math.asin(*argument*)	The arc sine of the argument
Math.atan(*argument*)	The arc tangent of the argument
Math.atan2(*argument1, argument2*)	The angle of polar coordinates x and y
Math.ceil(*argument*)	The number 1 larger than or equal to the argument
Math.cos(*argument*)	The cosine of the argument
Math.exp(*argument*)	A natural logarithm
Math.floor(*argument*)	The number 1 less than or equal to the argument
Math.E	Base of natural logarithms
Math.LN2	Logarithm of 2 (appx: 0.6932)
Math.LN10	Logarithm of 10 (appx: 2.3026)
Math.log	Logarithm of positive numbers greater than zero
Math.LOG10E	Base-10 logarithm of E
Math.LOG2E	Base-2 logarithm of E
Math.max(*arg1,arg2*)	The greater of the two arguments
Math.min(*arg1,arg2*)	The lesser of the two arguments
Math.PI	The value of pi
Math.pow(*arg1, arg2*)	*arg1* raised to the *arg2* power
Math.random	A random number between 0 and 1
Math.round	Rounds to the nearest number
Math.sin(*argument*)	The sine of the argument
Math.sqrt(*argument*)	The square root of the argument
Math.SQRT1_2	The square root of 1/2
Math.SQRT2	The square root of 2
Math.tan(*argument*)	The tangent of the argument

The arguments above are put together using the mathematics operators:

- **+** Add
- **-** Subtract
- ***** Multiply
- **/** Divide

For example:

```
<SCRIPT LANGUAGE="javascript">
Math.square(2*2)  //will return 2, the square root of four (2*2)
</SCRIPT>
```

Many of the preceding `Math.methods` that represent numbers can be used together to create mathematical equations. This line of code will return a random number between 1 and 50:

```
<SCRIPT LANGUAGE="javascript">
Math.round(50 * Math.random());
</SCRIPT>
```

You can find `Math`, and some of the preceding methods, used as part of a JavaScript example in Chapter 6, Lesson 33.

`navigator` Object

`navigator` is the overriding object containing all the information regarding the user's browser:

```
<SCRIPT LANGUAGE="javascript">
document.write("You're using " +navigator.appName+ ".")
</SCRIPT>
```

You can find `navigator` used as part of a JavaScript example in Chapter 1, Lesson 3.

See also: `appCodeName`, `appName`, `appVersion`, and `userAgent`.

`onBlur` Event Handler

`onBlur` is enacted when the form item loses focus, meaning cursor attention has moved away from the element:

```
<FORM>
<INPUT TYPE="text"
➥onBlur="alert('Stop!  Did you fill in your name?')">
</FORM>
```

You can find `onBlur` used as part of a JavaScript example in Chapter 2, Lesson 6.

onChange **Event Handler**

onChange will occur when data in a form item is changed or focus is moved away from the form element:

```
<FORM>
<TEXTAREA onChange="alert('Something wrong?')"></TEXTAREA>
</FORM>
```

You can find onChange used as part of a JavaScript example in Chapter 2, Lesson 6.

onClick **Event Handler**

When the mouse is clicked on a particular element identified by the Event Handler, onClick will be enacted:

```
<FORM>
<INPUT TYPE="submit" onClick="location.href='page.html'">
</FORM>
```

You can find onClick used as part of a JavaScript example in Chapter 2, Lesson 6.

onDblClick **Event Handler**

onDblClick is new to the HTML 4.0 code and can be used in a range of element including forms, tables, and the <SPAN> command that can encompass any item. But be careful using it because not all browsers support it yet. The Event Handler is performed when the mouse is clicked twice. This example shows the use of the <SPAN> flag:

```
<SPAN onDblClick="function()"><IMG SRC="image.gif"></SPAN>
```

The <SPAN> command is only there to carry the onDblClick. It alters the image in no other way.

You can find onDblClick and <SPAN> used as part of a JavaScript example in Chapter 2, Lesson 8.

onFocus **Event Handler**

onFocus will occur when focus is placed upon a form item, meaning it was clicked on or moved to through hitting the Tab key:

```
<FORM>
<INPUT TYPE="text" onFocus="window.status='Fill in your name'"
</FORM>
```

You can find onFocus used as part of a JavaScript example in Chapter 2, Lesson 6.

onKeyDown Event Handler

onKeyDown is a new Event Handler from HTML 4.0 code, so not all browsers support it yet. When the user presses a key, this event is enacted:

```
<FORM>
<INPUT TYPE="text" onKeyDown="alert('Filling in the form yet??')">
</FORM>
```

onKeyUp Event Handler

When the user releases the key, onKeyUp is enacted:

```
<FORM><INPUT TYPE="text" onKeyUp="alert('Thanks, that hurt.')">
</FORM>
```

onLoad Event Handler

onLoad appears mostly in the BODY flag of the HTML document:

```
<BODY onLoad="function()">
```

Its purpose is to act as a trigger for a function, or the JavaScript code that is attached to it, when the page loads.

You can find onLoad used as part of a JavaScript example in Chapter 2, Lesson 6.

onMouseDown Event Handler

onMouseDown is new with HTML 4.0, so not all browsers support it yet. This event occurs when the mouse button is clicked down:

```
<IMG SRC="image.gif" onMouseDown="document.pic1='image2.gif'">
```

You can find onMouseDown used as part of a JavaScript example in Chapter 2, Lesson 8.

onMouseMove Event Handler

onMouseMove is new to HTML 4.0, so not all browsers support it yet. When the user moves the mouse, this event occurs:

```
<BODY onMouseMove="function()">
```

onMouseOut Event Handler

onMouseOut is usually used in conjunction with the onMouseOver Event Handler in order to create an image flip effect:

```
<A HREF="http://www.cnn.com"
onMouseOver="document.pic1.src='menu1on.gif'"
➥onMouseOut="document.pic1.src='menu1off.gif'">
<IMG SRC="menu1off.gif" BORDER=0 NAME="pic1"></a>
```

You can find onMouseOut used as part of a JavaScript example in Chapter 2, Lesson 7.

onMouseOver Event Handler

When the mouse passes over top of the item, onMouseOver will occur:

```
<A HREF="http://www.cnn.com"
onMouseOver="document.pic1.src='menu1on.gif'"
onMouseOut="document.pic1.src='menu1off.gif'">
<IMG SRC="menu1off.gif" BORDER=0 NAME="pic1"></a>
```

You can find onMouseOver used as part of a JavaScript example in Chapter 2, Lesson 5.

onMouseUp Event Handler

onMouseUp is new to HTML 4.0, so not all browsers support it yet. This event, which takes place when the user releases the mouse button, is often used in conjunction with onMouseDown to create an effect of two events with one mouse click:

```
<A HREF="http://www.cnn.com"
onMouseDown="document.pic1.src='menu1on.gif'"
onMouseUp="document.pic1.src='menu1off.gif'">
<IMG SRC="menu1off.gif" BORDER=0 NAME="pic1"></a>
```

You can find onMouseUp used as part of a JavaScript example in Chapter 2, Lesson 8.

onSelect Event Handler

onSelect is enacted when some, or all, of the form element is highlighted:

```
<FORM>
<INPUT TYPE="text" onSelect="alert('function()')">
</FORM>
```

onSubmit Event Handler

The onSubmit event occurs when the form is submitted. This Event Handler goes best in the submit-button portion of the HTML form:

```
<FORM>
<INPUT TYPE="submit" onSubmit="document.bgColor='red'">
</FORM>
```

You can find onSubmit used as part of a JavaScript example in Chapter 2, Lesson 6.

onUnload Event Handler

Like the onLoad Event Handler, onUnload is often found in the BODY flag:

```
<BODY onLoad="function()" onUnload="alert('bye!')">
```

It is enacted when the user moves to another page, or unloads the current page.

You can find onUnload used as part of a JavaScript example in Chapter 2, Lesson 6.

open Method

You can use open to open a new browser window, in which you can load a whole new HTML document, or to create a second window from the original page. This code will open a new browser window and load page.html into it:

```
<SCRIPT LANGUAGE="javascript">
window.open('page.html')
</SCRIPT>
```

This example will create a new browser window and fill it with the text from the document.write statements:

```
<SCRIPT LANGUAGE="javascript">
function openWindow()
{
OpenWindow=window.open("", "newwin", "height=250,width=250")
OpenWindow.document.write("<HTML>")
OpenWindow.document.write("<TITLE>Welcome</TITLE>")
OpenWindow.document.write("<BODY BGCOLOR='pink'>")
OpenWindow.document.write("<H1>Welcome to my page!</H1>")
OpenWindow.document.write("</BODY>")
OpenWindow.document.write("</HTML>")
}
</SCRIPT>
```

This code sets the new window's HEIGHT and WIDTH to 250 pixels. The open method also allows you to set the window elements shown in Table B.2.

Table B.2   Window Elements That Can Be Set with the open Method

Window Element	Can Be Set to...
Toolbar	Yes or no
Menu bar	Yes or no
Scrollbars	Yes or no
Resizable	Yes or no
Location	Yes or no
Directories	Yes or no
Status	Yes or no

You can find open, and the commands listed above, used as part of a JavaScript example in Chapter 4, Lesson 19.

See also: window.

parent Property of frame and window

parent is used in hierarchy statements to denote the overriding document in a frame situation or the document that spawned the new window:

```
<FORM>
<INPUT TYPE="button" onClick="parent.location.href='page.html'">
</FORM>
```

See also: frames and window.

pathname Property

The pathname method is used to return the path portion of a URL without the root of the server:

```
<SCRIPT LANGUAGE="javascript">
document.write("You're at www.joe.com/" +location.pathname+ ".")
</SCRIPT>
```

See also: host, hostname, href, port, and protocol.

port Property

port returns the port the user is attached to during his or her Internet session:

```
<SCRIPT LANGUAGE="javascript">
document.write("You're using port: " +location.port+ ".")
</SCRIPT>
```

See also: host, hostname, href, pathname, and protocol.

prompt Method

prompt is used to display a JavaScript dialog box in order to gather information from the user. The prompt is always assigned a variable. The information offered by the user then takes on that variable name. If the user offers no information, the value for the variable is entered as null.

In the following example, the text in the first set of quotation marks appears on the prompt box. The text in the second set of quotation marks appears in the text area on the prompt box. If you do not want text in the text area, leave the quotation marks empty:

```
<SCRIPT LANGUAGE="javascript">
var name =  prompt("This is a Prompt Box", "write your name here")
</SCRIPT>
```

Figure B.3 shows what the prompt box looks like.

Figure B.3
The prompt box.

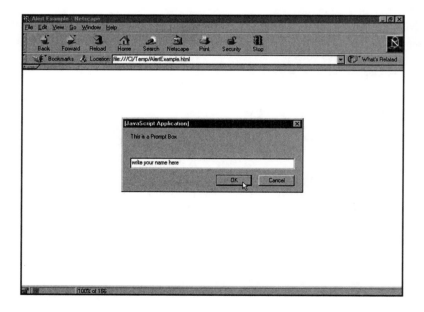

You can find `prompt` used as part of a JavaScript example in Chapter 3, Lesson 11.

See also: `alert` and `confirm`.

`protocol` Property

`protocol` is the set of rules used by the browser to deal with the page currently loaded or the file the hypertext link is pointing at:

```
<SCRIPT LANGUAGE="javascript">
document.write("This document is displayed using "
↪+location.protocol+ ".")
</SCRIPT>
```

Returned stings might include `http`, `ftp`, `mailto`, `news`, `file`, or `JavaScript`.

See also: `host`, `hostname`, `href`, `pathname`, and `port`.

`referrer` Property

`referrer` returns the URL of the document visited just before the current document:

```
<SCRIPT LANGUAGE="javascript">
document.write("You just came from " +location.referrer+ ".")
</SCRIPT>
```

You can find `referrer` used as part of a JavaScript example in Chapter 1, Lesson 3.

See also: `document`.

`self` Property

`self` denotes the current window. This example creates a button that closes the current window:

```
<FORM>
<INPUT TYPE="button" onClick=" self.close()">
</FORM>
```

`selectedIndex` Property

`selectedIndex` is used to return the number representing the index of a select item. For example, the following HTML form drop-down menu box is a series of select items:

```
<FORM NAME="FormA">
<SELECT NAME="SelectBox">
<OPTION> Red
<OPTION> Green
```

```
<OPTION> Blue
</SELECT>
</FORM>
```

The options Red, Green, and Blue are numbered 0, 1, and 2, respectively. To return that index number to a JavaScript, you would use this hierarchy statement:

```
document.FormA.SelectBox.selectedIndex
```

You can find `selectedIndex` used as part of a JavaScript example in Chapter 5, Lesson 27.

setDate Method

The method `setDate` is used to set a number representing the day of the month, 1 through 31, through the `Date` object:

```
<SCRIPT LANGUAGE="javascript">
var Millenium = new Date ()
var pointintime = Millenium.setDate("January 1, 2001")
</SCRIPT>
```

The date January 1, 2001 is now a set point in the future and can be used to figure the amount of time between a point in time and January 1, 2001.

See also: `setHours`, `setMinutes`, `setMonth`, `setSeconds`, `setTime`, `setTimeout`, and `setYear`.

setHours Method

`setHours` is used to set the current hour from 0 (midnight) through 23 (military format) as a specific point in time. The format is

```
<SCRIPT LANGUAGE="javascript">
var Millenium = new Date ()
var pointintime = Millenium.setHours("January 1, 2001")

</SCRIPT>
```

The format can be used to figure the number of hours until the specified date.

See also: `setDate`, `setMinutes`, `setMonth`, `setSeconds`, `setTime`, `setTimeout`, and `setYear`.

setMinutes **Method**

setMinutes is used to set the minute, 0 through 59, as a specific point in time. The format is

```
<SCRIPT LANGUAGE="javascript">
var Millenium = new Date ()
var pointintime = Millenium.setMinutes("January 1, 2001")

</SCRIPT>
```

The format can be used to figure the number of minutes until the specified date.

See also: setDate, setHours, setMonth, setSeconds, setTime, setTimeout, and setYear.

setMonth **Method**

setMonth is used to set the current month, 0 (January) through 11 (December), as a specific point in time. The format is

```
<SCRIPT LANGUAGE="javascript">
var Millenium = new Date ()
var pointintime = Millenium.setMonth("January 1, 2001")

</SCRIPT>
```

The format can be used to figure the number of months until the specified date.

See also: setDate, setHours, setMinutes, setSeconds, setTime, setTimeout, and setYear.

setSeconds **Method**

setSeconds is used to set the current second, 0 through 59, as a specific point in time. The format is

```
<SCRIPT LANGUAGE="javascript">
var Millenium = new Date ()
var pointintime = Millenium.setSeconds("January 1, 2001")

</SCRIPT>
```

The format can be used to figure the number of seconds until the specified date.

See also: setDate, setHours, setMinutes, setMonth, setTime, setTimeout, and setYear.

setTime Method

setTime is the base of the Date object. It returns the number of milliseconds since January 1, 1970 until the point in time set by you. The format is

```
<SCRIPT LANGUAGE="javascript">
var Millenium = new Date ()
var pointintime =  Millenium.setTime("January 1, 2001")

</SCRIPT>
```

The format can be used to figure the total time until the specified date.

See also: setDate, setHours, setMinutes, setMonth, setSeconds, setTimeout, and setYear.

setTimeout Method

The setTimeout method makes a function run again and again; in addition, setTimeout allows for some downtime set in milliseconds. The format is

```
<SCRIPT LANGUAGE="javascript">
function joe()
{
JavaScript events

var timer = setTimeout("joe()", 1000)
}
</SCRIPT>
```

This format will loop the function joe again and again, waiting 1 second before starting the loop the next time. Remember that JavaScript counts time in milliseconds, so 1000 is equal to 1 second.

You can find setTimeout used as part of a JavaScript example in Chapter 7, Lesson 42.

setYear Method

setYear is used to set the current year, minus 1900, as a two-digit representation. The format is

```
<SCRIPT LANGUAGE="javascript">
var Millenium = new Date ()
var pointintime = Millenium.setYear("January 1, 2001")
</SCRIPT>
```

The format can be used to figure the number of years until the specified date.

See also: setDate, setHours, setMinutes, setMonth, setTime, and setTimeout.

You can find `setYear` used as part of a JavaScript example in Chapter 7, Lesson 41.

small Method

`small` is used to alter text strings to display one size smaller than the browser default:

```
<SCRIPT LANGUAGE="javascript">
var textString = "Hello There"
document.write("textString.small()")
</SCRIPT>
```

See also: `big` and `fontsize`.

status Property

The status area is the lowest portion of the browser window. It's where `Document Done` appears when a page has finished loading. You can direct and alter the display in this space using this format:

```
<A HREF="page.html" onMouseOver="window.status='Click Here!'">
➥link</A>
```

You can find `status` used as part of a JavaScript example in Chapter 2, Lesson 5.

strike Method

`strike` is used to create a strikethrough effect on a text string:

```
<SCRIPT LANGUAGE="javascript">
var textString = "Hello There!"
document.write(textString.strike())
</SCRIPT>
```

See also: `big`, `bold`, `italic`, and `small`.

sub Method

`sub` is used to create a subscript like the *2* in H_2O:

```
<SCRIPT LANGUAGE="javascript">
var textString = "2"
document.write("H")
document.write(textString.sub())
document.write("O")
</SCRIPT>
```

See also: `big`, `bold`, `italic`, `small`, and `sup`.

substring Method

The method substring is used to return a portion of a text string between two indexes. For example:

```
<SCRIPT LANGUAGE="javascript">
var TextString = "Merry Christmas"
var TheString = TextString.substring(1,0)
</SCRIPT>
```

This JavaScript would return the first letter of the text string because the number 1 is the greater of the two indexes.

sup Method

sup works the same way as the sub method. It's used to create superscript text like the *st* in *1st*:

```
<SCRIPT LANGUAGE="javascript">
var textString = "st"
document.write("1")
document.write(textString.sup())
</SCRIPT>
```

See also: big, bold, italic, small, and sub.

title Property

title refers to the title of the HTML document. Used with document, you can return the page's title:

```
<SCRIPT LANGUAGE="javascript">
document.write("The Title is " +document.title+ ".")
</SCRIPT>
```

You can find title used as part of a JavaScript example in Chapter 1, Lesson 3.

toLowerCase Method

toLowerCase is used to change a text string to all lowercase letters:

```
<SCRIPT LANGUAGE="javascript">
var textString = "Hello There!"
document.write(textString.toLowerCase())
</SCRIPT>
```

You can find `toLowerCase` used as part of a JavaScript example in Chapter 5, Lesson 24.

See also: `toUpperCase`.

toUpperCase Method

`toUpperCase` is used to change a text string to all uppercase letters:

```
<SCRIPT LANGUAGE="javascript">
var textString = "Hello There!"
document.write(textString.toUpperCase())
</SCRIPT>
```

You can find `toUpperCase` used as part of a JavaScript example in Chapter 5, Lesson 24.

See also: `toLowerCase`.

userAgent Property

`userAgent` will return the HTTP protocol header used to load the current HTML document:

```
<SCRIPT LANGUAGE="javascript">
document.write("The header reads " +document.userAgent+ ".")
</SCRIPT>
```

You can find `userAgent` used as part of a JavaScript example in Chapter 1, Lesson 3.

See also: `appCodeName`, `appName`, and `appVersion`.

value Property

`value` represents the text that is written, or given, to an HTML form item. The value of a text box or text area is the text the user has written in. The value of a radio button or check box is a simple 1 (yes) or 0 (no) depending on whether the user has clicked the element or not.

In the following code

```
<FORM NAME="FormA">
<INPUT TYPE="text" NAME="Tbox">
</FORM>
```

the text a user wrote into the form's text box is represented by:

```
document.FormA.Tbox.value
```

You can find `value` used as part of a JavaScript example in Chapter 5, Lesson 23.

var Variable

`var` is used to assign a variable name to a string or set of JavaScript commands. The traditional method follows this pattern:

```
<SCRIPT LANGUAGE="javascript">
var navapp = navigator.appName
document.write(navapp)</SCRIPT>
```

Now you can call for `navigator.appName` throughout the remainder of the script with just the variable name `navapp`.

Actually, the single equal sign is enough to set a variable name. The `var` isn't required, but it's still a good idea to use it to help yourself when writing scripts.

You can find `var` first used as part of a JavaScript example in Chapter 3, Lesson 11.

See also: the descriptions of local and global variables in Appendix A, "JavaScript Basic Concepts."

vlinkColor Property

`vlinkColor` is used to return the current HTML document's visited link color:

```
<SCRIPT LANGUAGE="javascript">
document.write("The link color is " +document.vlinkColor+ ".")
</SCRIPT>
```

You can find `vlinkColor` used as part of a JavaScript example in Chapter 1, Lesson 3.

See also: `alinkColor`, `bgColor`, `fgColor`, and `linkColor`.

while Loop

The `while` loop is a format that allows a JavaScript, or a set of JavaScript statements, to run again and again as long as a condition has not been met. Traditionally, `while` loops are used when you do not know how many times the script will loop. This is a possible format for a `while` loop:

```
<SCRIPT LANGUAGE="javascript">
var loops=input from a prompt or other method within the script
var num=1
while (num <= loops)
{
JavaScript event
}
</SCRIPT>
```

Because the number that will be assigned to the loops variable is unknown, a while loop is used with a condition so that when the loop's variable number equals the number returned from the script (num <= loops), the looping should stop.

You can find the while loop used as part of a JavaScript example in Chapter 6, Lesson 36.

See also: for loop.

window Object

The window is the browser window. This is the highest-level object accessible in the JavaScript hierarchy (DOM).

You can find window used as part of a JavaScript example in Chapter 2, Lesson 5.

For examples of its use, see the frames, parent, self, status, and top properties.

See also: alert, close, confirm, open, prompt, and write methods, and the onLoad and onUnload Event Handlers.

write Method

write is used with the document object to write lines of text to an HTML document. Those lines appear on the pages just as written carrying no effects from the script. In this instance, the command is simply a delivery device:

```
<SCRIPT LANGUAGE="javascript">
document.write("Hello There!")
</SCRIPT>
```

You can find write used as part of a JavaScript example in Chapter 1, Lesson 1.

See also: writeln.

writeln Method

The writeln method works much the same way as the write method, except each new writeln statement is ended with what is equal to a break (<BR>) flag. However, the command is not understood by all browsers and can be buggy. It is better to use the write statement alone and add the <BR> commands to get line breaks.

```
<SCRIPT LANGUAGE="javascript">
document.writeln("Hello There!")
</SCRIPT>
```

You can find writeln used as part of a JavaScript example in Chapter 1, Lesson 1.

See also: write.

JavaScript Reserved Variable Words

When naming variables or functions, you must be careful not to use a word that already exists in the JavaScript language. The command words found in Appendix A, "JavaScript Basic Concepts," and Appendix B, "JavaScript Command Reference," are all off-limits.

In addition, here is a list of off-limits words. Although they might not be currently in use in the JavaScript language, they are reserved for later versions of JavaScript:

abstract	false	interface	super
break	final	long	switch
byte	finally	native	synchronized
case	float	new	this
catch	for	null	throw
char	goto	package	throws
class	if	private	transient
const	implements	protected	true
continue	import	public	try
default	in	return	void
do	instanceof	short	while
double	int	static	with
extends			

And, of course, var and function.

Scripts Available on htmlgoodies.com

The http://www.htmlgoodies.com/JSBook/ site offers more than 500 JavaScripts from many great authors. Each script is available for you to test, download, and use. Try your hand at altering some of these scripts. Make them better, change where the output appears in the browser window, or just use them as they are. They're ready to go.

The scripts are loosely broken into the following categories:

1. Alert scripts, such as button, link, and email scripts, all produce alert, prompt, or confirm boxes.
2. Buttons and email scripts deal with buttons and email scripts.
3. Clocks, calculators, and calendar scripts all deal with numbers, times, or dates.
4. Color scripts deal with color.
5. Game scripts either play games or deal with them as their topics. There are also some scripts that deal with leisure activities such as music.
6. HTML and developer scripts deal with HTML and the development of Web pages. These are a lot of scripts here that work "behind the scenes" to create a look or an event to help your Web pages or Web site. This is also where you'll find all the password protection scripts.
7. Image scripts deal with, display, manipulate, or create image animation.
8. Scrolling scripts scroll text in the document window, in text boxes, and in the status bar, among other places.

9. Text-based scripts all have one thing in common: They produce text and manipulate text on the HTML document.

10. Miscellaneous scripts didn't fit anywhere else.

Without further ado, here's the list of scripts.

Alert Scripts

These scripts all use alert, prompt, or confirm boxes.

No Clicking!: This script disables the user's ability to click on the page. *Requires Microsoft Internet Explorer 4.0.*

Alert Page Verification Form: This script posts a new page when a part of the form has not been filled out or not been filled out correctly.

How Long Load?: How long did it take your page to load? This script will tell you.

Screen Rez: Do you have the right screen settings for this page? Use this script to alert your users.

800×600 Alert: This script pops up an alert box if the user has their settings at 800×600, but you can change it to whatever settings you want.

Web-TV User Alert: This script pops up an alert box when a Web TV user stops by.

Update Alert: When someone enters the page, this script pops up an alert with the date and time of the page's last update.

No Go IE: This script will tell the user that they are not using Internet Explorer and that the following page has some IE-only elements. A choice to enter is then offered.

Multiple Alerts: That's what you get when you click.

Three Choices: This script gives an alert box that offers three choices to the viewer before going into your site.

Coming From?: This script produces an alert that welcomes the user from the page they just left.

Are You 18?: If yes, you go in—if no, too bad.

Chooser Script: This script gives you a list of pages to choose from. Choose one and tell the browser what to do with it.

Yes, No Script: Do you go in? Yes or no.

Thank You Link: This one gets your name and then sends you to the link of your choice with an alert message.

Personalized Welcome: As is, this script asks for your domain and then gives you a nice greeting. You can change it to ask for anything, and then give the same greeting.

Pop-Up Box: When someone logs in to your page, an alert box pops up. They see the page no matter what button they choose.

A Better Pop-Up Box: This script works the same way as the one above, but it won't allow the viewer in the page if they choose "Cancel."

Insert Name: This script pops up a prompt box asking for the viewer's name. What they enter is posted throughout the page.

Coming and Going: This script posts an alert when the person enters and again when they leave.

Anonymous Name: This script asks for the name the same as above. However, this script enables the view to remain anonymous if they so choose.

Mouse-Over Alert Box: This script produces an alert box when the mouse passes over a link.

Advanced Mouse-Over Alert Box: This script puts up a prompt box asking for the person's name. After writing it in, an alert box pops up saying "Hi."

Click For Alert Box: Clicking on the link brings up an alert box.

First/Last Name: This script pops up a prompt box that asks for the viewer's first and last name, and then posts it where you want it in the document.

Answer to Page: This script pops up a prompt box and asks a question. Depending on the answer, the viewer is sent to a specific page.

A Confirm Box: This script works pretty much like the previous ones, except this is a confirm box. It has a question mark rather than an exclamation point.

Buttons, Links, and Email Scripts

These scripts employ buttons, create links to other pages, or deal with email.

Click N' Go #2: This is a basic, well written, drop-down link menu.

Guest Book Prompt: This script prompts you for a name and then creates a guestbook for that name and associated email address.

Rotating Text Links: Text links rotate in a text box.

HotMail Fetch: This script grabs your HotMail email in the background while you do other things. (Contents are in a zip file.)

Email Button with Subject: You get a button that asks for a subject line. You then get an email with that subject.

A Drop-Down Menu Script: With a GO! button! Woohoo!

See Source: Here's a button that enables you to see the source of a page.

Link Message: Send them a message when they click!

Link Search: This script enables the user to enter a word, and then click on a link to choose which search engine gets the honor.

Drop-Down Link Menu in Frames: This script is what many have been asking for—a drop-down link menu that works with frames. Contents are in a zip file.

No Click Links: This script creates a link that works with no click. Just pass the mouse over it.

AOL Style Keyword: This script acts like the AOL keywords by taking a user to a new page depending on the word they put in.

Link of the Minute: Depending on the minute, you get a link.

Highlight Button: Pass your mouse over the button—it lights up. *Requires Microsoft Internet Explorer 4.0.*

Menu Links: This is a combination script of image flips and OnMouseOver that creates a nice navigation panel. See it in action. Contents are in a zip file.

Navigation Panel: This is a menu of links. Just click once to go.

Get a Cursor: This script is used with form commands. Use it and your first form element will get a cursor in the text box without having to be clicked on.

Go Box: Great script. This one allows for a description of the link and then the ability to see the page code.

New Window Search: This script allows for the search of multiple search engines. Results are posted on separate pages in new windows.

Mailto: Alerts: This script works with the basic mailto: forms. When the user clicks to send the mail, the script first asks if everything is okay, and then says thanks.

Total Cost Form: This script will enable your users to choose from a list of priced items. The script will tally the items, add the tax, and send the information to you.

MouseOver Color Buttons: These are link buttons that change color when you move over them. *Requires Microsoft Internet Explorer 4.0.*

Search Box: This is a nice copy and paste item that will enable your users to search multiple search engines from your page.

Linker: This script enables the user to choose a series of links. It then creates a page using just those links.

& Script: This script will tell you the & ASCII commands required to place nonletter and nonnumber characters on your page.

Layered Search Window: This script creates a layer window using a mouse-over. The new layer is the search window. *Requires 4.0 Browsers.*

Three Step Go Window Link: You'll need to seeit to understand the goofy title I gave it.

Scared Button: The button will not allow you to click it.

Radio Button Links: Clicking on the radio buttons sends you to a new link.

Scrolling Buttons: This script enables you to list multiple buttons that scroll through. Neat effect.

Plug-In Script: This script tells what plug-ins a person has on his or her browser.

Big Plug-In Script: Ditto, but offers more information about the plug-ins.

Running IE4?!?!: Are you? This script will tell you.

HREF Script: You put in the URL and off you go.

Fill All for Guest Books: This script will not let the user submit the guestbook form without filling in all the offered fields.

Fill All With Alert: Same as the previous script, but this one offers an alert on submit that asks for verification.

Multiple Form Check: This is a series of scripts that will check guestbook form fields for many different items including all fields being filled in, letters or numbers, too many spaces, capitalization, and more.

Multiple Random Emailing: One button chooses a random email address to send a letter to.

Status Bar Button: This is a button that posts text in the status bar. Not much worth, but great fun.

Headliner!: This is a button with text scrolling across. Each text scroll is different and each scroll carries its own URL. It is currently set up to run with frames.

Go There Button: This is a menu of links with a button that activates the browser.

Link Info: Great, great script. When the mouse passes over the link, information is posted in form boxes. Check it out.

Great Place: Here's a two-step link taking you to a great place.

Info Mail: This script gathers the user's name, email address, and URL and sends them to you with the click of a button.

Email Checker: This script works with the simple guestbook format.

Webring: This script allows you to start you own webring using another site's power.

Targets in Pull-Down Menus: This is how you add TARGET commands to frame page pull-down menus so the links you offer can change specific frames.

Blinker Button: One link—blinking text.

Static Words Link Button: Four links, static words.

Scrolling Link Button: This is a link button that scrolls the text.

One Button—Many Links: This is a link button with four links.

Mailto: Script Verification: This script acts like a CGI-based guestbook sending the viewer to another page when they submit the form to your email.

Check Email Address: This script allows you to enter an email address and verify if it is a true address.

I Sent It Already!: This script displays a personalized message telling the user that their mailto: guestbook data has been sent.

Random Link Pages: This script asks a couple of questions and takes you to a page based on your answers.

Browser Detector Buttons: This script tells all about the browser a viewer is using.

Scrolling Link Buttons: You get a scrolling list of links—choose one and click to go.

Random Link Generator: This script produces five random links.

Explorer Only!!!—Link Buttons: This script uses Active X technology to produce Explorer links.

Random Link Buttons: This script produces a random link.

Drop-Down Link Menu: This script does what the others do, but it flips around. Try it.

Two Images/Two Links: This script flips between two images. Depending on which one is up, that's the one that works when clicked.

Color Buttons: Click the button, change the color.

New Window Button: This is a button that opens a new browser window with a new page.

BACK and FORWARD Buttons: These buttons act just like the buttons at the top of the browser.

Jump Buttons: These buttons enable you to jump around within a page.

Link Reads Along Bottom: This script enables you to change what text appears in the status bar when the mouse pointer passes over the link.

Erase Status Bar: When words appear in the status bar, they tend to stay there until new words are called for. This script sets it so the words erase within two seconds after appearing.

Questions, Then Send: This script asks questions. Depending on your answer, you are sent to an appropriate page.

Countdown to Page Change: This is a counter that counts up until a preset time. At that time, that page changes.

Wait for Page Change: This script waits a preset amount of time and then changes to a page depending on your browser type.

Choose Link Destination: This script will post radio buttons underneath an HREF link. You choose the button and the link becomes that destination.

Jump Box: This is a pull-down menu that enables you to choose a link and jump to it.

Email: This is a button that produces an email window addressed to you.

Email with Subject and CC: This script creates an email button with the subject box and the CC box already filled out.

Email with Subject: Ditto above, but only the subject line is filled out.

Email with CC: Ditto above, but only the CC box is filled out.

Email Has Been Sent Alert: You attach this script to a simple guestbook form and it alerts the viewer that the email is being sent.

Button Box: This is a button that produces an alert box when clicked.

Reload Button: Here's a button that reloads the current page when clicked.

Auto Back and Forward: Using this script will automatically send people forward or backward one page, depending on how you set it up.

Radio Button Color Changer: Click on the radio button and the background changes color.

Color Button: Click on the button and the background changes color.

Question/Color Button: This button asks two questions. Depending on the answers, the background color changes.

The Three C's: Clocks, Calendars, and Calculator Scripts

These scripts all deal with numbers, times, or dates.

Quadratic Equation: This script does just what it says. *Requires Microsoft Internet Explorer.* Contents are in a zip file.

Time Zone Buttons: This script uses your computer's time to figure six other major time zones.

Calendar and Datebook: With one script, you get both. Contents are in a zip file.

Today Calendar: This script gets the date and posts the current month's calendar. It's a great script.

Square Root in the Status Bar: This script figures a square root and posts the answer in the status bar.

Loan Amount: Great math script. Use this script to know what your payments will be before the guy at the bank tells you.

Digital Clock: This one is exactly what it says. Contents are in a zip file.

Slope: You give this script four input points and it figures the slope of the line.

The Areas: Need to find an area? This is your script.

DHTML Clock: It is what it says—in big blue letters no less. *Requires Microsoft Internet Explorer 4.0.*

Tangent: All you triangle fans out there will love this one.

Sine: Ditto.

Cosine: Ditto. Ditto.

Count It!: You put in a number and the script counts up to it. Useless—but fun.

The Pythagorean Theorem: A squared plus B squared equals C squared. This little script will bear me out.

Circle Circumference: This one uses pi. Mmmmmm...pie.

Parameter of a Quadrilateral: Please have the width and length ready.

Area of a Quadrilateral: Ditto the information—different equation.

Another Great Science Calculator: Enough said.

Digital Clock: Three items displayed—time, AM/PM, date.

Number of Letters: This script is basically useless, but fun. You put in a sentence and it counts the number of letters.

Money Conversion Script: Pick from a long list of currencies. The conversion is done for you.

Area of a Triangle: Use this script to get through that math class.

Multiple Java Calendar: This script is a real work. Take a look at all the functions.

Running Calculator: How far—how fast?

World Clock—Daylight Savings Time: Just as it says...

Circle Calculator: This script will help a great deal with finding the area and other measurements of a circle.

Math Check: How good are your math skills? This script will check you over four levels.

College Tuition Chooser: Choose a college from the money you'll spend.

The Super Calculator: The author claims it's the greatest JS calculator yet! Please note, it will not work on Microsoft Internet Explorer. Maybe it isn't that great.

Percentage Calculator: Find the percentage of any number from another.

Power Calculator: Figure the power of any number.

Solve For X: This one will get you through high school algebra.

Nautical Calculator: This is a great script that figures a lot of stuff you're going to need to know next time you take the boat out.

Celsius to Fahrenheit: And back again.

JavaScript Clock Fix: This is a fix for some JavaScript Clocks that are displaying the wrong month.

Click Through Rate Calculator: This figures the percentage for you.

Graphic Enhanced Calculator: You have to see this script to believe it. You'll need to grab the script and a ton of little graphics to get it to function.

Celsius to Fahrenheit: That's what it does...differently than the one above.

Date and Time: This script puts up the date and time someone came in to your page.

Tells Time, Begs You to Stay: That's what it does when you try to leave.

Java Alarm Clock: You tell the script when you want to be alerted. It keeps track of the time and a box pops up when it's time.

Body Mass Calculator: Are you in good shape? Do you really want to know?

Simple Calculator(s): This can be one large calculator or four small ones. Take a look.

Your Age in Dog Years: Woof.

A Great GPA Calculator: This one recognizes + and -.

Basic Calendar: This script is just what it says.

Entire Year Calendar: It takes up space, but you get the entire year.

Calendar/Datebook: This script displays a calendar-type datebook you can fill in with your appointments.

A Calculator: Figure out math equations to your heart's content.

Another Clock: A basic digital clock.

Java Clock: This is a digital clock that displays the time plus AM or PM inside a small frame.

Click Displays Date and Time: This script produces a button. Click on it and you get the date and time.

Single Function Calculator: This script will only do one function. You can change what that function is, but it still will only do the one.

Equation Helper: This script takes just about any equation and solves for X.

Count Up: You set the length of time. This script then counts up and displays a message when time's up.

Count Down: Ditto above, but this one counts down.

Countdown to Page Change: A timer is set up that changes the page when a predetermined time is reached.

GPA Calculator: Figure out your grade right from the Web. This script will take your final marks and show you your all-important grade point average.

Conversion Calculators: One deals with distances, one deals with weights, and one deals with volume measurements.

A Stopwatch: Nothing fancy. It just counts up until you say stop or reset.

Color Scripts

These scripts display or manipulate color in some fashion.

Color Box: See boxes of color, click on boxes of color, get hex!

Color Gradient Test: You choose the color and this script shows it from dark to light and back again.

Show Color Cube: Great script! It lets you put in either the word, hex, or RGB code of a color. It then posts a small cube showing the color.

Get the Lights: This is a simple game where clicking the right radio button "turns on" the lights.

Red to Black...and Back: This script is annoying. Maybe that's why I like it. It flashes red to black a few times—and then posts the page.

Light Switch: This script is useless but really fun. It goes from light to dark with a switch.

Lights Out!: Click the button and the lights go out.

Color Wait: This script rolls colors when someone logs in to the page—but what's more, it posts text along the bottom of the page while the person is waiting.

Background Roller: This script rolls through a series of colors again, and again, and again, until you go nuts.

Background Flasher: Go easy or go silly. This is a fun script.

Random Background Colors: Add a little random color to your page.

Background Color Prompt: Allow your user to choose the background color before going in.

Hex to RGB and Back Again: Put in the hex code, get the red, green, and blue...and vice versa.

Background Table Color: Use the table to choose a color for the page depending on what mood you're in.

Color Change with Display: This script slowly fades in a background color. But while it is fading, the color codes display. Take a look. I like this one.

Color Start: This script tells you to wait for the page to load while you watch a color display.

Color Cube: You have to try it out to believe it. Many colors as you roll your pointer along.

Hex Coder: Great script. You type in the color name, and it gives you the hex code. Great for page development.

Large Color Script: Very useful. This script gives hex codes and color combinations.

All Colors: This one asks you about all the different items that you can do with colors. It then posts your answers. It's great for seeing how colors work together before using them on your page. *Netscape Navigator Browsers Only.*

Color Code Verify: Put in a color code—a window pops up showing you what it looks like.

Background Color Log: Try to get the last background color. This script plays along.

Background Color with Alert: That's what it does.

Chat Room Color Prompt: Do you go into chat rooms? Take this script with you.

Word = Background Color: A prompt box asks for a word and changes the background color by what you write. Any word seems to work.

Color = Hour: This script produces a different background color depending on the time of the day.

Pull-Down Color Menu: Use the menu to change the background color.

New Color Every 5 Seconds: Enough said.

An Interview for a New Color: Takes time, but it's fun.

Color Buttons: Click the button, change the color.

Pull-Down Colors: This is a pull-down menu of colors.

Background Color Changer: Using this script will make your page's background roll through colors of your choice before posting the text.

B&W Background: This script fades the background from black to white before the text appears.

Mouse-Over Color Change: You will offer color names. When the mouse passes over the name, the background changes to that color.

Mouse-Over Color Changer: This script changes the page to blue when the mouse passes over.

Text Color Changer: This script changes color depending on what the viewer writes to the page.

Radio Button Color Changer: Click on the radio button, change the color.

Button Color Changer: Click on the button, change the color.

Questions then Color: This button asks you two questions. Depending on your answer, it changes the background color.

Day/Night Script: During the morning hours, your page is black text on white, at night it turns to white text on black. It's a day/evening effect.

Game Scripts

These scripts either play or deal with games as their topics. There are also some scripts that deal with leisure activities such as music.

Ships at Sea: A two-player version of a sinking game.

Peg Solitaire: Jump over one—take it out. You've played this before—now try it on your computer. Contents are in a zip file.

Bridge: This script will help your game.

NBA Totals Projection: How will your favorite player do?

Magic Eightball: Remember that water-filled eightball that would tell you your fortune? Here it is in Java form.

Magic Eightball Two: This is another version of the magic eightball with a whole lot more graphical support.

Roundball: This is a basketball animation. Play college or pro.

Field Goal: Line it up and hopefully kick it through. *Requires Netscape Navigator 4.0.*

The Right Button: Can you find the button that will light when you click on it? No fair looking at the code.

Point Guard Stats: How's your favorite player doing? How are you doing? This script will tell you.

Super Bowl Game: Can you tell me who won, and who lost, the last 31 Super Bowls? (posted before Super Bowl XXXII).

Chinese Zodiac: What was the Chinese animal zodiac sign the year you were born?

Frame-Based Quiz with Timer: You're under the gun on this one.

Basketball Champ Quiz: How well do you know the champs from seasons past?

Social Security State: Give the first three numbers of your SS number and this script will tell you the state that issued it. There is no concern about giving the number. The script is self-contained and the first three numbers are basically worthless without the other six.

Jay's Game: Play this! It's a speed game where you try to check off numbers before time runs out. It's tougher than you think.

The Maze: You have to play it to believe it.

Text-Based Quiz: This quiz is more text-based than the other form-based quizzes.

Random Number Entry: The script picks a random number between 1 and 10. You guess at it. When you get it right—or after three tries—you get to go in.

Get to See Hanson: …or any other rock group. This is a game where you move forward to meet the group.

Graded Multiple Choice Quiz: This is a quiz that grades itself and places a check or an X if the answer is right or wrong. The only downfall is that the answers are pretty easy to locate before taking the quiz.

Slots: Play with someone else's money.

Insult Machine: Tell people what you think. They choose one of four insults and the script delivers.

Brick: This is a great copy of the old brick game.

Tic Tac Toe: Two players—one screen.

Middle School Quiz: A simple quizgame. You can change it to include your own questions, answers, and responses.

Football: Play football online.

Baseball: Ditto with baseball.

French Translator: Use this script to translate a phrase from English to French.

A Quiz: This is a four-question quiz that grades you. Welcome to high school.

Find Me!: This is a fun game created by a 12-year-old JavaScript wizard. Find the only working link!

Blackjack-21: Play the game. I like this script because it calls the dealer "The Idiot." Every played and felt that way?

Backspace Race: See if you can get rid of the text before the computer does.

Find Mr. Hockey: This is a great simple seek-and-find type game.

Check's Out!: Try to get rid of all the checks. I couldn't do it.

What's Your Sign?: Enter your birthday—and you get your sign.

Lottery Number Picker: Why play birthdays—use this script!

Golf Handicapper: This script figures the USGA handicap index.

A Mad Lib Game: Try playing!

Russian Roulette: Someone wins—someone loses...with a bang.

HTML and Developer Scripts

These scripts deal with HTML and the development of Web pages. These are a lot of scripts here that work "behind the scenes" to get a look or an event to help your Web pages or Web site. This is also where you'll find all the password protection scripts.

Got Frames?: This script goes into your page's BODY command. It will perform a redirect if the user tries to look at the page outside of the frame setting.

Monitor Detect: This is a redirect script that deals with the monitor settings set by the user. Contents are in a zip file.

Tag Pad: This is an HTML editor that works a lot like using Notepad.

Open C Drive: Click the button and get the contents of the C drive.

See Size Window: The user puts in the height and width of a new window, clicks a button, and the new window pops up. It's great for page development.

PC/MAC Detect Script: Depending on which operating system the viewer is using, this script sends the user to a specific page best viewed with that type of system.

Every Other Password: This is a pretty good password script that takes every other letter of the password and creates the page name. See it for yourself. Contents are in a zip file.

JavaScript Redirect: This script acts like a meta refresh in JavaScript.

The Same Size: This script opens a window the same size as the current window. *Navigator Browsers Only.*

A Good HTML Editor: Enough said...

Please Wait Script: This script posts a message telling the user to wait because the page is being loaded.

Version 4 or Not: This script recognizes the user's browser version number. If it's version 4, a specific page is brought up. Anything else goes to another page.

Stay Alive: If your server kicks you off after a couple of minutes of inactivity, downloading gives you headaches, right? This script makes sure you have activity within the time frame so you do not get kicked off.

Remote Control Window: The little one works the big one.

Password 33 Script: Password protect your pages. See it in action.

Immediate Page Load: This script enables the user to load two pages at once so the second comes in very fast when called for.

Transport or Password: This script enables the person to type in a word. If the word is a page, they are transported. It also works pretty well as a password script.

Page Depending on Browser: This script will note the browser and send the viewer to the page best suited for him or her.

PageMaker Clone: Make your own page with this one.

Multiple Search Engines: Search multiple Internet search engines with one click.

Remote Surfs Four Sites: This script enables you to surf four sites at once.

Four Search: This script enables you to search four search engines at once, all on one screen.

onMouseOver Layers: This script uses layer commands with the onMouseover commands. *Requires Netscape 4.0.*

onMouseOver Layers Menu: This script uses layer commands with the onMouseover command to create a pull-down menu. *Requires Netscape 4.0.*

Layer Toggle: This script uses JavaScript to toggle between layers. *Requires Netscape 4.0.*

HTML Editor: This JavaScript helps with HTML page construction.

3-Step Password: This is a pretty good password script that does its best to protect the password and the link it is going to. Tough to figure out from the script.

Password Script: Yet another nice password script.

Remote Control Window: This script pops a window up that enables you to control the first window.

Page of the Day: This script sets up a page of the day. You get 31 at the most, until they invent a month with 32 days.

Random Page: This script posts a page stating that a random page is to come, and then it goes to the random page from the list you offer.

Two Number Password: This script is great because it is difficult to grab the password from the script. Give it a try.

Simple Password: It doesn't get easier than this one.

Searchable Database: This is a script that acts as a search engine. It basically searches itself, but if you will take the time to enter all the titles and descriptions of your pages, it will search just like a personal search engine.

Who Came—And When: This script is a personalized counter.

Stops onMouseOver Text from Hanging Around: Use this script to ensure that the onMouseover text you use doesn't stay on the status bar after the user has moved on.

Verification of Guestbook Data: This script posts a virtual page when someone uses your simple mailto: guestbook.

Random Image Plus Link: This script produces a random image plus a link associated with that image.

Stops New Browser Windows: This script enables you to target to the same browser window to stop new windows from opening in your image maps and frames.

A Great HTML Editor: What more can you say?

Password: This script requires a password be typed in to enter a specific page. The password is the page's name.

Keypad Password: This script produces a key pad. The viewer enters a password number to get to the next page. The password is the name of the page. You can change the password number.

A Counter: This is a simple counter that produces an alert box count each time you enter the page. It also administers a greeting depending on the number of times. However, it only counts up to ten.

Cookie Counter: This is a fully functioning counter that uses the viewer's cookie to post a count on the page.

An HTML Editor: Now you can create your HTML documents right to your browser window.

Another HTML Editor: Choose your favorite.

Image Scripts

These scripts deal with, display, or manipulate images, or set images into motion.

Smooth Stop: This is an animation than brings images to a smooth stop, as if on ice. *Netscape Navigator 4.0 Only*.

Page Branding: This is a Geocities-style page brand.

Three to One Image Flip: This script is very clever. Three images sit on top of one another. When the mouse passes over one of them, it "blows up" to fill the space of all three. Contents are in a zip file.

Triple Flip Button: This script is a triple image, image flip.

Show Active Channel: This script looks at the user's browser. If it's an Explorer browser, the Active Channel image is posted to the page.

Multiple Image Flip: Three images are used to create one pretty cool flip.

DHTML Christmas Countdown: This is a clock that counts down to Christmas with a flying Santa. *Microsoft Internet Explorer 4.0 Only.*

Image Toggle: This is a basic image flip except the flip is enacted by the user pushing buttons.

Image Browser: Use this script to enable users to scroll through a list of images.

Stay Flipped Image Flip: After it's flipped—it stays.

Dual Image Flip: Not only do you get an image flip, you also get a secondary image popping up. Contents are in a zip file.

Image Option: Choose an image from a pull-down list. Hit the button and it displays.

Background Time: This script posts a different background color and image, plus a different image on your page, depending on what time of day it happens to be.

Flip Flap Image Script: This is a great multi-platform image flipping script.

Move the Image: This script enables you to make an image interactive. Your viewers can move it anywhere they want. *Microsoft Internet Explorer 4.0 Only.*

An Image Depending on the Date: Want a specific image on only a certain date or dates? This script will do it for you.

Floating Apple: This script employs layering to enable the Apple logo to break apart and fly around the screen. *Netscape 4 versions only.*

Black Hole: An image MouseOver starts a multiple page slide show.

Image Map Status Bar Message: This script uses mapping commands to make messages on different sections of an image map.

Multiple Image Flipping: Great script. Great effect. Take a look.

Image Mover: This is another image-moving script using Netscape 4.0 layer commands. *Requires Netscape Navigator 4.0.*

Image Search: This employs multiple images with a flip script to enable your readers to search five different search engines.

Four Movers: This script enables four images to basically fly all over your page. *Requires Netscape Navigator 4.0.*

Image Mover: Great script. The active image rolls all over the screen no matter what text is in its way. *Requires Netscape Navigator 4.0.*

Image Display JavaScript: This script enables your user to click on a link and see a picture pop up in a new, framing browser window.

Stop the Picture: If you have a large image downloading, this script enables your viewer to click a button and stop it.

Client-Side Image Map Script: This script works a lot like a client-side image map except it displays sections in a text box rather than the status bar.

Image Flipping Link: People have been asking for this one. On the MouseOver, the image changes, plus different text appears in the status bar. Really slick.

MouseOver for Image Maps: This script enables you to place text in the status bar for your image maps.

New Image Gif: This script places a new .GIF image where you want it—what's more, it keeps an eye on the date. When you want the image to come down, it removes it for you.

Random Image Plus Link: This script produces a random image plus a link associated with that image.

Random Number Generator—With Images: This script produces a random number that is displayed with images.

Random Pictures: An improvement over my script.

Another Random Picture Script: Ditto above.

Picture in Black: This script displays a chosen image surrounded by black in its own window.

Picture Changer: This script produces a picture change when the mouse moves across. Use small images.

Random Picture Display: This is a random picture generator. You will need 60 pictures to make it work correctly.

New Image Each Month: Depending on the month, this script displays another picture.

New Image Each Hour: Depending on the hour, this script displays another picture.

New Image Each Day: Depending on the date, this script displays another picture.

Scrolling Scripts

Scrolling text is very popular. These scripts scroll text in the document window, in text boxes, and in the status bar, among other places.

Left Right Scroller: This script scrolls text in from the left and the right inside a text box.

Easy Status Bar Scroll: Just what it says.

Bounce Scroll: This script bounces scrolling text all over the page. It'll get attention if nothing else. *Netscape 4.0 Required.*

Super Scroll: This is a scroll that sizes itself to your page and then gives the user a few options to play with.

Dual Scroll: Why did I post this script? I don't know—it just looked cool to me.

Letter by Letter Scroll: This script scrolls along letter by...oh, you know the rest.

Multiline Scroll: This script posts a message depending on the time of day and then runs a multiple-line scroll message.

Active Scroll: This script produces a scroll that is also an active link.

Netscape Marquee: This is a Netscape version of the Microsoft Internet Explorer Marquee. *Requires Netscape 4.0.*

Scroll to the New Century: Here's a countdown scroll to the year 2000...or to whatever date you want.

Scroll in Spanish: This is a scrolling JavaScript—in Spanish.

Spanish Form Scroll: This is a form scroll—in Spanish.

Spanish Backward Scroll: This is a scroll that goes the wrong way. It's also written in Spanish.

Controlled Scroll: This is a scroll that your viewers have some control over.

Four Scroll: This is a scroll employing four lines.

Ping Pong Visual: This is a ping pong visual that you can control.

Prompting Scroll: This script asks you for some text, and then scrolls it for you.

Replace Scroll: Take a look. It replaces letters in a scroll.

Flashing Words: This isn't exactly a scroll, but it's close. Words flash in the status bar along the bottom. Useless but fun.

Little Scroll: This script produces a scroll along the bottom, but only a little tiny one.

Pong Scroll: It's too hard to describe—just go see it.

Roll Scroll: The scroll comes in one letter at a time.

Scroll on Status Bar: This script produces a scroll down in the status bar where it reads "Document Done."

A Basic Scroll: This script produces a scroll on the document window.

One-At-A-Time Scroll: One-letter-at-a-time scroll across the status bar at the bottom of the browser.

Small Scroll: Here is a quick, easy to understand, on-page scroll.

Another Small Scroll: Ditto above with different scripting.

A Large, Involved Scroll: This script is a big pup. It will allow modification on every aspect of the text and the scroll. Detailed instructions are included.

Capital Scroll: This isn't a scroll per se, but it fits here. It takes a line of text and changes each letter from lowercase to caps. It looks like a wave.

Text-Based Scripts

These scripts all have one thing in common. They produce text on the HTML document.

Random Up To 50: This script produces a random number between 1 and 50, but you can set it to any upper limit you'd like.

Netscape Low Version: If your user is running Navigator version 2.0 or less, this script pops up text that offers a link to upgrade.

Status Scroll Count: The length of time you've been in a page just scrolls right by.

Add From Prompt: This script calls for information through a prompt and then enables you to post it in a text box through the use of a button.

Post Next Holiday: This script does what it says.

Hello in Bar: This throws up a prompt for the user's name and then offers a greeting in the status bar.

New Array Text Pages: This is a series of five different scripts that create "...Of the Day" type events wherein something happens each day or at a specific time of day. Where this script is different is that it uses a new type of array programming to get the effect in a simpler fashion.

Fun Text: It's like a Mad Lib game that plays for you.

Meta Tags: This script uses a prompt command to gather information in order to create your page's meta tags.

Headline Linker Script: This script is a little hard to explain. The idea is that you can get three headlines in a text box. Each is its own location too. You click the box to make it work. Go see it—it'll be easier than me explaining it.

Text Fader 1.3: This script is sooooo cool.

Transfer Data: Use this script to transfer data across pages. This is currently set up to transfer data from a form from one page to another.

Super Script Date: This script posts the date but also adds either the "st" or the "th" after the day number.

Message Plus Date: Two in one. This script is offered in two formats.

Remind Me: This script sits quietly in your browser until a specific date. Then it pops up telling you the time has come.

Tip Box: This script pops up a Tool Tip-style box when the mouse passes over text. Contents are in a zip file. *Requires Microsoft Internet Explorer 4.0.*

Make Me a Password: Great script. Need a password? This script will generate a random letter and number password at whatever length you require.

Mad Libber: This is a basic Mad Lib game.

Full Text Date: Just copy and paste and it's all yours.

Just the Date: This script posts the month (in text form) and the day.

Color Gradient Text: This is a great script that "rainbows" your text.

Highlighter: This script enables an onMouseOver to highlight a link. *Requires Microsoft Internet Explorer 4.0.*

Text Fader: This script is great. You'll have to see it to get the full effect.

You Came in...: This script tells the user something they already knew—when they came into the page. But it does so in such grand fashion that I had to post it. *Requires Microsoft Internet Explorer 4.0.*

The Updater: This script posts the date the page was last updated.

Pop-Up Tables: As your mouse passes over text, a table pops up to tell more. It's DHTML and has to be seen to be believed. *Requires Microsoft Internet Explorer 4.0.*

Flashing Warning: Just what it says. *Requires Navigator 4.0.* (c)Proclaim It!

This script posts two large lines of text to tell the world...something. *Requires Netscape Navigator 4.0.*

Personal Title Bar: This script prompts the user for a name and then uses that to post the title command for the page.

Date and Time in Status Bar: This script posts the date and time in the status bar.

Quote in New Window: Just what it says.

Follow the Moving Mouse: This script creates a block of color and text that follows your mouse around the screen. Think of it as a pet. *Requires Netscape Navigator 4.0.*

Hello in the Status Bar: This script asks for the user's name and then posts it in the status bar.

Layer Click: Click and the text follows you. Great effect. *Requires Netscape Navigator 4.0.*

Place the Message: This is a great script for developers to have around. It enables you to put in coordinates and then see where they fall on the page. *Requires Netscape Navigator 4.0.*

Moving Block of Text: This script will give you a colored block of text that flies around your screen. And who wouldn't want that? *Requires Netscape Navigator 4.0.*

Count the Seconds: This script counts the seconds a user has been in your page. It also posts alerts at certain times.

Random Link Script: This script posts a random link to follow.

Age Update Script: This script posts an age and automatically updates it when the birthday passes.

Status Bar Clock: Tell them what time it is—in the status bar.

Link Change: Run your mouse over the link—It changes. *Requires Microsoft Internet Explorer 4.0.*

Get Back to Frames: This script displays a message that the page the viewer is looking at should be in a frame setting and will not run by itself.

Bigger Text: Make text jump out when the mouse moves over. *Requires Microsoft Internet Explorer 4.0.*

Flipping Burst: The textwill become much more brilliant when your mouse moves over. *Requires Microsoft Internet Explorer 4.0.*

Multicolored Text: Every letter is a different color. It's very Saturday morning.

Copyright and Last Updated: This is a good quick script that you can paste onto your documents to give a bit of good information.

Fade Out: This script fades text in and out. You have to see this! *Requires Microsoft Internet Explorer 4.0.*

Many, Many Quotes: 160 sayings to get you started on your day.

Random Fact: Useless knowledge finally has a home.

Everyday Script: You get a different color scheme and message every day of the week.

All About: This script tells the user all about his or her machine and browser.

Goodbye Window: This script posts a goodbye window with links when your user leaves the page.

Sesame Street: This script will make your page brought to you by a random letter and a random number.

Which President?: You need this script for high school. Pick a number between 1 and 42 and this script tells you which president it was.

World Time: This script displays the current time and times for multiple locations around the world.

Time Stamp: This time stamp is an update of earlier versions. Here you will get a 12 at midnight instead of a zero.

How Many Days Until Christmas?: This script will tell you.

Browser and More: This script posts your browser and operating system and tells you if there is an update available to you. If there is, you get a link to go and get it.

Tips For the Day: This is ascript that offers your viewers some tips. You choose the topic.

Lots of Stuff Script: Take a look at this one. It posts all kind of stuff about your visit.

Pass the Text: This script is really silly, but you can't seem to stop doing it.

Date/Time in Spanish: This script posts the correct time and date in Spanish.

Rainbow Text: Enter your text. This script makes it a rainbow color.

James Bond: Use this script, answer the questions, and you'll get the famous James Bond line.

Update Message: This script displays the last time the page was updated and then a message to the viewer.

Day-to-Day Message: This script displays a different message depending on the day of the week.

Java or Not?: This script displays whether the browser is JavaScript-enabled or not.

Microsoft Explorer 4.0 Link Color: This script will change the link color on MouseOver. *Requires Microsoft Internet Explorer 4.0.*

Post the Date in Numbers: That's what it does.

Coming From Display: This script displays the page that referred the user to your page.

Who Came—and When?: This script prompts the viewer and then tells her how many times she has been to the page before.

Text in Status Bar Delay: This script enables the text in the status bar to stay for a short time—about a second—then goes away.

Lose Text in Status Bar: This script makes status bar text go away quickly.

Text in Status Bar: This script puts text in the status bar whether the mouse goes over a link or not. Use it to announce your home page.

Displays Date and Time of Arrival: Enough said.

Displays Family: This script is good for small children. It enables them to answer questions about their family and then posts their answers equaling a happy family.

A Mad Lib Game: Try playing!

Stops onMouseOver Text from Hanging Around: Use this script to make it so that the onMouseOver text you use doesn't stay on the status bar after the user has moved on.

Last Modification: This script posts when the page was last modified.

Date Page: This is a great script that creates a link to a page depending on the date. You could write pages forever...but don't.

Blinking Greetings: This script posts a greeting depending on the time of day. Plus it blinks! Woohoo!

Display a Message Depending on the Time: That says it all. You can change the messages you will display.

Displays the Browser Version: Post this script and the reader will see what type of browser (Netscape or Explorer) he is using.

Displays More Browser Info: This script does the same as above, but also displays browser type, version, and a few other items.

Get Name, Post Name: This script ask for the viewer's name and then posts it anywhere you want throughout the document.

Get Name, Post Name, 2: This is a different look than the one above.

Date Stamp: This script posts the date on the page showing the last time the page was modified.

New Message at Bottom: This script displays a new message along the bottom of the browser.

Cleans Up URL: This script breaks the URL reading along the bottom of the page into Domain: and Page:.

Message Depending on the Date: You set the messages and, depending on the date, one pops up.

Animated Text on Status Bar: What more can I say?

Mouse Produces Words: You can set the words that appear when the mouse moves over a link on your page.

First/Last Name Post: This script asks for the viewer's first and last name and then posts them anywhere in the document.

Do You Have JavaScript Capabilities?: This script will post a message to the page whether the browser has JavaScript capabilities or not.

Random Sentence Generator: More like a random story generator. This script creates a new story every time someone logs in to the page.

New Greeting: Depending on the time of day, this script produces a new greeting.

Miscellaneous Scripts

These didn't really fit in any of the other categories.

Script Tester: Use this script to paste in and then test your scripts.

Something of the Day: This is a great joke of the day script that you can change to be "anything" of the Day.

No Right Click: This script disallows the right-click properties while the viewer looks at your page.

Holiday MIDI: This script lies in wait until a specific date arrives. Then it pops to life, posts a message, and plays a MIDI. *Requires Microsoft Internet Explorer 4.0.*

Build Your Own Computer: This script was built for a site that builds computers. That site was nice enough to allow me to post it here. Contents are in a zip file.

No Tripod Banner: The author claims this script will rid you of them.

Random MIDI Player: Try this one out.

Guitar Notes: You put in the string and fret and this script tells you the note.

A Constant MIDI: Want a MIDI to keep playing whether or not the user stays in the frames of your page? This script will do it.

Digital Clock Jumpers: This script sets up a table which shows you how to configure the jumpers in a PC case to adjust the LCD digits for the proper clock speeds.

Same Size Window: This script opens a window the exact same size as the viewer's screen.

Multi-Button / Multi-Platform Sound Player: The author claims it's the only one of its kind. See it work.

Hello and Goodbye: This script pops up a window that disappears on its own.

Quick Window: This script pops up a window using a MouseOver command.

Cross-Browser Sound Script: This script sees the browser and then chooses the EMBED or the BGSOUND option for the user. No more soundless pages.

Show Me the MIDI!: This is a random MIDI player that also posts the name of the MIDI being played.

Embed Sounds Through Java: This is an onLoad script that will work across platforms to embed a sound.

Another Random MIDI Script: Just like it says...

Two Frames at Once with Radio Buttons: You are offered eight choices in two columns. Choose one from each, click the button, and the two pages you chose load in two frames at once.

Download Script: Here's a button that starts an FTP download for you.

Adding Choices Script: This script enables your user to choose from a list of items—then adds them up.

Chi-square: For all the statistics people out there—use this script to figure a 2×2 Chi-square.

Date Verification: Enter a date. This script tells you whether it exists or not.

Learning Tool: This script enables you to click boxes, and then shows you the JavaScript to create what you did.

Random MIDI: This script plays a random MIDI file.

Chat Room Scripts: I have no idea how these work. There are seven of them and they do things in chat rooms.

Guitar Chord Chart: Another great guitar chord chart.

A Chord Finder: This script is great for guitarists trying to find that darn chord.

Sees Browser: This script tells you about your browser.

Age Verification: This script is not very functional. It simply asks your age and lets you in. It might scare off younger viewers though.

Play a Music File: This script calls for, and plays, a .WAV file.

Auto Reload: This script reloads the page automatically.

Guitar Chord Chart: This is a script that shows the fingering of a chord you select. The root of the chord blinks.

Index

Symbols

, (separates commands operator), 263

' ' (single quotation marks), 27-28

" "(double quotation marks), 10, 27-28

!= (not equal to operator), 160, 263

<!- - tag, 69

% (divide and return remainder operator), 140, 262

& (and operator), 263

& script script (HTML Goodies Web site), 307

&& (and operator), 263

(((or operator), 263

( ) (double parentheses), instance, 10

* (multiplication operator), 140, 262, 284

+ (addition operator), 19, 140, 262, 284

- (subtraction operator), 140, 262, 284

- -> tag, 69

/ (divide operator), 140, 262

/ (division operator), 284

// (comments), 58

</SCRIPT> command, 10

; (ends lines of JavaScript operator), 263

< (less than operator), 160, 263

<= (less than or equal to operator), 160, 263

= (assignment operator), 154, 263

= = (equal to operator), 154, 160, 263

> (greater than operator), 160, 263

>= (greater than or equal to operator), 160, 263

? (conditional operator), 160, 263

3-step password script (HTML Goodies Web site), 318

800 × 600 alert script (HTML Goodies Web site), 304

A

abs( ) method, 151, 283

acos( ) method, 151, 283

action property, 265

active scroll script (HTML Goodies Web site), 322

add from prompt script (HTML Goodies Web site), 323

adding choices script (HTML Goodies Web site), 329

addition operator (+), 140, 262, 284

advanced mouse-over alert box script (HTML Goodies Web site), 305

age update script (HTML Goodies Web site), 325

age verification script (HTML Goodies Web site), 330

alert boxes, 33, 116-117

alert page verification form script (HTML Goodies Web site), 304

331

335

351

T

X - Y - Z

I don't have time for learning curves.

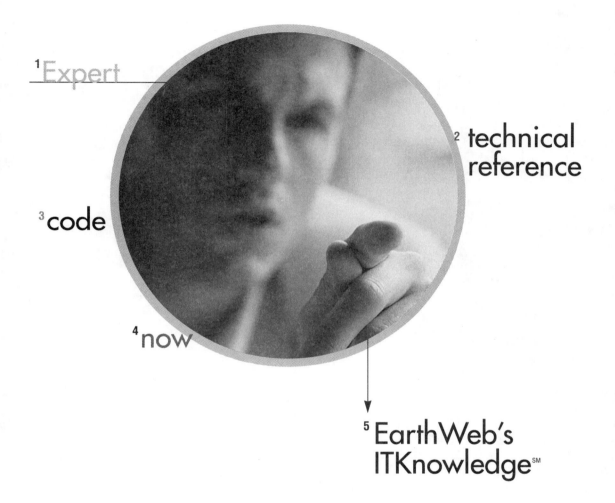

¹Expert

² technical reference

³code

⁴now

⁵ EarthWeb's ITKnowledge℠

They rely on you to be the ❶ expert on tough development challenges. There's no time for learning curves, so you go online for ❷ technical references from the experts who wrote the books. Find answers fast simply by clicking on our search engine. Access hundreds of online books, tutorials and even source ❸ code samples ❹ now. Go to ❺ EarthWeb's ITKnowledge, get immediate answers, and get down to it.

Get your FREE ITKnowledge trial subscription today at <u>itkgo.com</u>.
Use code number 027.

EARTHWEB
Go further *faster*

Other Related Titles

Sams Teach Yourself Java 2 Platform in 21 Days Complete Compiler Edition
Laura Lemay
ISBN: 0-672-31647-1
$49.99 USA/$74.95 CAN

Creating Killer Web Sites
David Siegel
ISBN: 1-56830-433-1
$49.99 USA/$74.95 CAN

The Waite Group's Java 1.2 How-To
Steve Potts
ISBN: 1-57169-157-X
$39.99 USA/$57.95 CAN

HTML Goodies
Joe Burns
ISBN: 0-7897-1823-5
$19.99 USA /
$28.95 CAN

Sams Teach Yourself XML in 21 Days
Simon North and Paul Hermans
ISBN: 1-57521-396-6
$29.99 USA /
$44.95 CAN

Sams Teach Yourself Java in 24 Hours
Rogers Cadenhead
ISBN: 0-672-31630-7
$19.99 USA /
$28.95 CAN

www.quecorp.com

All prices are subject to change.